EXPLORING U2: IS *THIS* ROCK 'N' ROLL?

Essays on the Music, Work, and Influence of U2

EDITED BY SCOTT CALHOUN

THE SCARECROW PRESS, INC.
Lanham • Toronto • Plymouth, UK
2012

Published by Scarecrow Press, Inc.
A wholly owned subsidary of The Rowman & Littlefield Publishing Group, Inc.
4501 Forbes Boulevard, Suite 200, Lanham, Maryland 20706
http://www.scarecrowpress.com

Estover Road, Plymouth PL6 7PY, United Kingdom

British Library Cataloguing in Publication Information Available

Library of Congress Cataloging-in-Publication Data

Exploring U2 : is this rock 'n' roll? : essays on the music, work, and influence of U2 / edited by Scott Calhoun.
    p. cm.
  Includes bibliographical references and index.
  ISBN 978-0-8108-8157-0 (cloth : alk. paper) — ISBN 978-0-8108-8158-7 (ebook)
  1. U2 (Musical group) 2. Rock music—Ireland—History and criticism. I. Calhoun, Scott.
  ML421.U2E97 2012
  782.42166092'2—dc23   2011026157

For Garilyn—thank you for
your hope, patience, and love along my way.

CONTENTS

Part II: Don't Expect, Suggest

Part III: Take This Soul

Part IV: When I Look at the World

Foreword: U2—Contents and Discontents

ANTHONY DECURTIS

THIS FOREWORD ORIGINATED AS MY KEYNOTE address at "U2: The Hype and the Feedback," a conference devoted to U2 at North Carolina Central University, Durham, October 2009. At their best, in my estimation, keynote addresses are more exhortatory than detailed analyses filled with scintillating insights. The real hard work, the carving out and defining of new directions and the reexamination and challenging of long-standing but perhaps wrong or no-longer-useful assumptions, occurs in panel presentations and discussions—and in the bar. Most certainly, in this case, in the bar. Keynotes should be exactly what the term denotes: the statement of a primary theme. It should serve as a reminder of why all have come together. It should be a statement of purpose and, in some broad sense, a call to action.

Sounding a keynote involves a certain amount of rediscovering the obvious. After all, on the most superficial level, all who attended the conference knew why we all had come there: to celebrate and explore the music and meaning of U2, a band that, for many of us, had been part of our lives for nearly thirty years and a significant source of pleasure and inspiration. The conference provided an opportunity to revivify that pleasure and re-energize that inspiration. And now this book arrives to document much of the good work that took place.

As in any decades-long relationship, it's easy to take our connection to and understanding of U2 for granted. As we all know, U2 rarely does anything in a quiet way, so whenever the band is active, we have plenty of opportunities to engage it. We can buy the music, see the videos, read the interviews, watch the television performances, and, as has been increasingly true in recent years, assess the ongoing success or failure of the group's elaborate marketing gambits—an aspect of U2's public identity that Bruce Springsteen hilariously punctured when he inducted the band into the Rock and Roll Hall of Fame in March 2005.

Referring with mock envy to U2's iPod ad, which featured the song "Vertigo" and for which the band did not take a fee, Springsteen remarked, "Smart, wily Irish guys. Anybody . . . anybody . . . can do an ad and take the money. But to do the ad and *not* take the money . . . that's smart. That's wily."

What Springsteen was getting at, what he was having fun with, is U2's tendency to walk right up to a line of ethical or political or aesthetic or musical compromise and dramatically fail to cross it. It is virtually a U2 hallmark to push everything as far as it can go but no further. It is one of the band's signatures to acknowledge and even respect a world in which total purity is impossible, in which keeping your hands perfectly clean is simply not feasible, but somehow to still remain refreshingly pure and clean. "Pure" and "clean" aren't words that the members of U2 would necessarily apply to themselves or their actions, but they are true nonetheless.

One of the obvious truths about U2 that I rediscovered in the course of preparing for the conference is how much has been written about the band. And a strange corollary of that for me was reencountering how much *I've* written about the band, beginning with a very enthusiastic review of *The Unforgettable Fire* for *Record* magazine in 1984. But as much as has been written about U2 and as much of it is strong, original, and varied, at least one theme emerges over the course of time: the sense of U2's bringing itself to a critical crossroads, with everything—the band's commercial viability, critical credibility, and moral standing—at stake.

Of course, at least some of that impression is the result of rock critic posturing: It gives a story a much greater sense of occasion if a writer can somehow define a story's peg as not merely the release of a new album but a make-or-break moment of truth for the band and all that it represents. U2's relentless sense of drama plays into this as well. Bono's sheer enthusiasm ensures that no U2 release will ever be merely quotidian. Beyond that, his hyperarticulate rendering of the band's aesthetic and personal motivations makes every album sound like a dramatic departure from its predecessors. Finally, the simple fact is that U2 has reinvented itself a number of times, pushed certain styles to the breaking point, and then switched directions. Each of those moves won new fans and disappointed others, got praised or pilloried by critics, and genuinely put some aspects of the band's ongoing success at risk.

The first crisis to confront U2 was the question of whether or not the band could live up to the scale of its audacious ambitions. Before U2 had ever performed in the United States and before the band's first album, *Boy*, was even released here, Bono told Jim Henke of *Rolling Stone*, "I don't mean to sound arrogant, but even at this stage, I do feel that we are meant to be one of the great groups. There's a certain spark, a certain chemistry, that was special about the Stones, the Who and the Beatles, and I think it's also special about U2." The story ended with Bono declaring, "It is my ambition to travel to America and give it what I consider it wants and needs."

"I don't mean to sound arrogant": oh, heaven forfend! That statement should probably be appended to all of Bono's public declarations, as he would likely be the first to admit. That story would hardly be the last time that Bono's mouth raised issues about U2's self-importance and position in the world—and it wouldn't be the last. But it called valuable attention to the band. Having your band written about in *Rolling Stone* under the semi-ironic headline "Here Comes the Next Big Thing" obviously incites certain expectations, as decades of artists blessed and cursed with the title of "New Dylan" can attest. But it also makes it impossible to be ignored, and it forces people to at least give a listen—a state of affairs that any band just starting out and desperate to be noticed would find desirable. That U2 was capable of cashing the check of Bono's claim is precisely what has made the band's excesses seem charming rather than off-putting over the years.

The release of *War* in 1983 generated more controversy. Addressing "the troubles" in Ireland—overtly but without really taking a hard stand, except in favor of peace—caused some to view the band as exploiting a subject that demanded a position on one side or the other of the Catholic-Protestant line. "This is not a rebel song," Bono would announce in introducing "Sunday Bloody Sunday," a song that referred in its very title to a 1972 attack by British soldiers on unarmed civil rights demonstrators in Northern Ireland. Bono waving a white flag that meant, what exactly, confused matters further—but only for anyone who genuinely cared. For most fans, particularly in the United States, the intricacies of Irish politics could not have seemed more remote from their lives. The flag and the declamatory, military-march drumming in "Sunday Bloody Sunday" were read as indicators of commitment, and the vagueness of their focus only allowed fans to sketch in whatever inchoate views and values they held important onto that blank white screen.

More meaningful, the pain, suffering, and frustration that everyone in Ireland felt came through palpably—and that emotion proved universal. "The trench is dug within our hearts / And mothers, children, brothers, sisters torn apart," Bono sang, and who could not relate to that? That Bono himself was the product of a mixed Catholic-Protestant marriage only lent the song greater poignancy. And, finally, there is the spirituality of the song: "The real battle yet begun / To claim the victory Jesus won." Again, it was a controversial declaration but one that proved reassuring to many listeners.

I confess to paying relatively little attention to U2 during those early years. I was living in Atlanta at the time and heard and liked the band's singles on WRAS-FM, the Georgia State University college radio station I listened to almost exclusively. I saw the band's evocative videos on the various fledgling cable video stations, including MTV, that kept popping up around that time, and I enjoyed those too. But I failed to listen to the albums closely and consequently missed important aspects of their depth and complexity. The brightness and surge of songs such as "I Will Follow" and "Gloria" made them immediately accessible to me, but as with U2's singles to this day, they weren't necessarily reflective of the full range of what the band had on its mind at the time. Today, *Boy* and to a lesser extent *October* are among my favorites of the band's albums. As with people, you know you're truly in love when an album's flaws only make you love the album more deeply—that's the way I feel about *Boy*. I hear other people's reservations about it, and I understand them and even occasionally agree. But their complaints have no impact whatsoever on my affection for it.

By 1983, *War* had come to define U2, and that's an album I still have trouble with—trouble that was even worse back then. As I mentioned, I was living in Georgia in the early eighties, which meant that I was obsessed with REM, whom I was able to see regularly and whom I came to know. At the time, the two bands seemed to have virtually nothing in common. While Bono was marching around onstage waving a flag at the end of a long pole, REM was doing shows in which the lighting design made it virtually impossible to even see the band.

REM also seemed at the head of some kind of American underground rock revival. Despite my long-standing Anglophilia—dating back to the Beatles and, beyond that, to my love for and study of centuries of English literature—anything from the United Kingdom seemed slightly suspect to me. While Bono was making pronouncements about U2 being one of the great bands like the Stones, the Who, and the Beatles and bringing America what it wants and needs, REM was putting out important singles, such as "Radio Free Europe" back with "Sitting Still," on which none of the bands members could even bring himself to look directly into the camera for the cover photo shoot.

I was much more drawn to the vagueness and mystery of REM's sound, as opposed to what I heard as the sonic bluster of U2. Two album titles—*War, Murmur*—say it all. At the time, Michael Stipe was essentially helping to invent a new persona for lead singers—the reluctant rock star, the front man for whom getting onstage seemed a kind of torment or at least embarrassment, as if you could just incidentally, through no fault, motivation, or reason of your own, mysteriously find yourself the leader of a rock band, standing onstage in front of adoring fans. It was a stance that he would eventually abandon—and how!—but that for better or worse would go on to be enormously influential to this day. Bono, meanwhile, was dangling off the rafters at the Us Festival, doing whatever he could or had to do to win U2 an audience.

I had occasion to discuss some of these issues with the Edge when I went off to Dublin and London in 1987 to do my first big story on U2—a *Rolling Stone* cover pegged to the release of *The Joshua Tree.* One late night when the interviews were over and I was out to dinner with the Edge, Adam Clayton, Paul McGuinness, and various other friends of the band, the Edge and I, over whiskey and cigars, got on the subject of other bands. I brought up REM, and he seemed intrigued but mystified. He would never have put it in these terms, but he identified what might be regarded as a failure of nerve in REM. He seemed particularly perplexed by Stipe and his reluctant rock star posture. It reminded me of a conversation I read about between John Lennon and Brian Jones and Keith Richards of the Rolling Stones in the early sixties in which Lennon pointed at each of them and said, "You're OK, and you're OK," but expressed, shall we say, doubts about Mick Jagger and what he would later describe as Jagger's "fag dancing."

Characteristically, the Edge was not nearly as acerbic as Lennon, nor were his views as harsh. But in the way that bands are inevitably dependent on their front men, the Edge clearly viewed Bono as the man who could deliver U2 where it needed to go, and he clearly viewed the band's job as giving Bono the confidence to say and do everything that he felt he needed to do to get them there. To get up onstage and be reluctant about what you're doing there seemed to make no sense to him, an absolute contradiction in terms. Plus, the Edge had probably had enough of reluctance on his own side of the pond, with the dozens of punk and postpunk UK bands who were condescending about going to America and doing the hard work necessary to become successful there, while U2 was desperate to prove that it could play on the same big stage as all its idols.

What I would only come to understand later—and what has become clear to the world at large—is how many similarities there are between U2 and REM and how many there were even in the early eighties. Far from being bombastic, *Boy* and *October* are searching and complex albums, as shrouded in shadows as anything REM was doing at the time. While REM was never as determined as U2 to become a commercially successful band, a great deal of ambition was concealed within the group's seeming diffidence. Both bands represented a refreshing blast of optimism in a cynical time, and both went to great lengths to achieve whatever they could entirely on their own terms.

And they would, of course, go on to become great friends and mutual admirers. Peter Buck has credited Bono with revealing to him the secret of successful child care: two nannies. And it was clear how much things had changed in the world when Bono, who was just beginning to spend a considerable amount of time in New York, confided to me that Michael Stipe had been essential to introducing him to the city and its innumerable aspects. He spoke in awe of Stipe's confidence, connections, and social grace and described himself, in comparison, as fumbling and inept as he sought to become a New Yorker.

After *War*, U2's next controversial move, of course, was choosing to work with Brian Eno and Daniel Lanois on *The Unforgettable Fire*. This was the moment when I got fully involved with U2. Bono has talked about how Eno initially met with the band to explain how he didn't want to work with it. However, like so many people who walked into a room with Bono thinking one thing only to leave thinking exactly the opposite, Eno has now been working with the band for a quarter century.

But for fans who loved the more muscular U2 of *War*, *The Unforgettable Fire* was a abrupt departure—and a disappointing one at that. But "Pride (In the Name of Love)" proved enough to keep many of those fans engaged, and, of course, U2's live shows continued to be riots of energy, celebration, and emotion. And, of course, *The Joshua Tree* would come

along a few years later and raise the band to the level of superstars. In suc-
ceeding years, many more moments came for which some fans lost faith
and others climbed on board. The media onslaught of *Rattle and Hum*—a
film! an album!—alienated some fans. It seemed as if, having gotten big,
U2 did not know when to stop.

In my view, *Achtung Baby* and the Zoo TV tour represent the pinnacle
of U2's career. At that point, the band managed to reinvent its sound, reinvent not only its own live shows but many aspects of live performance
in general, and shed its image as dour do-gooders without succumbing to
silliness. The Zoo TV tour is the only one in my experience that got better
as it got bigger. When I first saw the show at Madison Square Garden, it
was great, but both the performances and the ideas seemed cramped, too
big for the space. Later, at Giants Stadium and on the Zooropa tour to
follow, both fully flowered. The concerts were fun, smart, and completely
exhilarating.

As they had with *Rattle and Hum*, however, U2 overshot the mark
with *Pop*. It's as if the band had taken as its motto one of William Blake's
"Proverbs of Hell": "Enough, or too much!" It's one thing to explore
ideas of media and mass culture as the band did with Zoo TV and *Zooropa*;
it's quite another to attempt to celebrate its most meretricious aspects as
the band seemed to be trying to do with *Pop* and the PopMart tour that
followed. If you've built an entire career radiating caring, hope, and optimism, it's a dangerous business to suddenly be trading in irony and detach-
ment. Was this the reward, fans wondered, for having believed?

All this might have been forgiven had the album been stronger musically. But as the band has subsequently revealed, a tour had been arranged
before the album was completed, and recording was ultimately rushed. To
this day, *Pop* sounds unfinished—though Bono, whose commitment to the
Pop project never faltered, has insisted in his inimitable rhetorical way that
the songs were completed on the road. Whatever. The album and tour left
a bad taste in the mouths of many fans.

So the next moment of reckoning came with *All That You Can't Leave
Behind*—a title that in many ways speaks eloquently for itself. To a great
degree, Zoo TV, *Zooropa*, *Pop*, and PopMart were projects that attempted
to create art out of excess and indulgence—often successfully. They were
conceptual gambits, ultimately about their ideas. In contrast, *All That You
Can't Leave Behind* was about essences, about songs.

I had occasion to spend a few days with Bono as the band was working
on that album. I was writing an article, one of the first, for *Rolling Stone*
about his efforts to have impoverished countries relieved of their debts

to wealthy nations. We spent a few days together in Washington, DC, in conference rooms saturated with fluorescent light and in dingy hotel bars. When we entered the well-worn lobby of the hotel where we were staying, Bono turned to the woman accompanying him from Principle Management and said, only half-jokingly, "If the next album doesn't do well, we're always going to stay in hotels like this."

Between his meetings with African finance ministers and White House officials, Bono and I talked about U2. Jimmy Iovine, the head of Interscope Records and one of U2's producers, had been talking to the band members about, among other things, doing more promotion when their new album came out. Bono, an enthusiastic and talented mimic, re-created the truculent whine of Iovine's New York accent as he rendered their dialogue.

> *Iovine:* Look at the rappers, they're not afraid to get out there when they have something to sell.
>
> *Bono:* Well, we do as much as we can.
>
> *Iovine:* Yeah, but I don't have to tell them. They *want* to do it.

I thought about that conversation when *All That You Can't Leave Behind* came out and Bono sang about (U2's being?) "The last of the rock stars / When hip-hop drove the big cars."

Bono also described a conversation with Iovine about sequencing the order of songs on the album—a vexing problem for every band and particularly for ones as obsessive as U2. As Bono was describing his grand theory of sequencing, Iovine interrupted him: "You want to know how to sequence an album? You take the best song, and you put that one first. You take the second-best song—that's next. The third-best song? Third. Fourth-best song? That goes fourth." And so on. Again, without getting too reductive or overthinking it, that isn't a bad description of the way that the songs on *All That You Can't Leave Behind* are sequenced.

As we were saying good-bye at the airport, Bono described to me how the album would be about songs, and he sang a few verses of what I think was "Beautiful Day." He asked me what I thought. What are you supposed to say? "Actually, I'd alter that image a bit—it's not really working." Not likely. He also told me that the Edge had returned to some streamlined guitar sounds that he hadn't used since the band's earliest albums. That all sounded good to me.

All That You Can't Leave Behind restored a great deal of faith in U2, and it turned out to be the perfect album for the cataclysm that would arrive not long after its release: the terrorist attacks on September 11, 2001. I had gotten married on September 8, 2001, a gorgeous Saturday in upstate New York, and U2 had sent a case of champagne and a case of Guinness to the reception. Earlier that summer, Bono had dedicated a brief version of "Unchained Melody" to my wife and me at a show in Albany, New York. So, along with being a native New Yorker who was preparing to leave for his honeymoon on the morning the planes hit my beloved home-town, U2 is extremely bound up in my feelings about that day, the worst day of my life.

When U2 came to town to play Madison Square Garden not long after September 11, the city was still reeling. "Walk On" had, quite ap-propriately, become one of the anthems of the city's resilience and survival. During the band's performance, in a magnificent gesture, the names of all the victims of the September 11 attacks scrolled on the video screens. After the show, at a reception for the band, Bono told me that some people had advised the group not to run that scroll, that the city's feelings were still too raw, that it might be seen as exploitative. In fact, it was a bold and perfect gesture, exactly what the city needed, and it was gratefully received and appreciated. Everyone in the audience was moved.

When Bruce Springsteen first played New York after releasing *The Rising*, he opened his show by simply saying, "How are you doing? I've been thinking about you." New Yorkers wanted to feel precisely that—an assurance from the artists they loved that the city was in their hearts and on their minds. U2 and Bruce Springsteen are at the top of that list, and they were quite possibly the only artists at that time who had the moral and emotional standing to speak so directly about an experience that ripped into the city's soul.

In the decade since then, U2 has continued its process of upping the stakes, making risky—or wily—moves, and still managing to come out on top. I love "Vertigo" but wasn't crazy about *How to Dismantle an Atomic Bomb*—another album that seemed unfinished to me. I didn't much like "Get On Your Boots" but very much enjoyed *No Line on the Horizon*, which seems unfinished to me in the right way, a way reminiscent of *The Unforgettable Fire*. Of course, *No Line on the Horizon*, like everything else these days, hasn't sold as well as I'm sure U2 hoped it would. And as I'm writing this, Bono and the Edge's score for director Julie Taymor's Broadway musical

Spider-Man: Turn Off the Dark has embroiled U2, if only indirectly, in yet another make-or-break proposition.

Characteristically, though, U2 is still insisting on playing on the big stage—both literally and figuratively. Regardless of your preferences for this or that album, this or that song, U2 has done some great work in this decade—arguably more great work than any other band at its level. When *Greatest Hits + B Sides 2000–2010* arrives, as it inevitably will, that set will be able to stand credibly alongside its two predecessors. Along with the music, Bono, as everyone knows, has become a philanthropic activist of international importance.

For all these reasons, U2 is the perfect band for what we hope may still become the age of Obama. They remain inspirational figures, beacons of hope in impossible times. Their belief that divisions can be bridged by the strength of rhetoric and vision confounds the frustration that we sometimes feel with the band. Despite all the temptations to succumb to cynicism, the members of U2 continue to believe that we can be better people and that we can build a better world. Their music, even the beautiful, ghostly atmospherics of *No Line on the Horizon*, continues to be a call to action— action in the world and action in the fertile realms of our imaginations. For this band, there truly is no line on the horizon—no line between Earth and sky, between young and old, between the fates of the poorest and the richest, between who we are and who we aspire to be.

The last time I interviewed Bono was about four years ago for one of the fortieth-anniversary issues of *Rolling Stone*. When I appeared at the door of his New York apartment, I surprised him. The interview was supposed to have been done by *Time* columnist, Harvard professor, political consultant, and Irish firebrand Samantha Power.

I have no idea what happened with her schedule, but when I sat bleary-eyed that morning at my computer after rising brain-numbingly early with my then-twenty-month-old daughter Francesca, I opened an e-mail from *Rolling Stone* that simply read, "Can you interview Bono at 11:00 this morning?" My reply was equally direct: "Oh, absolutely." I sometimes joke about certain artists that you could wake me up in the middle of the night and ask me to interview them and I'd be able to do it without the slightest problem. I never thought I would have to test the truth of that claim, but this time, with Bono, was as close as I've ever gotten.

Bono emerged bleary-eyed himself. I noticed four champagne flutes on his coffee table from the night before, which likely explained the problem. I greeted him with the words, "No fancy Harvard professors for you. You'll never escape the music press!"

We embraced and caught up a bit. He seemed genuinely pleased to hear that I had become a father. He asked if he could give my daughter a gift. Once again, what do you say? He went and got a copy of the edition of *Peter and the Wolf* that he had illustrated as part of a collaboration with his old running buddy Gavin Friday.

Because my daughter's birthday is Christmas Eve, Bono drew a large Christmas tree on the bottom of the page. Then he wrote her a message that says a lot about him and U2. I took it to heart, and I hope that one day, when she's older, Francesca will too, for its honesty, simplicity, and openheartedness.

"Francesca, welcome to Planet Earth," he wrote. "There's so much for you to do." Turn off the dark, indeed.

Acknowledgments

THIS COLLECTION OF CHAPTERS IS LIKE A LEAF on a branch of a tree planted, what feels like, long ago. I have been cultivated by many gardeners, which in turn brought about the creation of the U2 conference and these resulting contributions. U2 itself, of course, is a sort of rootstock nourishing the development of its fans—through delights and provocations—only a few of which are presented here between these covers. And for U2, I am thankful. With regard to this specific leaf, this book, whatever strengths and welcomed expressions of the tree there are here are the result of the labors of the following growers, to whom I'm grateful.

I am indebted to Amanda Satta for her brilliant work and enthusiastic help with editing and preparing the manuscript during a school year, which for her was full of many important projects and enticing diversions. I wish to thank my first-year seminar and American literature students for their patience and goodwill. Thank you to Monique Muncy as well, for her administrative support. Thank you to Donald Deardorff, Kelley Eskridge, Dara Fraley, Tim Frame, Stephen Judge, Ben Kouba, Sherry Lawrence, Alan Light, Beth Maynard, Matt McGee, Robert Milliman, Angela Pancella, Misty Phillips, and Robert Winn for their work in helping create the conference where these works were first shared. I am exceedingly grateful for Bennett Graff at Scarecrow Press for accepting this project and guiding it with his humane professionalism to its completion. I thank Christen Karniski at Scarecrow as well, for her assistance and expertise. Thank you to all my contributors, of course—with a special thanks to Anthony DeCurtis and Neil McCormick for their writings, and to David Butgereit, who contributed his enthusiasm. I appreciate the help that Beth

Maynard, Marylinn Maione, and Arlan Hess gave in reviewing the bibli-ography. Many thanks to Garilyn, Madeline, Lillian, Emily, Vivian, and Rose for the sacrifices you made, whether you knew it or not, so I could finish this work.

I wish to thank Principle Management for fielding my questions and being of assistance for both the conference and this book. And I cannot offer enough thanks to the entire staff behind the superb website @U2 and its affiliate sites for their camaraderie and integrity and for being the best resource on this planet for all things U2.

Introduction

SCOTT CALHOUN

To be a thing of study or not to be . . . I doubt that question is on the mind of any rock band when meeting up for the first day of practice. It has to be one of the least compelling reasons for forming a band, and, anyway, it seems a lot of what motivates someone to get into rock 'n' roll isn't governed by a mental process at all. Even one thousand gigs later, the goal for most groups is to stay together, keep making music, and hold on to fans. Does a point ever come when someone looks up and says, "I hope there will be a book or two that takes a serious look at what we've done. Then, maybe some brave college will offer a class on us. And who knows, maybe there will be a whole conference about us?" Once in a while, for a few acts, it must sink in that they have altered the course of things . . . but who would actually speak the thought?

Cue Bono, and cue him well in advance of U2's one-thousandth gig.

Late in 1980, as the plastic in U2's first album was cooling, Bono said to Jim Henke at *Rolling Stone*, "I don't mean to sound arrogant, but at this stage, I do feel that we are meant to be one of the great groups. There's a certain spark, a certain chemistry, that was special about the Stones, the Who, and the Beatles, and I think it's also special about U2." Henke heard Bono's humility but recognized his confidence all the same. What he heard in U2's music was proof enough to call it "a band to be reckoned with" and for *Rolling Stone* to title its February 19, 1981, profile of U2, "Here Comes the 'Next Big Thing.'" In Bono's estimation of what U2 was meant to be, we hear what has propelled U2 to be what it has become. It's the sound of a dreamer with both feet on the ground, reaching for the sky. Henke heard it; I hear it; we hear it too, as have millions by now. In

U2, both then and now, we hear the sound of humans who have not given up; we hear songs of great expectations.

While becoming a thing of study was not one of U2's stated goals, joining the ranks of the Beatles was. Along the way, U2 moved through the last thirty-five years with a disruptive force such that when critics, analysts, historians, and academics examine the history of popular music and culture, they find that U2 matters. There have been serious books about U2, and its work has been brought into the classroom. U2 has become a topic of study. Many academic gatherings examine the types and nuances of popular music, of course, and there have been symposiums or conferences dedicated to just the Beatles, Bob Dylan, the Grateful Dead, and Bruce Springsteen. Now, there has been a conference about U2, from whence the chapters in this book came. Here we are again, dancing, so to speak, about architecture. But in this case, we are responding to what Springsteen called "some of the most beautiful sonic architecture in rock and roll" when he inducted U2 into the Rock and Roll Hall of Fame. I wonder if just as Bono's early self-assuredness now sounds as prescient as it still sounds unsettling, he did not also think that someday people will explore his band's music, work, and influence to see what it has done.

U2 lived up to the hype surrounding *Boy*, its debut album, and the story of its popular and critical success in the 1980s is now well known. Scholarly interest was scant until the mid-1990s, when academic papers began appearing. A few things coalesced early in the twenty-first century to create what is now called the field of U2 studies. First, Bono began spending a good deal of his undeniable rock-star capital on humanitarian and philanthropic issues. He was appearing at the White House, the Vatican, G8 meetings, Davos with the world's economic leaders, on a bus tour through the American Midwest, and on your church's video screens. If you missed seeing him on the evening news, you were reminded of his influence every time you saw another white ONE bracelet on the wrist of a hand toggling a Product (Red) iPod or holding a cup of Starbucks Product (RED) coffee. Even if you tried to avoid U2, perhaps because of what it did to you after *The Joshua Tree*, its front man was unavoidable. And then U2, knowing a lot of its fans tuned them out in the 1990s, brought many of them back with *All That You Can't Leave Behind* and memorable, moving post-9/11 concerts, such as at Madison Square Garden and the 2002 Super Bowl halftime show.

Second, thoughtful fans and academics were gaining perspective on the 1990s and could appreciate U2's leap from hugely successful band of the '80s to extraordinary early '90s phenomenon in and of popular culture and the nascent digital entertainment industry. Not only was U2 producing culture but its product was a delicious, intelligent critique of the inherent limitations of a consumer-centric approach to life and the "stuff" we turn to for satisfaction. All of this intrigued students, teachers, and critics enough to put their thoughts in writing that began to appear outside the mainstream music press. As university departments were formed around culture studies, what had been the side projects of teachers and scholars working in traditional, mainstream disciplines found new audiences and new legitimacy as valuable inquiries into the popular art a society makes. The questions of culture studies were not new, but the places in which academics were finding freedom to search for answers were no longer regarded as temporal, ephemeral, or otherwise void of the human experience.

The path to being what Bono called "one of the great groups" entails, as it must, mastering the conventions of rock 'n' roll, which paradoxically includes learning how to reject something of rock's tradition so you can establish a new chapter in its history. Your chapter, your transformation of the form while you carry it with you, becomes the template for not only what will be your own future but also for what all subsequent contenders will want to leave in the past. The next band wishing to be among the greats will need to master rock 'n' roll as it is now, because of what you've done, and then learn how to reject something of it. When done excellently, such a band becomes an inevitable reference for all future bands, as U2 is, and frustrates the young creatives into rebelliously refreshing the form. After all, rock 'n' roll is, as Bono will quip from time to time, the sound of revenge.

What U2 has done excellently is advance into its own better future as it took us into ours. They will joke, sometimes quite seriously, that they came from nowhere, with no musical roots, no pedigree, no skill. No past; just future. Improvement should come easily to a band starting with so little, then, but to the extent this was really true for U2, its deficits were mostly unapparent for its surplus of determination to be a band and its love for performing live. It's written somewhere in U2's DNA the unshakeable conviction that where there is not, there can be through the collective efforts of those who want it and are willing to work for it. It's an amoral approach to life in itself, and U2 has chosen to want and work for the good. When the band takes the stage, its faith in the collective becomes animated by the possibility of its exponential growth, motivating U2 to want to turn whatever despair or longing is the room into a mobilizing hope. When Henke was in England in 1980 to see U2, Bono told him, "We're playing to an audience in Britain that ranges in age from seventeen to twenty-five.

There is massive unemployment, and there is real disillusionment. U2's music is about getting up and doing something about it." It has been this emphasis throughout U2's career that has inspired many of its fans to work toward improving the worlds they live in. U2 has engendered a loyalty in listeners that goes beyond following tours from town to town or claiming one of the four band members as a favorite.

The loyalty can sometimes get mistaken for a kind of mania or fanaticism because, I think, it's so rare for a rock band to have such a powerful hold on so many people at one time. And speaking of time, it's extremely rare for a rock band to last ten years with its original lineup, let alone for over thirty-five years, as U2 has. (Or consider this: To date, U2 has been performing with an unchanged lineup for about half of the entire history of rock 'n' roll.) When I was interviewed about the inaugural U2 conference in 2009, the well-intentioned reporter called me a U2 obsessive for what I think he saw as my taking fandom to an unusual level. The term struck me as suggesting I had an unhealthy interest in the subject and might benefit from seeing someone about it. But we all have our obsessions, and I've heard the term in play more frequently since, with regard to interests academic and personal. My obsession, if that's what it is, comes from finding in U2's music what I find in other artists who address the grand topics of life at the levels of both the bold and sublime. At any rate, I think the reporter didn't quite know what else to call me.

A few books in recent years have taken up U2 as an occasion for philosophical or spiritual explorations, and within their aims they have enriched their conversations by bringing U2's lyrics, mainly, to bear on aspects of the human condition. This book presents views from diverse disciplines and professions, which I believe not only helps us learn more about what U2 has done, to date, but also helps us imagine the next questions we could ask of U2's work and of ourselves. These essays were first shared in Durham, North Carolina, either as a part of the conference program or in the conversations obsessives tend to have when gathered for such a weekend. From the many excellent presentations, I selected what I thought would show the angles from which students, scholars, critics, and fans explore U2. I also knew these presentations were new, unpublished attempts, in part or in whole, to understand something about U2. Even as I finished that last sentence I winced a little, because U2 is best understood in decibels and LED lights seen through fog machines, not by reading a book. Still, what happens after listening to a U2 album or attending a concert is just as real as the music itself, and U2's fans know that things have changed for the better because of U2. What makes this happen, why and how it happens, and how U2 has become so good at doing it are the guiding questions here. In this book, I feel I am in the good company of obsessives, and it is a delight to present them as furthering the field of U2 studies.

Though U2 is, without a doubt, a rock band and is best experienced as such, it is also more than rock 'n' roll, of course. As is the case with U2's work within the form, the band has redefined the role of the rock star and the rock show such that we do well to ask, "Is *this* rock 'n' roll?" Anthony DeCurtis's keynote address from the conference opened this exploration, noting from his estimable vantage point U2's unique substance and ways of frustrating the rock paradigm. As many of the conversations went at the conference, so the following chapters ask big questions and seek with objectivity to say something equally big. Some of those doing the talking here are fans unattached to an academy, while others work as scholars, teachers, critics, or clergy. All fit the description of intellectually curious fans who were sufficiently obsessive about U2 to come to a conference about what Henke once described as "pop music with brains."

Of course, as Neil McCormick said at the end of his chapter on how Dublin's forces formed U2, "It's not the whole story. You can read this whole book, and you will never get the whole story. But there's truth in it all the same." So a book such as this can only take us closer to the whole story. The following sixteen chapters help do that by exploring what shaped U2 and how U2 shapes listeners; how some of U2's best-known performances and signature aesthetics have evolved, along with the creation of its brand; the spiritual dimension in U2's repertoire and live performances; and how U2 has introduced its great expectations into contemporary cultural dialogues. A bibliography indicates how small the U2 studies library still is, and though it is a good beginning, it is not enough for gaining a critical understanding of the past thirty-five years of U2's art, activism, and achievements. I hope this book supplies some answers but is more effective at raising new questions and starting a few conversations for you. I hope it is not long before your voice is in the sound.

EIGHTEEN YEARS OF DAWNING   I

Boy to Man
A Dublin-Shaped Band

1

NEIL MCCORMICK

S O HERE I GO AGAIN, writing about U2.

In 2009, I was invited to address the first U2 academic conference, which I accepted with some reservations. For one thing, I'm not an academic. I'm an art school dropout who played in a rock band and wound up as a music critic, more by accident than design. For another thing, I'm not strictly a fan of U2, at least not in the obsessive sense of fandom so prevalent in pop culture.

So the very idea of talking about U2 to a room full of academic U2 fans was intimidating because, I figured, most of them would probably know more about U2 than I did. That's no joke. I've had too many conversations with U2 fans either expressing surprise at my lack of familiarity with obscure B-sides or peppering the conversation with lyrical references that fly right over my head. For a lot of dedicated fans (and I guess you'd have to be pretty dedicated to turn up at a conference in Durham, North Carolina), their appreciation of U2 forms a significant and even central part of their lives. For me, U2 has been more of a background to my life. Crucially, it is not a group I chose for myself; it more or less chose me. We went to school together; I watched the band form; I saw the members rehearse; I witnessed their gradual yet astonishing transformation from ramshackle teenage band to white-hot sci-fi rock group, all the way to the stadium-busting superstars they are today. I love them because they formed my prime musical experience. I love them almost despite myself, like you love your family and friends: unequivocally yet not without reservation.

My unique qualification when it comes to U2 is that I was there, and I still am here. That's been a blessing and a curse, as anyone who has read my memoir *Killing Bono* will know. I wrote a book about my dismal musical career struggling in the shadows of superstardom, and Bono liked it so much that he asked me to write U2's own book. So just when I thought I had exorcised all my angst about being Bono's doppelganger, I spent two years as his ghostwriter, helping put together the autobiography *U2 by U2*. U2 is the group I cannot escape, even if I tried. Not that I try too hard.

Which is all a slightly long-winded way to explain why I chose to address the conference on how growing up in Dublin in the 1970s shaped U2. Because that's the bit that I could guarantee that I knew better than anyone else in the room, because I was there, growing up with them.

As a band, U2 has many more dimensions than what the stereotypical flag-waving, lighters-aloft image allows. It can be epic and intimate, political and emotional, embracing high art and low culture. U2 is a confusing group, and I mean that as a compliment. For some critics, U2 is pompous and overblown, representing a rock nadir, the triumph of the blockbuster tendency over rock's primal roots, yet there is a stranger, more subterranean side to the band with a streak of dark irony that mocks such simplistic criticism. It is hardly surprising that the band represents so many different and often completely contrasting things to different people. During the conference, I listened to Stephen Catanzarite's lecture about the "conservative voice in U2," discussing *Achtung Baby* as "a metaphor for the fall of man" (you can discover his views for yourself elsewhere in this book). Despite the conviction that he brought to his arguments, the whole thing sounded so ludicrous that it just seemed to me an example of how, when it comes to music, people hear what they want to hear. But then I spoke to Bono, and while I was having some fun at Stephen's expense, Bono remarked, "Both theories sound bang on."

So if we hear what we want to hear, this is what I hear when I listen to U2: I hear the greatest rock band of our times—the most modern in terms of the way that it drags the primal musical template of the sixties into new sonic terrain, the most creatively ambitious in the way that it constantly endeavors to keep its sound and artistic focus evolving, the most politically bold in the ways that it attempts to use commercial popularity for a greater good, and the most emotionally and spiritually sincere in the way that it tries to make rock that is bigger and more meaningful than the band members themselves could ever be as individuals. They have had an extraordinary career, and one of the most extraordinary things about it (possibly even unique, in the history of popular music) is that there is only one U2. The same four individuals that make up the band now were all present at the first, fateful gathering in 1976.

There is a particular dynamic to the personalities that constitute U2, a kind of internally strong, beautifully balanced yet somehow fluid form that facilitates both change and consistency. When I was working on *U2 by U2*, I came up with the idea of the band as a diamond configuration, although the actual geometry is suspect and certainly more complex. But here goes: Bono is the vertical point of the diamond, stretching out front, which is where you have always been able to find him. You don't need me to tell you that he is an incredible character. He was already a bit of a star in the corridors of Mount Temple, when he was known as Paul Hewson. He was the kind of boy people wanted to know, with lots of young acolytes and hangers-on. Bono has many layers: an intense curiosity, a huge appetite (for food, ideas, people, life), a passion that can veer toward rage, and a speedy, explosive creativity that contains within it a kind of restless overexcitement and impatience (every new idea is always the greatest idea), bundled with the egotism of someone who believes that he can make a difference yet counterbalanced by a strong sense of humor (he is a funny guy) with qualities of loyalty and humility—for a rock star, Bono pays a lot of attention to the feelings of other people. Bono is the psyche of U2: he gives the band much of its complexity of character; he drives it forward by leading the way (often recklessly) as it charges over the edge because he himself cannot stop going forward. His restlessness comes, I think, from a secret fear of repose. There is a black hole in Bono that is the very engine of U2, one that dates back to the sense of loss and injustice that overwhelmed him with the death of his mother when he was fourteen years old.

Let's shift to another point of the diamond: the Edge. Clearly, he is the musical genius in U2, not just because he is the most talented musician in the band, but because he has a particular way of hearing sounds and looking into musical patterns and finding something unique to him. And then, rather crucially, he has the analytic curiosity and scientific bent to discover ways of capturing this unique vision, along with the Zen-like patience required to really work things through to the last detail. His quality of calm, studious focus makes him an ideal counterweight to Bono's more immediate and explosive creativity. Those two are the Lennon and McCartney of U2, although possibly even better matched than John and Paul in that their collaboration is not poisoned by competitive rivalry. They might have been a productive musical partnership whoever else was in the band with them, which is not to diminish the roles of the people who actually are in the band.

Larry Mullen Jr. is the bottom point of my diamond, on which everything balances. Bono once described him to me as "the brakes in U2," but his point was that you need brakes when the rocket is veering wildly off course. Larry is a guy who likes to say no, who needs to be convinced of the worth of an idea (in many respects: artistically, financially, morally) before he will commit to it, although once committed, he is 100 percent in. For me, Larry is a complicated character who masquerades as a simple one. He sometimes says that he plays drums because he likes hitting things, but the underlying question might be exactly why he likes hitting things. He has a need to express himself as great as Bono's, which springs from a similar sense of loss (Larry's mother also died when he was a teenager) but to which he responds in a buttoned-down manner. Larry is conservative in a nonpolitical sense: he wants to keep the world, or at least his world, tightly in control. He is really the yang to Bono's yin—if I can mix up my geometrical balancing forces. Where Larry expresses himself most fully is behind a drumkit.

And then there's Adam, which is where my diamond analogy falls apart. He's a kind of wandering point in U2, which members themselves often refer to as their wild card. This sometimes refers to his playing, which, in the early days especially, was untutored in a way that led to the band's adjusting around him, which in itself created a unique musical character, his bass lines forcing his fellow musicians to react in unexpected ways. But everything about Adam, his urbane personality and sense of style, seemed different in the early days to most Dublin teenagers, which helped define and shape the personality and originality of U2. Here was a teenage boy who turned up on his first day at a new school wearing a hippy-style afghan coat and a yellow workman's helmet. For Adam, it was always kind of *rock stardom or nothing!* and back at the beginning of things, his ambition gave the band a sense of purpose and direction. Although his role has changed over the years, he acts as a kind of social lubricant, a man whose polite, easygoing ways and instinct for conflict resolution make the functioning of this complex dynamic possible.

So actually I am not sure what shape that makes. I tried looking it up, but all I could come up with is some kind of unstable nonequilateral four-sided polygon. Just as it is nonequilateral, it is not quite equal either. Conceptually, Bono is the leader of U2; musically, the Edge is the leader. But U2 has a democratic band structure in that everyone has a vote and everyone has the right of veto, but, as Larry is wont to point out, it's a democracy in which some votes count more than others. Perhaps some voices are just louder than others.

The rise of U2 is a great rock-and-roll story, and like most such stories, it has become distorted by time and retelling. Bono in particular is a storyteller, a mythmaker, a very unreliable narrator. Working with the band on *U2 by U2*, I constantly had to check his timeline of events and research his quotes. We ran ino a bit of a problem with a beautiful and elegant Nietzsche quote: "The night is even darker than the day knows but joy is deeper than despair, because joy seeks eternity." I had the Nietzeshe society delving into the philosopher's most arcane corners, only to declare that he never said any such thing, despite being an elegant summation of an aspect of Nietzschean philosophy. So maybe we can all look forward to a new philosophical treatise someday: *Thus Spake Bono*.

He is also rather fond of declaring, "As Sam Shepard said, 'Right in the center of a contradiction, that's the place to be.'" He sometimes expands it to "That's where the energy is, that's where the heat is." Only it turns out that all Sam Shepard said was something like "Contradiction is interesting." I told Bono that he could stop attributing this to the great American playwright and claim it for himself. But it may be too late, as it turns up everywhere now as a Shepard quote, whose source is . . . Bono.

At any rate, contradiction is an interesting place to be, and it is certainly where U2 resides. "I have read a lot of rubbish about U2," Larry told me while I was working on the book. "Sometimes when I see us described in some mythic sense or called corporate masters of our own destiny, I have to laugh out loud. Being in U2 is more like riding a runaway train, hanging on to it for dear life." Larry's point is that U2 was not preordained. It's easy to look back at the story and think that A followed B followed C and that it was all as it was meant to be. Bands are often great believers in destiny, usually because they have fulfilled theirs. They set out with the intention to become rock stars, and lo, it comes to pass. From the point of view of anyone who hasn't had it quite so easy, it can seem a somewhat egotistic belief, but I suspect that the notion actually serves quite a healthy function in terms of ego—a belief in fate, destiny, or a higher power shifting responsibility for everything that happens, from the self to some outside force. I am not sure if U2 believes in destiny, but it certainly believes in God. Personally, I prefer to think of a band's formation, growth, original-ity, and success (or not) as a process of unfolding accident allied to creative evolution. Some of it comes from the individuals; some of it comes from outside forces; and combined, it owes much of its impetus to that rather dreadful and horribly overused pop culture term *zeitgeist*, creating the right thing, in the right place, at the right time to give the world what it doesn't even know it needs. And somehow the circumstances in our little school in Dublin in the 1970s were primed to make this group of individuals coalesce in a special way and give them the tools to conquer the world.

Dublin has changed a lot since we were growing up there, some of it for the better, some for the worse. After the economic boom years of the Celtic Tiger (in which the success of U2 certainly played a part), the explosive growth of the 1980s and 1990s, the triumphs of the political peace process, and the boost of creative confidence in the nation's psyche, the country of Ireland seemed so transformed that, to me at least, it became barely recognizable. When I returned from my new home in London to visit family and friends, I found myself getting lost, confused by all the new roads and buildings. Indeed, when a film was made of my book *Killing Bono*, filmmakers shot most of it in Belfast, because they thought that the rather smaller, poorer Northern Irish city looked more like Dublin in the seventies than Dublin itself did. But then came the global economic crisis of the first decade of the twenty-first century, in which the bubble of Irish prosperity burst so spectacularly that it had to be bailed out by the European Union and the International Monetary Fund. With collapsed property prices, rising unemployment, and crippling national debt, the capital city is almost becoming, once again, the Dublin I called home.

Ireland was a poor country in the seventies, the poorest nation in Western Europe. It was also a small and insulated country. It was not culturally mixed—the population was almost 100 percent white and over 95 percent Catholic (in the southern republic at least, with the British territory of Northern Ireland being very different and very separate). And in many ways, it was a repressed country, partly because there was little separation between church and state. The Catholic lobby was massive and powerful in ways that we now know (and, to be honest, suspected even then) led to a great deal of horrific abuse. There was no divorce, no (legal) homosexuality, no pornography—no sex basically, or at least that's how it often seemed to frustrated teenagers. Most primary school education was left to the Christian Brothers and the nuns, and in the experience of many, it could be pretty brutal and almost unbelievably ignorant. I had girlfriends who had been taught that they should spread a newspaper on a boy's lap before sitting on his knee; otherwise, they might fall pregnant.

I don't want to paint exaggerated pictures of poverty, neglect, and abuse, however. I loved growing up in Ireland, but even in our teens, my friends and I understood that it was not a fundamentally modern country. Unemployment was high, and the prospects for young people were not good. Emigration was so entrenched that it was said that the country's population was shrinking every year. Mostly young people headed off to Britain in search of jobs, which was just a ferry ride across the Irish Sea, but there was also huge traffic to the promised land of America and much talk of how to get a precious green card. The Irish diaspora reached out to most corners of the world, and it was commonly held that there were more Irish people living outside of Ireland than within it. A 2000 US census found forty-one million Americans claiming to be wholly or partly of Irish descent, one in five of the white American population. Meanwhile, there were only around three million Irish in Ireland. This meant that there was two-way traffic with the world, with people coming home for Christmas and holidays and bringing news from outside, but there was also a kind of void in the country, with generation after generation leaving. It meant that we were always looking to the outside, in particular to the United Kingdom, not just for work but for art, inspiration, hope. For the future, really.

There was, of course, Northern Ireland, home to "the Troubles," still part of Britain, and rent by conflict between the Catholic and Protestant populations. It is fair to wonder how they might have affected our lives, but the answer might surprise you: not at all really. Older generations might have had strong political feelings about the legitimacy of the struggle, but politically and economically, the Republic of Ireland had its own issues to deal with, and there was more of a sense of paying lip service to the notion of a united Ireland than actually getting one's hands dirty doing something about it. Certainly, we were taught about it, and we talked about it, but there was no bombing in the south, no sectarian murder, and no soldiers on the street to contend with, so it wasn't really vivid or present in our lives. Indeed, in Ireland, I recall that there were some objections to the very idea of U2 writing about the Troubles as specifically as it did on "Sunday Bloody Sunday" in 1983, on the grounds that the band members were from the south, so what the hell did they know about it? I suppose our closeness to that conflict and the debate about it as part of our history did incubate a sense of political awareness. We might not have been personally affected, but it was impossible not to hold a position. Yet the sense I always had growing up in Ireland was that most people in the south rejected both the presence of the British in Northern Ireland and the paramilitary response to it. Peace seemed possible through only a third way: a rejection of things as they stood. So in a sense, the presence of the Northern Ireland Troubles helped shape a political character that rejected the status quo, a character that is apparent in U2.

Dublin was a little different from the rest of Ireland, anyway. It was sometimes referred to as West Britain, retaining a greater sense of the power structures that existed before the 1916 rebellion (in terms of architecture, political liberalism, and, among some of the wealthier elements of the population, genealogic descent). Rather crucially, certainly from a young person's point of view, we picked up BBC television and radio, those precious airwaves crossing the Irish Sea from Wales. Most of the rest of the country had access to only RTE (Radio Telefis Eireann), which was low budget, amateur, and deeply conservative. We might have had to put up with some wavy lines and static, but at least we got *Top of the Pops* and saw the kind of long-haired, sexually threatening pop stars who were censored to the point of invisibility elsewhere in the country. With Dublin being a cosmopolitan city, we had lots of cinemas, although moral censorship was so ridiculously enforced that I frequently found it impossible to follow the plot of the film. I remember seeing Brian DePalma's *Dressed to Kill* with the murder scenes removed. But in a way, all these tantalizing glimpses of an exotic and free popular culture worked more powerfully on the teen imagination than complete unfettered access because we were forced to fill in the blanks, reimagine things by ourselves. When U2 came through, it was different from any of the British groups who might have been called its contemporaries, not necessarily because it chose to be, but because it had to be.

When it came to rock and roll, international bands rarely visited. We could hear the records, sure, in our elder siblings' collections or in certain very macho "heavy rock" discos, but we rarely got to see it up close, because there was little in the way of big specialized music venues for visiting artists. There were some theaters, some big pub venues, and a boxing ring billed as the National Stadium. Ireland just wasn't part of the international touring circuit. What we did have, though, were ballrooms, where uniformed showbands played cover versions of popular hits and country and western music. This scene was repressive toward creativity, youth, energy, anything that threatened the established promoters' and bands' mafia-like domination of what was, to a few, a lucrative live music circuit. Some of the more ambitious Irish rock musicians kicked against the pricks, so to speak, and forced the showband venues to open up to an Irish-flavored rock music: there were local heroes Rory Gallagher and Brush Shiels (who had a band called Skid Row, who almost made it internationally and originally took Phil Lynnot under his wing), Thin Lizzy and Horslips, with their Celtic rock flavorings; but to enjoy any kind of real success, they had to do what the Irish had been doing for generations—leave the country. For those less-celebrated rock bands left behind, the only options were pub gigs (dominated by often pedestrian blues bands) or surrendering to the showband lure of playing cover versions. So when punk came along and U2 started to emerge with it, those of us tiring of this suffocatingly repressed music scene really had to make it happen for ourselves. We had to make our venues in church halls and community centers and, famously, for U2, in a car park beneath the Dandelion flea market. But necessity is not just the mother of invention; it is the mother of originality, because if you have to do something but don't know how it is supposed to be done, then chances are, you are going to do it your own way. Indeed, its own way was the only way for U2.

But that was all ahead of us. In the early seventies, Mount Temple Comprehensive School was a bit of a progressive oasis, just by virtue of its being mixed sex (unusual in Ireland) and nondenominational (the only such nonprivate school in Dublin that I was aware of). It was a secondary school (for ages thirteen to eighteen), free of the pernicious influence of Christian Brothers and nuns. In fact, the majority of pupils were probably Protestant because there weren't too many other educational options for them. The pupils came from a huge catchment area because the school appealed to parents who were uncomfortable with the orthodoxies of Irish education. Only Larry lived close to the school. Adam and Edge came in from the satellite town of Malahide, seven miles away.

You cannot overstate the importance of that school in the incubation, nurturing, and flourishing of U2. It was an enabling institution, a place where you were encouraged rather than repressed, and as I have tried to demonstrate, repression (philosophical, religious, psychological, sexual) was one of the defining characteristics of Irish life. Some of the teachers at Mount Temple were extraordinary, perhaps because it was the kind of school that would naturally attract people with open spirits. Our history teacher, Donald Moxham, was perhaps key in the U2 story. He was just a great enabler, an avuncular, bearded, jolly giant always on the side of the pupils. He was the guy you went to when you needed help sorting something out, and he was a huge supporter of the young U2 in terms of getting the musicians a room to practice in and just helping the group exist within the school framework, which at the time seemed really unusual in itself. It may be the case that there are bands in every school now, and you can take university courses on how to become a roadie, but it certainly wasn't the case in seventies Dublin. Everything about rock and roll felt against the odds, against prevailing winds, and against the established ways of doing things.

Albert Bradshaw, the music teacher, was another important facilitator for generally encouraging not just a love and appreciation of music but an active involvement with it. Albert was a gentle character who ran an accomplished choir in which all pupils were encouraged to participate. Bono, Edge, and I all sang, and Albert had a keen ear for where and how your voice could fit in. You couldn't get away with much. It always amazed me that with thirty or more pupils singing, he could pick out a suspect note with unerring accuracy. It is a big part of U2's story that band members were not particularly virtuoso musicians and that they only really bloomed when they took on the punk ethos of playing to suit their primitive abilities, but it is also true that they had to believe that there was music in them, and Albert is one of the characters that incubated this belief.

Jack Heaslip played an important role in the U2 story and indeed still does. He was an English teacher and, significantly, a guidance counselor at Mount Temple in the seventies. As Bono relates in *U2 by U2*, Jack helped see him through a kind of breakdown in 1974 following the sudden death of his mother. Bono recalls the period as turbulent, with angry outbursts in class, knocking over chairs and tables, his mind raging with fundamental questions about life, the universe, and everything. Jack was someone whom the kids could talk to because he really listened, and he gave Bono a lot of time and space to work things out for himself. Many years later, Jack experienced his own religious crisis or epiphany and left teaching to become an Anglican priest. He officiated at the marriage of Bono and the lovely Ali, his school sweetheart; he baptized their children; he helped bury Bono's father; and he still fulfills a role as a spiritual counselor to Bono. What makes Jack a particularly interesting and influential person in this context is that there is nothing dogmatic about him; he has an open, creative, and poetic approach to life and faith. I can remember him reading in class from Leonard Cohen and overseeing sex education classes so explicit that it caused one nervous girl to faint. He was a long way from the Christian Brothers. And it is an openness that is reflected in Bono's own faith and its practical interactions with the corporeal world.

Sophie Shirley was the religious teacher, but again, in the context of a nondenominational school, her approach was undogmatic and creative. I was the bane of that woman's life, being the school's most vocal atheist. But for Bono and Edge, she was an inspiration, a gentle soul who was wordly enough to acknowledge that life was not always beautiful but included, as Bono recalls, "God's fingerprints everywhere." In Ireland, there were only two responses to the near religious fascism that dominated the Catholic state: like it or lump it. But in Mount Temple, we were introduced to a third way. A great wave of born-again fervor swept the world in 1976, and in this most undogmatic of schools, a lot of pupils, inspired by Miss Shirley, got caught up in it. Bono and Edge were among them, and later they drew Larry into the fold (although, ever practical, he wasn't as unwavering in his devotion to the more lunatic fringe that began to dominate for a while and subsequently almost broke up U2 by demanding a devotional rigor every bit as unbending and unquestioning as the most orthodox aspects of Catholicism).

Even if you don't accept the notion of God's hand guiding U2 to glory, the importance of deep spiritual commitment in U2 (or three-fourths of the band anyway) cannot be underestimated. First it was something other than the band that bound members together, giving them a sense of higher purpose, indeed a mission. It was a concept made explicit in the title of their first great unrecorded song, "Street Mission," even if the actual lyrics ("some say, maybe tomorrow, a resurrection, hello") were fairly inscrutable. But crucially, the young U2's faith also served to keep it steady as the hurricane of a pop career swept it up. Life on the road breaks many a band, distracting them from artistic purpose, burning out young spirits with the often exhausting decadence that fills up those boring hours between adrenaline-busting gigs, when the hedonistic pleasures of sex and drugs become the automatic partners of rock and roll. U2's spiritual zeal in the early days in particular offered a peculiar kind of protection, like an amulet warding off dangerous spirits. The young U2 may have been, at times, almost humorlessly squeaky clean, but members were able to do a lot of growing up before they embraced the decadence of their chosen profession, with irony and humor, as the adult rock stars who created *Achtung Baby*.

U2 came together at Mount Temple School and had its first gathering in Larry Mullen's kitchen on September 25, 1976. The reason why we know the date is that my brother Ivan was there and made the now-legendary entry in his diary: "Watched TV. Joined a pop group with friends. Had a rehearsal. Great." Sadly, he did not record for posterity exactly what he watched on television.

As we know, Ivan didn't last long in the group. He was mainly tolerated at first because he had the best electric guitar, which Dave Evans (who had made his guitar from a DIY kit) used to liberate him of during rehearsals. The first gig, in Mount Temple's school gym late in 1976, featured the same four musicians who are still playing in U2 now. To put it into perspective, the four Beatles lasted less than a decade together. There are enough ex-members of the Rolling Stones to form another group altogether. But Bono, Edge, Adam, and Larry have been together from the very beginning, bonded by a deep and abiding loyalty and love. You can probably offer up lots of different theories about why and how that has come to pass, but really it is a mystery, perhaps the greatest mystery of U2. Rock music is not particularly complex, bearing little relationship to classical compositions carefully transcribed for trained musicians to play. A rock band is really a summation of the personalities in the group and how they express their character through their instruments. They don't have to be the best musicians. They just have to be the right musicians. They have to fit together. Most bands, at some time or another, alter their chemical makeup by replacing an original with another musician (often removing the weakest musical link for a putatively stronger one) and somehow losing everything in the process. U2's togetherness is its greatest strength—the musicians' recognition that they are one but not the same. They get to carry one another.

Feedback, as U2 announced itself in 1976, played three songs at that first gig: Peter Frampton's "Show Me the Way," a Beach Boys medley, and "Bye Bye Baby," by the popular Scottish teenybop band the Bay City Rollers. Not particularly auspicious beginnings. I don't know if there was anything in that performance that would make an experienced observer think that he or she was witnessing something special. But as a fifteen-year-old fellow pupil, I was utterly blown away. What did I know? I had never seen a rock band before. And for that matter, I don't think U2 had either. As I have tried to make clear, that is a huge contributory factor to the originality of U2. We were cut off on our little island. We didn't have much firsthand exposure to popular music, so we had to concoct our own version. A lot of that, of course, was disastrous. There were plenty of extremely poor Irish groups offering up watered-down versions of sec-ondhand trends. Indeed, that is exactly what U2 (in its early incarnation as Feedback anyway) was trying to do at first.

Those early gigs were crammed with really weak versions of the kind of overcomplicated progressive and heavy rock songs that were popular with older teenagers at the time. The worst I ever saw was a comically inept version of the Moody Blues' "Nights in White Satin" in St. Fintan's school, with my sister Stella on backing vocals and her friend Orla Dunne contributing a flute solo. This was the kind of music heard in the heavy rock discos that teenagers in Dublin could get into, and it was just too technically demanding for the young U2 to play. The band was really be-ing confronted with its limitations, which was so dispiriting that it might have done them in. But it was 1977, rock's year zero, when the Ramones, the Sex Pistols, and the Clash reset the clock; virtuosity was (temporarily at least) tossed out with the garbage, and all that really mattered was passion.

U2 was saved by punk. The musicians were the right age to buy into the whole ethos, to get carried away with the spirit of revolution. But punk in Dublin was not like punk in England or, for that matter, New York. It was, like everything else in Irish pop culture, a secondhand affair,

viewed from a distance. We read about it in imported magazines such as
the *NME* and *Sounds* (when we could find them), and we made up our
own versions, interpreting often fanciful journalistic descriptions for ourselves, so it was more about the idea that these groups represented rather
than the actual music they were making. And the music that Irish punks
were rejecting wasn't the overblown, overly technical, sci-fi-and-fantasy-
infected progressive rock of the 1970s, nor disco, nor pop. It was the
cheesy cover versions of the showband scene. Our whole musical argument was essentially different and localized. Interestingly, there were really
no out-and-out angry punk rock groups on the emerging Irish scene. The
bands that first appeared were either heated up R&B retro (Boomtown
Rats, Revolver, the Radiators from Space) or much more angular and arty
(the Atrix, DC Nien), already adopting the more sophisticated postures of
new wave. There was a homegrown originality to the scene because bands
were assembling ideas as best they could without much exposure to the
source material, like kids building models without the plans.

It would be misleading to overstate our isolation. We could find records imported into a few hip backstreet stores, and we had some rebel
rock radio, notably the Dublin pirate radio show of a DJ called Dave Fan-
ning, who was the Irish answer to Britain's legendary pioneering DJ John
Peel (whose show dedicated Dubliners could tune into through the static
every night after 10 p.m.). We found what we needed and shared it by going round to one another's houses and listening to new vinyl imports. But
there was nonetheless a scarcity to it that made it more precious and more
baffling, like a series of dots that we had to connect ourselves.

For U2, the traffic of ideas from the United Kingdom may have been
a little more pronounced than for others because there was an Anglo-Irish
element to the band. As I have said before, Dublin was considered by
many in Ireland to be West Britain, and Mount Temple—having an un-
usually progressive, liberal aspect and being populated mainly by Protestant
pupils—would have been the most West British of schools. The Edge is
of Welsh origin, and while he spent almost his entire life in Ireland (the
Evanses relocated when Edge was just one year old), it still meant that he
had strong family connections with the United Kingdom. Adam was of
an English family, and although he too arrived in Ireland at an early age,
his persona (perhaps partly adopted as a childhood defense mechanism, the
ways in which an essentially lonely guy could project individuality into
hostile spaces) seemed imbued with a quintessentially eccentric English-
ness: he wore dressing gowns at home, drank coffee from a flask in school,
and had a manner of sophisticated faux-adult politeness that enabled him to

bamboozle elders. His father was a pilot, so Adam was well traveled, with much more exposure to the foreign world than what would have been the norm for working- and middle-class Irish kids. Crucially, in the summer of 1977, Adam got a school holiday job working in London, right at the moment when punk was gripping the city's music scene, so he came back to Dublin bearing albums and singles and an abundance of ideas about the direction of the group.

You can certainly hear in early U2 the influence of David Bowie—from quite early days, the band played "Suffragette City" from *Ziggy Stardust*, a song that imbued punky energy—and it took on board elements of Television and XTC, the more intellectual art punk bands. Patti Smith's *Horses* was an important record in our social group, one that I think Adam first brought back from London. I remember a party in a fellow pupil's house, where many of us crowded around the stereo, listening to this album and refusing to relinquish control to our friends who understandably just wanted to hear something they could dance to. We all saw the Jam on *Top of the Pops*, and that made a big impression on Bono and many other Dublin punks—its driven, jerky performance being quite a talking point for a while. And occasionally, a punk band would venture across the sea and play in Dublin, and those gigs were holy occasions, when every like-minded soul would congregate in a basement club or a converted cinema or student bar to worship, going absolutely mad at the presence of heroic aliens such as the Buzzcocks, the Ramones, and the Clash.

Here, I'd like to mention another important person in the story: Bill Graham. He was a journalist for Ireland's only music paper, the *Hot Press*, a haphazard, amateurish, but zealous organ that announced its mission as "Keeping Ireland Safe for Rock 'n' Roll." We all read it avidly, and I wound up working there after school. Bill was its most intellectual and fanatical character, a wild and brilliant theorist and prose stylist who saw something in the passion and hunger of Bono and took the young U2 under his wing. Bill would play the band records and feed them music history, information, and theory.

A strong element of punk was the rejection of the past, and, of course, it is easy to reject the past if you don't actually have one. We'd be like "Yeah, f*** it, we're not into lead solos, man!" when what we really meant was that we had never fallen in love with solos in the first place and we couldn't play them anyway, so let's just ditch them and move on. U2 was essentially a band without strong musical roots. But there's something deeper here: U2 may not have had a binding sense of a musical past, but Ireland was all about the past. It was a young country forged in adversity and utterly awash with history, almost as if it were creating its identity by force-feeding the past to its population. It seemed at times that the past was all one ever heard about: the famine, the rebellion, the evil Brits, Oliver Cromwell (the way that some people spoke about the seventeenth-century British military leader, you might have thought that he had personally come round their houses and slaughtered their children), and, always, the overbearing presence of Jesus and all his Saints, witnesses to every injustice and misdeed along the way. And that is really what U2 and many of our generation were rejecting. U2 was rejecting the very idea that Ireland should be dominated by its history. Firing ahead under the rocketeering leadership of Bono, U2 was all about the future. (The past would come later, on *The Joshua Tree* and *Rattle and Hum*.)

If necessity is indeed the mother of invention, then it was just as well that the young U2 had a real inventor in its band. The fact that the Edge turned up at the first rehearsal with a homemade guitar was just a tantalizing hint of what was to come. He began developing a lateral guitar style from an early point, responding to Adam's bass lines but also developing his own highly personal theories about the "sex" of guitar strings and creating chords that left out certain "male" notes to give them a more fluid "female" character—which is, from some viewpoints, completely nuts but also utterly distinctive, demonstrating the kind of bold thinking from which true originality can emerge. The technical key to the young U2's sudden and explosive development was the Edge's acquisition of a Memory Man echo unit, which is a primitive device by the standards of today's digital guitar effects. But his use of that gadget was just phenomenal, manipulating it so that notes repeated and proliferated while he added harmonic notes on top, creating chords that couldn't exist in any other form, until these silvery guitar sounds built up into an extraordinary Edge orchestra, not so much a Wall of Sound as a Sea of Sound, a storm of notes ringing out of the thundering dynamics of Larry and Adam's propulsive rhythm section. Man, I loved to see that band play. To my teenage ears, it was transcendental what the Edge was doing, the sheer dynamic range of sound, making it hard to believe there was only one lead instrumentalist on stage.

There were a few bands trying similar things out at the time. Echo and harmonics were features of the Scars and the Skids from Scotland, while the extraordinary Durutti Column in the United Kingdom (really just guitarist Vini Reilly) was investigating the more ethereal effects of guitar echo, albeit quite divorced from the kind of rock template that made U2 so accessible. These were, I think, parallel explorations rather than direct influences. The most important bands for U2 were local bands. First there was the Boomtown Rats. Driven by Bob Geldof's enormous ambition and charisma, the band showed that it was possible to get out of Ireland and take on British bands on equal terms. Second were the Radiators from Space, who had one sensational Irish punk single, "Television Screen" (a speeded-up twelve-bar rock-and-roll song with the refrain "I'm gonna smash my Telecaster through the television screen, 'cause I don't like what's going down"), because the band was aggressive yet arty, and more important, its frontman, Steve Averill, was an ex–Mount Temple pupil who was available to offer much practical advice. Steve was a talented graphic designer who came up with the name U2 (a big improvement on both Feedback and its successor, the Hype) and went on to be U2's principal sleeve-and-poster designer, helping to define the band's distinctive aesthetics throughout its career.

Just as the Edge was exploring his ideas of what the guitar was for, Bono was exploring the role of frontman. Again, our Irish isolation from rock trends was surely a huge advantage in compelling him to find original ways to solve the age-old stage conundrums of communicating with an audience and personifying the band. His approach at first was highly theatrical, in ways that U2 didn't really revisit until the Zoo TV period. There were mimes and a routine in which he attempted to cadge a cigarette during a musical interlude but would then have to abandon it before lighting so that he could get back to the microphone. Of course, many others had taken theater into rock, and what he was attempting had been investigated by David Bowie, Peter Gabriel, Alex Harvey, and more. But as I keep pointing out, we had never seen these for ourselves. We had caught glimpses in brief perfomances on British music television shows perhaps, but the rest we just had to imagine. Fortunately, Bono was blessed with a vivid imagination and aided in his endeavors by his friendship with a bizarre bunch of bold and arty individuals, foremost of whom were his lifelong friends Gavin Friday (Fionan Hanvey) and Guggi (Derek Rowan). The pungently peculiar names (like Bono's) were self-invented, demonstrating allegiance to an imaginary place or gang known (for no reason that any of the participants can remember) as Lypton Village. They were self-styled Dadaists and Situationists, before any of them would have even understood those terms, getting up to maverick and surreal pranks. They used humor in an artistic way, to define themselves and reshape the world. There was a lot of laughter around that band, so it is odd to think of how humorless the young U2's image became as it really got going, overburdened perhaps with missionary religious zeal, although band members certainly rediscovered the subversive power of humor with Zoo TV, which was almost like the full flowering of Lypton Village.

There are a lot of odd and unique elements to the U2 story, but the existence of Lypton Village is among the most extraordinary. Everyone has a childhood gang, but the notion of a surrealist, arty gang of outsiders coming together on a lower-middle-class Dublin housing estate in the seventies seems too outlandish even for fiction. Is there something inherently Irish in this? Perhaps in terms of Ireland's fantastic poetic tradition, you can view Lypton Village as a young person's poetic rejection of reality, finding the confidence to conjure up an entirely alternative universe deemed preferable to the dullness of everyday life. At any rate, it is an indication of just how bold and original Bono's response to the world was, before he even became a rock singer. Lypton Village, of course, spawned more than just the leader of U2, because Gavin and Guggi went on to form the confrontational cult band the Virgin Prunes (who featured the Edge's brother Dik, when he had been ejected from his part-time role with the Hype), with Gavin going on to carve out a highly individual and artistically strong career in music, while Guggi developed into a profoundly gifted fine artist.

So there we have the young U2 in late-seventies Ireland, making it up as the band went along, combining Bono's poetic, theatrical, and surrealist artistic instincts with the Edge's lateral, scientific musical bent in a primal-colored rock group infected with the self-inventing spirit of punk and new wave, perfecting its art in a kind of rock culture vacuum, bonding emotionally because members shared a school, a liberal sensibility, a rejection of repressive Irish religious and political orthodoxies while being protected by a blossoming spiritual faith.

There is another key element that is part and parcel with this evolution in relative isolation: for the crucial early years of the band's development, U2 was allowed to just get on with it. There was a relatively short period in which U2 rose to the top of the pecking order in the local Irish scene, simply on account of being so much more urgent and exciting than any other local band. It won a one-off single deal with the Irish branch of CBS (in a battle-of-the-bands competition) and released its debut EP, *U2-3*, in 1979, just a year after band members had left school, when all were still teenagers. They were featured on the cover of *Hot Press* magazine. They were Ireland's great rock hopes. And yet the United Kingdom ignored them completely, with the parent branch of CBS declining to pick up the option on the band despite the recommendation of the company's Irish rep Jackie Haydn. Because nobody outside of Ireland took Irish rock music remotely serious. And for that, U2 has cause to be grateful.

The United Kingdom has an accelerated hothouse approach to pop music. Bands get an idea, do something interesting, and the voracious music media pounces at once, declaring them the next big thing, then writing them off as has-beens if they fail to live up to the media's own hyperbole. America has a different curve, because bands have to fight their way to the top of a local city or state scene before moving out across the vast country; so, they tend to get better by increments, certainly perfecting technical and musical craft along the way, building a reputation by degrees. But Ireland was not on the rock music map at all. Between the birth of rock and roll in the fifties and the arrival of punk in the late seventies, the country produced precisely three rock acts who registered in any notable way outside of Ireland: Northern Irish genius Van Morrison, Cork's phenomenal guitarist Rory Gallagher, and Dublin's superb hard rocker Thin Lizzy (which was actually, during its most successful years, a multinational line based in the United Kingdom). London-based record company A&R people weren't exactly hopping on the ferry and getting their pulses racing as they crossed the Irish Sea to discover the latest great white hope. The British music papers turned their noses up at our little country's parochial offerings (although there was a flurry of interest in the Northern Irish punk scene that gave us the Undertones and Stiff Little Fingers, romanticized by the notion of punk in a war zone). In general, Irish people weren't considered cool, certainly not in hip rock-and-roll ways. The Irish, instead, were the punch line of cruel jokes, the humor of stupidity. Comedians on mainstream British television shows told gags about thick Irishmen that would be considered racist in today's more politically sensitive times. So how likely was it that a group of dumb Paddies might turn out to be the biggest rock band on the planet?

A consequence of this is that U2 was able to develop past that first teenage rush and just keep getting better. It was able to hone its artistry and gain confidence from local triumphs invisible to the wider world. By the time one lone A&R man (Nick Stewart, known as the Captain, who had served as a soldier in Northern Ireland) from the small indie record label Island actually made the effort to come to Dublin to see the band in February 1980, U2 was a phenomenal live act who had just won five categories in the *Hot Press* Readers' Poll and was playing the largest venue in Dublin (the National Stadium) to a hugely enthusiastic and devoted audience. U2 had become unstoppable.

Let's go back to my dubious diamond shape. It is probably, in reality, a five-sided pentagon, because you have to find a point in there for the band's visionary manager Paul McGuinness. He was an urbane Anglo-Irishman, educated at Trinity College in Dublin, involved in advertising, dabbling in band management, ten years older than the members of U2, and concocting theories about how he could take a "baby band" out into the world. He was also a friend of fellow Trinity graduate Bill Graham, who brought U2 and McGuinness together. And then everything became possible because the best young band in Ireland had just hooked up with the most ambitious manager in Ireland. McGuinness had a mad idea that an Irish band could skip over the innate prejudices and parochialism of the UK music scene by making it in America. While the rest of Irish rock had its face fixed toward a London music business that just didn't want to know, McGuinness was already exploring notions of the interconnected-ness of Ireland and the United States, a country where, as I pointed out earlier, forty-one million people claimed Irish descent and dumb Paddy jokes weren't the currency of every cheap comedian. McGuinness didn't just take U2 out of Ireland; he brought the band to the world.

So let's throw away my speculative diamond altogether and just call U2 a Dublin-shaped band who could have come together only at that particu-lar time, in those particular circumstances, in that particular configuration. U2 has changed a great deal over the years, of course. We all do. The band has gone out into the world and changed the world too. But at the core of the band, in its essence, the same dynamics still operate. You always take your past with you; that really is all that you can't leave behind.

Loyalty and friendship are valued highly in Ireland, where bonds formed in youth and in adversity are among the strongest bonds of all. Maybe even stronger than family. U2 is still together, the same four people who convened for a common cause thirty-five years ago. That kind of thing is precious and rare in life, let alone in rock and roll. U2 genuinely recognizes that it is stronger as a group than as individuals, and band mem-bers actively subsume their egos to the needs of the greater whole. And maybe some of that is simply because, being Irish, U2 has always been an outsider in the iconography of rock, which has not just helped keep the band members connected to one another but helped them maintain a grasp of the bigger picture, a life that doesn't just center around the ego satisfac-tions of stardom.

U2's Irishness is the essence of why it has negotiated such an original and personal way through the minefield of pop culture—because, in some deep underlying way, it is impossible for an Irish person who grew up in Dublin in the seventies to really believe that rock stardom was one's birthright. From the beginning, U2 has had to make it all up as it went along. And the band is still doing it. By now, U2 should have detached itself and floated off into the egosphere, adrift in guitar-shaped swimming pools. Instead, the band is still working hard, sticking together, making records, challenging itself artistically, relentlessly touring, pushing forward political and charitable activist agendas.

When I mentioned to Bono that I was going to address an academic conference to discuss the deeper meaning of U2's works, he laughed. He was flattered and he was curious, but he was skeptical too, and that, to me, is a healthy response—because U2 still lives by a mantra that I have heard every member utter at some time over the past four decades and that every Irish person would understand: "We're four chancers from Dublin who got lucky."

It's not the whole story. You can read this whole book and never get the whole story. But there's truth in it all the same.

My Voyage of Discovery
Returning *October*'s Lost Lyrics

DANIELLE RHÉAUME

> *Has anyone found a brown leather bag? It's a brown leather kind of a case—tannish brown—because I lost it. I think it was twenty years ago this week . . . here in Portland. Two very beautiful girls walked out of our dressing room with a tannish brown bag. It had lots of important stuff in it . . . lyrics to the next album. . . . I'm ready for forgiveness.*
>
> —BONO, APRIL 15, 2001, PORTLAND, OREGON

BONO'S LOST LYRICS CAME INTO MY LIFE DURING the autumn of 2003, when I was working as an office assistant in a government agency best described as the Land of Beige. Beige walls. Beige floors. Beige ambition set to the droning, draining hum of low-spectrum fluorescent lights. The environment gave new meaning to Springsteen's lyrics to "Dancing in the Dark": "Man, I ain't getting nowhere just sitting in a dump like this / There's something happening somewhere."

I just knew that there was. At least it felt like there should be, and, more than anything, I needed there to be. The modest paycheck might have been reliable, but a lifetime spent editing mass mailings written by middle management was not what I had in mind for my life. The answer for some might have been to navigate their way up within the organization; I needed to find my way out.

After a few restless months contemplating law school and laboring over so-called logical reasoning puzzles for the Law School Admissions Test, I erred on the side of impractical and enrolled in two part-time writing classes at my alma mater The Evergreen State College in Olympia, Washington.

Evergreen is known for its progressive, interdisciplinary approach to education, written evaluations instead of grades, and, because of the students' collective unabashed love of cannabis, number one placement on *High Times* magazine's "List of Counterculture Colleges." Matt Groening, the creator of *The Simpsons*, graduated from there in 1977 and returned in 2000 to deliver the commencement address for my graduating class.

By the time I accepted my diploma, I'd identified writing as the one activity that consistently held my interest and challenged me—no matter what subject I was studying. The problem then and in 2003—as I soon discovered through my writing classes—was that I simply did not understand the amount of discipline and determination that writing, or any other artistic endeavor, required. I naively assumed that most successful artists, like Bono, for instance, just sat down and wrote lyrics. It was a linear, inspired process fueled by a reliable, unending well of creativity.

I was just another casualty of modern American "final product culture"—a culture where nearly everything you desire is immediately available twenty-four hours a day, seven days a week. This level of immediate gratification makes it easy to forget that there is a creative process behind the existence of everything.

Growing up blue-collar also contributed to my naïveté. Most of the influential adults in my life made very little for how hard they worked each day. This led to a persistent resentment toward more successful or affluent people. I regularly heard comments like "All those pencil pushers do is sit around all day while the rest of us actually work" or "I'd sure love to make millions dancing around like a clown, singing into a microphone." Nobody thought, or was brave enough to ask, "Well, if it's that easy, then why don't you do it?"

My supposition—even if only drawn subconsciously as a child—was that the people who were successful at white-collar jobs or artistic endeavors were just doing what came naturally. It wasn't real work. That's why it was terribly easy for me to lose hope when writing proved challenging and the right words didn't come. It didn't matter that I'd always been an avid reader. A book was just another final product that entered my hands, with a different world sealed neatly, effortlessly between its covers. I thought this was also true of the albums I listened to attentively, retaining every lyric as though it offered a clue about the special realm from where it came.

One of these albums was *The Joshua Tree*, which my older brother brought home on cassette tape in early 1987. He'd listened to it all the way home from the record store and couldn't wait to share it with me. He had a feeling.

"You're going to love this!" he said, handing me the itchy foam-covered headphones to his Sony Walkman. I placed them over my ears, listened for a moment, and then, just moments after Bono started singing "With or Without You," announced, without a hint of self-consciousness, "I'm going to know that man someday." I was only ten years old, and I still don't know where that idea came from. It wasn't as though it nagged at me to do something. It was just there, occupying a portion of my psyche like an unanswered question.

Along with that thought came a feeling of awe so moving it was as though my center of gravity shifted. Until then, I hadn't fully appreciated or understood music. I'd just been flirting with lyrics and enjoying some of the kitsch that defined most popular music of the time. U2 immediately stood out as being different—its sound traveled far beyond the temporal level, igniting my emotional, intellectual, and spiritual response. Of course I didn't have those words to describe how I felt at ten years old. I just knew that U2's music was unlike anything else—not to mention the fact that the lyrics stirred my already dramatic, often described by adults as overactive, imagination.

"She makes him wait on a 'bed of nails'?" I thought, listening closely and imagining a macabre circus act. "No wonder he's wailing!" I still had a thing or two to learn about metaphor. Fortunately, "that man" would prove to be a reliable mentor on that subject for days, weeks, heartbreaks, moments of celebration, months, and years to come.

Answer

U2's music had been part of my life for more than sixteen years when, on an ordinary Thursday in the Land of Beige, my coworker Cindy Harris e-mailed me to make weekend arrangements to attend a Halloween fund-raiser at a haunted house. In our e-mail exchange, she gave me her home e-mail address, which included her name and the alphanumeric "U2."

"Are you a U2 fan?" I wrote.

"Kind of. Why?" she replied.

"Because you are speaking with the biggest U2 fan you know," I wrote back.

Being a fan of U2 in Olympia, Washington, the self-declared indie music capital of North America, did not make me cool. What was cool was to "out-obscure" other people—something I saw as just another form of one-upmanship, exaggerating the already-tense relationship between art and success. Then again, it was always easy for me to be critical of that social dance because I was almost always on the losing end. My taste was decidedly mainstream by comparison to my peers. The irony was that openly liking U2 among a crowd of people that claimed to dislike the band was a rebellious, independent act.

"If you're a U2 fan, then I have a story for you," Cindy wrote back.

"Why? Did you meet them?" I responded, pushing Send with the excitement of a child releasing a shiny Mylar balloon and looking up. *How far will this go?*

A response arrived just moments later: "Not exactly . . . I'll just have to tell you the story sometime. . . . " The ellipses implied that now was not the time, that there was work to be done, but I simply couldn't let it rest.

I immediately picked up my phone and called her desk. She answered with a laugh. She was amused and probably a little annoyed by my persistence.

"I can't wait—I just have to know!"

I pressed her to tell me more until she explained. In 1983, her husband, David, discovered a brown briefcase that seemed to belong to U2, or maybe even just a fan of U2, in the attic of a house they rented near Tacoma. As she explained more, I vaguely recalled hearing or reading something about Bono losing lyrics sometime early in his career. That literally was all I knew: Lyrics had been lost. I didn't know the well-established legend about his briefcase being stolen in 1981 by two girls who snuck backstage after a show at the Foghorn Tavern in Portland, Oregon. I also didn't know that this briefcase contained all of the lyrics that Bono had prepared for U2's second album, *October.*

Cindy told me that she'd emptied the briefcase not long after they found it so that David could use it for his job as a long-haul truck driver. I was prepared for her to then say something about throwing the contents away, but she surprised me by offering to bring them into work the next day.

"What, you still have everything?" I asked.

"Yeah, I just have to get it out of my garage."

I was thrilled and immediately launched into online research. Almost every site I found stated that losing these lyrics had caused U2 to struggle terribly while recording *October.* This is why the album didn't do well commercially or critically and, as some sites suggested, U2 almost broke up soon after it was released. All this speculation, combined with my admittedly unrealistic expectations, led me to imagine that Cindy would arrive the next morning bearing a lost masterpiece of Bono's finished, or nearly finished, song lyrics.

The "Masterpiece"

If a masterpiece is supposed to be an artist's greatest achievement, I can safely say that what I found sitting on a conference table the next morning near Cindy's desk was not Bono's masterpiece. Instead it was a disorganized collection of letters, photos, colorful postcards, notebooks, calendars, and other papers—the sort of things you might find abandoned in a cluttered desk drawer.

Resting on top of the stack was an American work visa for Paul David Hewson, a then-twenty-year-old citizen of Ireland. Underneath it was a small black day planner for 1981 with a Dublin address embossed on the cover. I opened it to the first week of the year and read:

> *Monday, January 5:* Meeting with Paul McGuinness, followed by rehearsal each day for the next week and a half.
> *Wednesday, January 14: In the studio with Steve Lillywhite through Saturday.*
> *Friday, January 23: BBC broadcast and live show in Belfast, followed by a week of shows in Scotland and England.*

Hewson . . . Dublin . . . McGuinness . . . Lillywhite . . . Belfast . . . BBC . . . Even though my appreciation for U2 was largely visceral at that time, I'd read enough liner notes to know that these details were uniquely related to the band.

I placed the planner on the table and took a closer look at some of the photographs and proof sheets. One of the proof sheets featured small amusing pictures of Bono looking surprised while holding a burning copy of *Hot Press* magazine. There were also proof sheets for each band member, as well as some group shots. The most striking print featured all four band members bundled in heavy wool coats, standing on the forefront of a jetty that disappeared into white-capped waves behind them.

"The Irish Sea," I thought. I'd traveled that body of water just four years earlier during a solo trip through Ireland that helped me gain insight into my own Celtic ancestry.

Minutes later, I noticed the edge of a small blue spiral-bound notebook slipping out from the middle of the mess. I removed it and lifted the cover, where I found a to-do list that included "Write to me daddy—ring Ali." I could almost hear the Irish cadence in the use of "me" instead of "my." There was no question what I was looking at: the remnants of Bono's lost briefcase—an unintentional time capsule. I immediately began to feel a bit obsessive, like Gollum from *Lord of the Rings* with his "precious" ring. I didn't want to let my precious go—at least not back to Cindy's garage, where it could spend another twenty-two years collecting dust and growing mold in the dank, damp Pacific Northwest air.

"We need to get all of this back to Bono," I told Cindy, expecting she would resist. Before she could respond, my mind began to jump from one fear to another with the swiftness only panic can incite. *What if she decided to get it appraised or sell it online? What if she told friends about it and they offered her money beyond what I could afford? What if that person decided to publish or sell it? What if? What if? What if?*

But without even a hint of hesitation, Cindy brought me back into the moment by not only agreeing but also offering that I could take everything home. Her one condition was that she'd get a chance to meet Bono when his belongings were returned.

In that moment—when I accepted Cindy's offer and assumed responsibility for Bono's lost items—I stepped from the Land of Beige into an adventure that I never could have imagined when I first heard U2. My first step on the adventure didn't involve any pulse-quickening perils or glamorous brushes with fame. It started quietly, at home with Bono's creative process, which was abruptly and unintentionally frozen in time. The date: Sunday, March 22, 1981.

Anything but Boring

As the Internet legends of the lost briefcase predicted, there were lyrics in Bono's blue notebook. Most of them were just ideas or a progression of ideas, but some were more substantial. The most highly developed song, from what I could tell, was "I Fall Down," which made it onto the *October* album, despite the loss of his notebook. By the time that the lyrics were lost, the song must have taken on a life of its own, and the band was probably already practicing it. There were also some entries and ideas that seemed to be out of step with *October*. For example, there was a note of "Sunday Bloody Sunday—a single" on the same page as the word "War." The *War* album, which contained the song "Sunday Bloody Sunday," wouldn't come out until early 1983, more than a year after *October* was released in, yes, October 1981.

"What happened was, as a result of losing this notebook, we diverted to *October*. . . . So, had I not lost [the briefcase], we would have just gone straight into making *War*," Bono later explained.

I was especially drawn to entries that revealed awareness of a higher purpose or calling. Bono had written, "Hey, did you hear the one about the Irish man who grew up, blew up, got on a boat to tell the world they're running out of time not petrol?" And "What do you call someone who believes he has hope, a future—a madman or a fool?" Bono told me later that he was "really taken with [the idea] of the Shakespearean fool, who is a character that can change the world or shape the world, by making an idiot out of himself."

A lot of Bono's thoughts also went into stage directions, such as where to stand, how to handle the microphone, and what to wear during specific performances. A couple of my favorite, rather amusing, notes were a list of lost items—including a check, two shoes, and a guitar—as well as a series of introductions that started confidently with "Hi, my name is Bono. I'm the singer for U2 . . . " but ended self-consciously with "Is this boring?" *No, Bono—this is anything but boring.*

I found Bono's papers to be perfectly human and relatable. They were not the products of my admittedly absurd idea of an artist following a linear, inspired process fueled by a reliable, unending well of creativity. Having those expectations replaced with a more realistic appreciation of the messy and often unpredictable creative process gave me the insight that I needed to approach writing with what was, for me, an unprecedented patience.

Despite what I'd learned in school, "expressing myself"—whatever that even means—was not enough. Neither was expecting things to come naturally, as my upbringing suggested. Being a writer didn't mean sitting around with creative ideas, waiting for the perfect time to write or be "discovered." It also didn't mean posturing in coffeehouses, scrawling in journals, and trying to look "artsy." It meant taking time, working diligently, and appreciating the creative process. When I eventually explained this realization to Bono, he said, "C'mon, admit it—you took two looks at my shite and thought, 'If he can make it, so can I!'"

Navigation

I sent a few pictures of the collection to an acquaintance in England who knew people who could connect me with U2's "inner circle," as he called it. It took only about a week before I received an e-mail from one of U2's representatives. The subject line read "Bono's stuff," and the body of the e-mail was, to my surprise, just as casual. Finally, after more than twenty-two years, Bono's lyrics were on their way home.

Cindy and I assumed that it would be only a matter of days or weeks before we would meet him. Surely, he couldn't wait to be reunited with what he'd lost so many years earlier. We never imagined that it would take an entire year—a year full of intermittent communication and responses to e-mail that often took weeks or months to arrive. Sometimes, during extended periods of silence, I wondered if I had done something to make U2's management suspicious of us. If anything, I might have come off as overzealous, but who wouldn't? These were extraordinary, almost unbelievable, circumstances. Perhaps that is why, upon hearing about the discovery of his lost lyrics and our desire to return them, Bono wondered, "What's the deal? How much?"

If there was a "deal," it was that Cindy and I wanted to meet Bono in person. He was the one artist I'd always wanted to meet and, after having his lyrics, I was sure we'd have plenty to talk about. Neither Cindy nor I expected a reward or even considered asking for one.

By the time the first quarter at Evergreen finished, I was voluntarily assisting one of my professors and mentoring my peers. The professor asked me to continue volunteering the next quarter, and I jumped at the opportunity. I didn't want to borrow more money to pay for school, but I also wanted to be there. School had become my sanctuary—a place where I didn't have to squeeze my personality and passions into the confines of a cubicle.

About a month into teaching at night and working as an office assistant by day, I came across a manila folder titled "Rheaume, Danielle" on the desk of my new manager, who was out of his office for the day. I shouldn't have, but I looked inside. There was a handwritten note from the human resource manager saying that I did a good job but was "too sensitive"— a criticism that stung because I'd received it so many times in my life. I spent the following hours feeling embarrassed and ashamed, mustering just enough energy to finish the day.

When I arrived at school that night, a student in her midforties intercepted me at the door. She was carrying the story that I had reviewed and returned to her two days earlier. "You 'get' me," she said, holding up the paper and pointing at the evaluation I'd written in the white space on the last page. "I've never had a teacher really 'get' me before. Thank you!"

As the embarrassment and shame from earlier in the day evaporated, I had a simple but important realization: The exact same qualities that brought disapproval and apparent failure in one environment brought approval and success in another environment. The same sensitivity that had attracted criticism from childhood bullies and lousy office managers (all too often the same people) was what helped me "get" her. This sensitivity is also what motivated me to return Bono's lost lyrics. That and having a conscience.

Of course, my desire to return Bono's lyrics wasn't completely altruistic. I knew that I had far more to gain long-term by doing the right thing and being in Bono's good graces than I ever did by being greedy or exploitive. This is not to say that I was living in affluence or even comfort at the time. My home was a tiny, 180-square-foot partial garage that had been converted into a studio apartment. It had a cold concrete floor and heat that came from only an electric radiator on wheels. I had a car payment that I could barely afford and only one piece of furniture. Selling or publishing his lyrics might have brought money that would have made life a lot easier for a while. But then what would have happened? My sweet windfall would have eventually transformed into a nasty, acrid aftertaste. U2's music would become a persistent, painful reminder of how I did the wrong thing, and I'd eventually feel compelled to distance myself from a consistent source of pleasure in my life. It was a price I was unwilling to pay.

Returning *October*

Around October 17, 2004, I discovered that Bono was scheduled to speak at the World Affairs Council of Oregon on Wednesday, October 20. I wrote an e-mail to his representatives, asking if he might have time to meet in Portland the same day. They responded quickly, stating that it was a possibility, although they wouldn't be able to confirm anything until the 19th. By then I was living more than three hundred miles north of Portland, in Vancouver, British Columbia. The distance made it difficult for me to drive down at the last minute, so I departed early, as though the meeting was already confirmed, and I met Cindy in Olympia the evening of the 19th. Together we drove the final 121 miles to Portland, still not knowing whether we actually would meet Bono the next day. We were determined, however, to be nearby if he did have time.

That evening, while Cindy and I enjoyed cocktails with a dear friend who was letting us sleep on her couches, I received a phone call from Bono's personal assistant, confirming that he could meet us in the lobby of the Benson Hotel in downtown Portland the following afternoon. My persistence had finally paid off. I was going to meet "that man" after all. And even better than meeting him, I had the opportunity to give back a fraction of what he, through his art and perfectly imperfect journal entries, had already given me.

The first person Cindy and I met at the Benson Hotel was Bono's personal assistant—an attractive, friendly woman who sat with us before he arrived. She asked if we were nervous, and I piped up, telling her that I was, but I was also really excited about seeing him react to his lost items. I'd imagined and looked forward to this experience each day for one week short of a year. I hoped that he would at least be as delighted as I was the moment his lost items came into my hands.

An art history class I took while earning my BA taught me that it is impossible for museumgoers to ever view famous and widely published pieces of art with fresh eyes. They always have expectations. Sometimes those expectations are exceeded and other times they fall short. Rarely do they ever match up exactly with what they initially imagined. This is probably also true of how people view and experience those who have achieved celebrity status. They assume that the celebrity will be a certain way, but their assumption is based on a sliver of information or, more likely, misinformation. Bono's lost items contained a portion of the spirit that gave impetus to U2, and I was naturally interested in knowing more about the man who was once the boy who lost them. If I expected anything from Bono, it was that he had more to teach me.

Bono's assistant rose from her seat to take a phone call and stated that Bono would arrive momentarily. I sat in a chair facing Cindy. Just behind her was a tea and coffee service cart partially eclipsed by a wood pillar. As we waited in anticipation, I saw Bono approach the cart to make himself a cup of tea. There was something about his posture and the subtle way that he pushed back his hair before reaching for a small white teacup that made me flash on his powerful performance of "Sunday Bloody Sunday" in the *Rattle and Hum* film.

Cindy must have noticed my gaze because she turned to see Bono just as he emerged from the other side of the pillar with the cup of tea in one hand and a picture of the U2 iPod in the other. Cindy and I simultaneously rose to our feet to greet him. As soon as we finished introductions, he showed us the image of the iPod, explaining that he intended to send one to each of us. He then placed the picture on a small table beside the chair I'd been occupying before his arrival. He stated that he had to be very careful not to forget it because Apple hadn't yet released the image to the public.

He was very warm and accommodating, although I did detect a measure of initial cautiousness—healthy cautiousness. I respected that reserve as soon as I recognized it. No matter how connected I felt to his work, he barely knew me from a stranger on the street. He told us that when he heard that we had his belongings, he decided, if we were trustworthy enough to want to return his stuff, we were trustworthy enough to hold on to it until he came to us. I wished I'd known that in advance. If I had, it would have saved me countless hours and days of worry.

In the three months preceding our meeting, Cindy had started to question whether Bono really cared about his stuff anymore. She wondered if it might be better if she just gave everything to her daughter who "kind of" liked U2. I couldn't blame her for feeling concerned and wondering, but the thought of passing Bono's lost items over to a fifteen-year-old with passing interest in U2 horrified me. I reassured her that it was only a matter of time before he would meet us. I didn't admit that my confidence was also starting to wane.

As Cindy, Bono, and I settled into chairs, Bono asked how we'd found his lost items. Cindy responded, explaining how her husband had found the briefcase in the attic of their old house. As she spoke, I readied Bono's items. The day before I'd organized and divided everything into several resealable plastic sleeves usually used for art prints and photographs. Then I placed them in an inexpensive black art folio case. The case was beside my chair, leaning against the small table where Bono had placed the picture of the U2 iPod. On the other side of it, he sat listening to Cindy. As she spoke, I sensed that his cautiousness was subsiding a bit. Then, when the story transitioned to where Cindy passed his items into my hands, he turned toward me. I explained that I'd been an admirer of his work since I was ten years old. He said "thank you" and reached for my hand. As he held my hand, I explained the rest of the story—how Cindy had passed his lost items into my hands and how I had spent the past year trying to get them back to him. I admitted that I wouldn't do that for just anybody. My drive was fueled by an abiding appreciation of his work.

When I finished telling my part of the story, I asked him, "Are you ready to see what we have?"

"Yeah, let's see it!" he said, sitting up attentively.

The first sleeve I passed him contained photographs. As he peeled it open, I couldn't help but watch and read his reactions with the excitement and attention of parents watching their child open gifts from Santa on Christmas morning. I wondered, *Would he like what he found? Was it what he expected?*

I'd placed the group photo on the jetty at the top of the stack. Bono let out a long, soft "wow" as soon as he saw it. After quiet examination, he explained that the photo was taken either right before or right after U2's first ever trip out of Ireland. He then sorted through all of the proof sheets, noting the *Hot Press* shoot that he'd done with his friend Neil Mc-Cormick, as well as a series of photos where he joked that Adam "looked like a male model."

When he first held his blue notebook and flipped through the pages, he became quiet and focused, reviewing the lost ideas, lyrics, and other notes. I helped him find the pages of practiced introductions. He laughed as soon as he came across "Is this boring?" and read it aloud before explaining that he still doesn't like introducing himself. "After all of these years, that is still the one thing . . . ," he said.

Then he looked at small symbolic items, such as handwritten tour itineraries and set lists, as well as receipts for hotel rooms that cost less than $30 per night. "Twenty-eight dollars?" he said, marveling over one hotel receipt. "Wow!" Each of these items underscored the fact that U2 really was in a different place back in 1981 (a run-down inn near the Portland International Airport, to be exact).

After an hour visiting with us and reviewing his items, Bono had to leave and prepare for his speaking engagement. Cindy and I took a few photos with him, and he signed her U2 CDs. On my way to the Benson Hotel that afternoon, I'd purchased a first-edition LP copy of *Boy* for about $8 at a nearby record store. I'd hoped for a copy of *October*, for obvious reasons, but it didn't have any in stock. *Boy* was also a good choice, since U2 was touring on that album at the time that the lyrics were lost. I realized much later that October 20, 2004—the day his lyrics were returned—was the twenty-fourth anniversary of the release of *Boy*.

Bono signed the front of my LP "1981–2004, Just a hop and a skip . . . " and then the back with lyrics from U2's then-upcoming album *How to Dismantle an Atomic Bomb*: "'I'm alive, I'm being born. I just arrived, I'm at the door of the place I started out from and I want back inside. . . .' Thank you, Danielle, for helping me return." He also drew a caricature of his face—cleft chin and all—with the words "this notebook does not belong to Bono" inside my black moleskin notebook. "I use the same type of notebook," he said, handing it back to me.

After Bono said good-bye and started to walk away, I turned back to my chair and noticed that he'd left the picture of the U2 iPod on the table. I grabbed it quickly and called out, "Bono, wait!" He stopped and turned back to look at me. "You forgot something . . . ," I said, holding out the picture. I couldn't have choreographed a more perfect ending to our first meeting.

That evening, Cindy and I picked up tickets Bono left for us at will call at the Theatre of the Clouds so that we could attend his speech for the World Affairs Council of Oregon. When Bono took the stage, he said,

> It's been an extraordinary day. I can't quite believe that a funny thing happened to me today on my way to the Theatre of the Clouds. I can't quite

believe I said that, but it's true. I came across something I haven't seen in twenty-three years—since the first time I came to Portland, Oregon, and played a little place called the Foghorn.

When rowdier members of the audience howled at his mention of the Foghorn Tavern, Bono laughed and said,

> You can't remember the place! You can't remember the gig, because as far as I can remember, there were only eight people at the gig, and four of them were the band! The fifth was the bartender, the sixth was security, and the seventh and eighth people were thieves. I'm not kidding you!

Laughter filled the theater, and Bono paused, creating space for the response before continuing,

> And if there's only two people who come to your show, you have to meet them. We were so honored that we didn't notice them walking out with my briefcase. In it were lyrics and notes for U2's second album. The album was to be called *October*.

Howls of praise for *October*, mixed with long, snakelike hisses about the thieves. Bono continued, "Well, this October—twenty-three years later—this very day—I was given them back."

My heart pounded in loud, heavy beats against the audience's massive response. When the cheering and stomping calmed just enough for his voice to break through again, Bono asked, "How cool is that? People who could have published or sold my back pages, for absolutely no reward, handed them back. An act of grace. An act of goodness. You can never know how much that means to me . . ."

And you will never know how much it means to me . . .

His announcement set in motion a media frenzy, which led Cindy and me to do interviews with the *Today Show*, BBC, CBC, local news stations and newspapers, radio stations, and even a Canadian fanzine. These were mostly enjoyable, often even fun, experiences that kept my attention right up to the second week of December, when I started the master of fine arts in creative nonfiction writing program at Antioch University Los Angeles.

Writer's Christmas

When I started at Antioch, my colleagues might have thought that I had swallowed the Luxor Sky Beam. I was still glowing from the experience of returning Bono's lyrics and blasting my enthusiasm in every direction. I couldn't help myself—nor did I want to. When his lost items were in my possession, I was singularly, energetically focused on getting them back to him. Once they were returned, that energy and focus didn't just evaporate. It transformed into fuel for a new mission to understand and write about the circumstances surrounding the loss of his briefcase. My life had been so profoundly changed by those circumstances that I couldn't help but wonder exactly what happened on March 22, 1981. Eventually, my pursuit gained momentum through my time at Antioch, coloring nearly all aspects of my academic life and prompting me to begin a book-length manuscript, *The Return of* October.

There were times when I could tell that my unorthodox academic focus puzzled and even irritated some of my peers and faculty members. To more traditional academics, it seemed silly—almost unscholarly—to focus so much on popular musicians. They might have wondered, "What does a rock band have to do with writing?" To those who saw me as just another starstruck fan, I was embarrassingly uncool. "Doesn't she realize how crazy she seems talking about U2 all the time?" To those with a deep, abiding reverence for music, mystery, and metaphor, I was onto something.

That "something" was what one of my colleagues described as a "writer's Christmas." The process of uncovering what really happened on March 22, 1981, brought me all of the challenges and rewards that a writing student could ever ask for . . . and then some. There were intriguing characters, strange locations, research challenges, unusual circumstances, tests of character, and even banal, boring details that tested my attention span. It was the ultimate interdisciplinary education—one that I was experiencing all because Bono's briefcase disappeared the night that U2 played a nautical-themed sports bar full of rednecks, taxidermy starfish, and wooden seagulls.

The more I uncovered about the circumstances around the loss of Bono's briefcase, the more I came to see its loss as an essential test that U2 had to withstand on its route to being the resilient, determined band that it is today. Then again, if U2 hadn't already possessed those qualities, Bono's briefcase might not have gone missing in the first place. Therein lies this paradox: I have since learned that there is compelling reason to believe that Bono's briefcase was hidden backstage by an embittered local crew member retaliating against U2 for being too particular about its technical and artistic details. Another crew member had attempted but failed to return it to Bono a few days after the show at the Foghorn. Here was another case where the same qualities that brought disapproval in one environment brought approval and success in another environment.

My desire to learn more about the loss of Bono's briefcase and report what I had discovered eventually led me to interview Bono on December 19, 2005, in Portland, Oregon, as part of my academic field study at Antioch. U2 was in town for a concert at the Rose Garden, and Bono made time for me just before the show. That evening, Bono thanked me from stage for returning his lost lyrics during the introduction to "I Still Haven't Found What I'm Looking For." I was touched by his thank-you and slightly amused by his song choice because that is the same song that tortured the conscience of the crew member who attempted but failed to return Bono's briefcase to him in 1981.

If my colleagues hoped that getting the interview with Bono would cool my academic interest in U2, they were sorely mistaken. Something that Bono said during our interview about all art aspiring to the condition of music intrigued me and eventually led to my master's thesis, "Writing with Music in Mind: Aspiring Toward the Condition of Music in Creative Writing." From that paper came a preliminary structure for *The Return of October* and an ongoing, unquenchable desire to research and write about many subjects, including, of course, the fascinating phenomenon of music that U2 continues to inform, and be informed by, to this day.

I am encouraged and excited by the knowledge that other writers and academics see the significance of U2—not just as fans of its music but also as observers and appreciators of its greater cultural contributions. U2 is not just a band. The band members are not just rock stars with posh clothes and swagger. They are, possibly just by accident, although I doubt that could be entirely true, the mentors that some of us intellectual and creative misfits needed all along.

Potent Crossroads **3**
Where U2 and Progressive Awareness Meet

RACHEL E. SEILER

I DON'T HAVE TO TELL YOU ABOUT THE CROSSROADS. You already know. I'm not just talking about a place where two or more roads meet, although that's part of it. Even if you don't buy into the stories whispered in juke joints and country towns spread across the American South about soul-selling, trick-laying places of dusty boots and penitence, of conjuration, rootwork, and hoodoo, where many a bluesman struck a deal with the devil for guitar virtuosity, your intuitive mind understands the power of this kind of locale. Crossroads populate religious and folkloric belief all around the world. Stories of an intersection of dimensions as well as of roads where a guardian-trickster deity awaits to carry human desires to the gods are widely encountered in European, Caribbean, and West African lore. It's no wonder the selling-your-soul-for-guitar-prowess story has become a staple in blues and rock legends.

Whether you believe these kinds of tales or not, the symbolism of the crossroads speaks directly to the part of you that innately recognizes it as a charged metaphoric space. It's a locality where realms touch, a liminal place, a place literally neither here nor there, betwixt and between where strong forces are met and decisions are made.

Ron Sakolsky, coeditor of the influential *Sounding Off! Music as Subversion/Resistance/Revolution*, writes of the powerful place where music meets resistance:

> Speaking as a writer, while rebel musics have not been my exclusive focus, they have been my constant companion. They have nurtured my critical consciousness, sparked fresh intellectual insights, uplifted my spirits, reinforced my anger at injustice, and fueled my utopian dreams for a better world.[1]

His words could be my own. The experiences and insights that have arisen during my own frequent stops at his favored intersection and my immersion in the body of literature related to it led me to look into the relationship between U2's music and listeners' progressive awareness—the marriage of critical consciousness and action for social justice and change.[2] Such an inquiry has special relevancy now, I believe, as our times are ripe for change and as music—particularly U2's music—has a long history of converging with other forces of change.

I carried out an in-depth study of six listeners' experiences at the potent crossroads of their developing progressive awareness and their encounters with U2's music. My findings shed light on how U2's music played out in their day-to-day lives and made ripples in their perceptions and actions. I collected my data in the form of stories from the six listeners, working within the methodological framework of narrative inquiry, which holds as a tenet that stories are a basic communicative, meaning-making approach pervasive in the human experience.

To share here the six individual narratives I collected, I have created a composite story—a distilled, creative synthesis of the individual narratives. This condensed and consolidated story is imbued with collective meaning that conveys the participants' experiences using their own words and style of speech and encapsulates the major themes that emerged from my inter-pretation and analysis of the individual narratives. This composite story is an ideal introduction to my findings and illuminates the meanings that the participants constructed and ascribed to U2's music.[3] It reveals what it is about U2's music and the participants themselves that enabled the dynamic interplay between the music and their progressive awareness. Following the composite story, I share some connections between my findings and developmental theories and indicate possibilities that this work has in the areas of radical education and action for social change, along with some special applications for youth contexts in the real world.

The Approach and the Participants

My research was of a qualitative nature, with narrative inquiries that cross-cut disciplines and subjects and took a naturalistic approach by attempting to make sense of phenomena in terms of the meanings that people bring to them. My main objective was to learn how individuals experience and interact with their social world and the meaning that it has for them. Accordingly, I emphasized the subjective aspects of participants' lives, and I attempted to enter into their conceptual worlds. A benefit that I see to the methodology of narrative inquiry is that it employs feminist research values: it is a voice-centered, relational approach to research. It refutes the positivist presumption of a stable, unchanging reality that can be studied using the empirical methods of objective science.

I regard U2's music as belonging to a broad category of music called "contemporary conscious popular music," which includes music of any genre that focuses on social issues and perceived problems in society and may or may not include music that carries an overtly political message. It is music that is accessible to a wide audience, distributed through the mass media as a commercial product; it resides primarily in Western cultures and is of the late-twentieth and early-twenty-first century.

My study was not about discovering or making explicit what the words or sounds of U2's music mean and then extrapolating from these meanings the music's potential impact on people and society. Instead, I worked with the constructivist perspective that meaning is made socially as a person interacts with the world, and so my focus was on apprehending the mystery of the relationship between music and listener. From this perspective, positivism is a naïve approach in that it holds that there is a reality out there to be studied, captured, and understood. Subjectivity, however, is not static and unchanging but "a continuous process of production and transformation . . . a 'doing' rather than a being."[4] Therefore, the meaning and impact of music are contingent on listener constructions. Songs have no absolute meaning or value and can't be assessed according to what the lyrics say or what the performer believes; rather, a song's influence on a listener is a matter of what the music represents and expresses and how it is received. Only then does the music take on meaning, and only then might its social and political aspects become evident.

I worked with a small nonrandom sample of six participants because I sought to qualitatively understand their particular experiences in-depth through personal detail, as opposed to looking for what would be true for the many and promoting context-specific extrapolations. The three men and three women who volunteered for my project ranged in age from the early twenties to the late fifties and represented relatively diverse ethnic and religious/spiritual backgrounds. Four resided on the East Coast of the United States between New York and Florida; one lived in the Midwest; and one lived in California. Their educational levels ranged from having a high school diploma to having a doctoral degree.

My main data collection method was one in-depth semistructured interview that lasted for approximately sixty to ninety minutes with each participant. I began with a loosely structured prompt designed to activate narrative production. During their storytelling, I asked the participants en-gaging, focused, yet open-ended questions to encourage them to expand their stories in the direction of most interest to me. I also conducted a follow-up interview to discuss reactions to the primary interview and seek any further insights or questions the participants had.

I performed several open-ended readings of the interview transcripts and identified a large number of emergent themes. Using research sub-questions to conduct a targeted series of rereadings helped me identify the narrative material most directly relevant to my research. I used qualita-tive procedures to establish and evaluate that the results were an accurate interpretation of what participants meant, so that different voices were included, so that there was a critical appraisal of all aspects of the research, and so that I was self-critical as an investigator. I took data and tentative interpretations back to the participants and asked if they were plausible; I was critically self-reflective of my assumptions, worldviews, biases, theo-retical orientation, and relationship to the study. I spent enough time col-lecting data such that my report became saturated, and I provided thick, rich descriptions to persuade readers of the trustworthiness of the findings.

Meeting at the Crossroads

The resulting composite story is a tapestry woven from the individual nar-ratives resulting in a larger integrative level of meaning. It allows you to be present with the participants as they were present with me at the crossroads of U2's music and their progressive awareness. It offers you entrée to their worlds in their voices to help you understand their experiences and how they interpret them, and it presents the major themes, in concentrated form, that emerged from the narratives as a whole.

Organic researcher Jennifer Clements writes, "Stories offer an *interplay* whereby the reader experiences the parallel between his or her own story and the one on the page."[5] As you filter the story through the sieve of your own context, perhaps something within you will be subtly shifted by it, thus changing your story and creating new insights into your own experi-ences with U2's music.

The Composite Story

I grew up with music in a socially aware atmosphere—it's that much a part of who I am from the cradle, probably from the womb. I think you have these sort of formative years—when you're really sort of developing your worldview and your view about your place in the world—that for me just happened to coincide with the years of *War*, *The Unforgettable Fire*, and *The Joshua Tree*, and a lot of those early childhood lessons were mirrored in the lyrics.

I would not be the person I am today if I had not encountered the music. U2 completely catapulted me to adulthood. With U2, I'd like to think that those lyrics and music were little seeds that were planted in me; U2 started permeating my life, and social consciousness came, and that's when all those seeds, like, exploded, really. And they became something like plants inside of me. That's what we're put on this place for; it's not about this consume, consume, consume, buy more stuff, grow the economy, blah, blah, blah. No, we are here to meet other people's needs.

I think the first thing that U2's music requires of me is awareness. We're holding a mirror up and what do you see? The *Pop* album really does sum up the period where I was sort of understanding that a lot of how I look at the world has been offered to me—and in kind of meager, puny ways of seeing the world. I never saw things the same. Never ever. Never ever. In some ways I'm jealous of my friends who just go out on a Friday or Saturday night; I think once you become aware, you become responsible.

"Pride" was definitely my introduction to Martin Luther King, which was my introduction to racial injustice. My apologies to my former history professors, but it wasn't until U2 that I really became aware of the history of US involvement in Central America. "Bullet the Blue Sky" . . . what America the myth is . . . but you got the crooked crosses.

U2 wasn't the only band that was writing topical songs or whatever, but for me, it was the window, you know what I mean? It's fun and enjoyable music, with self-provoking lyrics. So I like it. It's not just because I know it's good for me or it's my medicine.

It personalizes the Other for me. Like in "Miss Sarajevo," I'm like, "Wow, what a silly thing to put on a beauty pageant in the war zone." But at the same time there's that need for normalcy and that desire, so it's not just people whom I don't know who are literally off in some other part of the world fighting about old things that I don't have any interest in. They're actual, real people.

From the first time I heard U2, there was something like, you know, the world is not the way it should be. If you come to that conclusion, the next logical step is, why not? And then hopefully you take the next step, which is, what can we do about it? Why am I here, how am I using my resources, how am I using my, you know, influence? It challenges you to get uncomfortable and grow.

Simple and essential, but powerful. U2's music is, here is the word for it: canonical. Universal themes that can be revisited over and over again of love, of peace, of something that's not gonna go away. So I think there's this politics of making peace, of tolerating differences. Basically, when you get to it, it's about love.

So now this music is fully a part of me. You carry it but not like a burden. It's not necessarily that I'm going through my day and all of sudden I say, "Oops, wait a minute, I'm slipping off track, let me hum a line from a U2 song." It's just something that's there. I have the values that are projected through music; it becomes a mantra—you go out in the big bad world and just live your life based on those basic beliefs.

I find it to be reassuring, comforting, because of the idea that we're not there yet; there is a place where the streets have no name, and I haven't found what I'm looking for, but there is that belief that it's there, out there; it exists, so when I listen to the music, I'm encouraged. I mean, it's one of those top, top things in my life that provides stability, a point of reference, a foundation for me. It sings to my soul. It keeps it alive, keeps it vibrant, moving like a stream or like a river. It keeps it flowing. It's almost as your heart keeps your blood flowing, you know? It's this *de dum, de dum, de dum* empowering somebody like myself, giving people like me a bigger voice. And so what if it's idealistic?!

I can't really separate the sort of spiritual elements of U2's music and my own life, so the first time I saw U2, I would say I had a spiritual experience. The audience was almost like an organism. I was at the concert at Madison Square Garden right after September 11—I couldn't tell you what it was specifically when U2 steamrolled into New York and just embraced the city and gave eight-million-plus people the will to carry on. Everyone in that audience was sister and brother that night. The electricity was hanging in the air, like a sixty-thousand-person sing-along. Ecofeminists would say that there's a unity of experience where you have . . . I felt a connection, a greater connection beyond myself.

U2 is very successful at just creating this kind of arc, hoping that people will travel through some of the same emotional experiences. It's really sort of a moment of transcendence, like a "come to God" moment. I mean, I'm high afterward and I've been sober for over ten years. Everyone just lets go. Church. When I say *church*, which is a collection of all kinds of people from all kinds of economic backgrounds, racial backgrounds, and, uh, spiritual backgrounds . . . ah, that's why I love going to see U2. I mean, I go to church and I love the people in my church, but I . . . yeah . . . seeing U2 feels more like church, the way it should be in my head. I think a really good encounter with, you know, the metaphysical aspect of life leaves you with a desire to be a peacemaker.

So I think when that is transmitted in a concert that filters through the skin, you don't have to be, you know, a "social justice person" as long as the message is there and you're able to connect with it.

I think that U2 fans really and truly are different from fans of, you know, whoever—pick an artist; we're probably more politically aware and more likely to be active in personal acts of engagement. There's something we identify in one another; there is kind of this feeling of equality, camaraderie, holding one another accountable and caring for one another—like a huge family of different ages and stages of development, everybody is affected by everybody.

I mean, you start out with "A Day without Me" and then you move to "Sunday Bloody Sunday"; that really is sort of like the two ends of the spectrum in terms of being completely introspective versus very outwardly thinking. The world changes, we impact the world, it impacts us, and it's a corevolutionary process. I've also tried to become a better human; U2's music has shown me that is also a way of doing humanitarian work for the world.

And that's another thing I absolutely love about U2, which I think is so important: they do not tell you what to think—they want you to come along for the ride and to do what you think is socially responsible. A song can't change the world. It's a song triggering something in someone. The music and, specifically, Bono's activism and speeches provide a spark to not go home and just watch television. Get up off your ass and do something! Through U2, I very quickly was able to find the kind of organization that would be my home—specifically, Amnesty International.

If all the U2 people are working in the same direction, it doesn't have to be the same organizations or efforts or whatever. When we're all working in the same direction, I'm, like, not off track. There are many different things that people are involved with because of U2. "The community" is an intangible thing, yet, I mean, I can point to things that have been accomplished, you know, tangible things that have been accomplished. You are one person who feels a certain way that a million other people feel too, and if you could find others and get together, you can change the world.

Findings, Theory, and Practice

The participants shared several characteristics that, when taken together, can be used to sketch a profile of this group and build a tentative theory

of how a connection between U2's music and their progressive awareness arose. U2's music is part of the basic subsoil of their essential, mineral
selves from which their progressive awareness springs, which nourishes and
shapes their meaningful being and action in the world. Five compelling
themes emerged in the participants' narratives that serve as starting points
for my wider theoretical reflections and ideas about how music intertwines
with forming one's progressive awareness: the profile of a conscious listener; consciousness raising; developing, expressing, and reinforcing values;
enhancing connections; synthesizing ways of meaningful being and action.

The profile of a conscious listener outlines common personal traits and
shared life experiences among the participants that may be seen as predis-
posing them to have U2's music significantly impact and influence their
lives; this profile also identifies markers of the U2 community that they
believe define it as a "conscious" community.

Adolescence was a time when the participants remember U2 colliding
with their emerging sense of self, their place in the world, their values, and
their progressive awareness. Their formative experiences with music often
occurred in the context of their families of origin. Music was an organic
part of their lives from youth, serving socializing and bonding functions
to the extent that perceiving links among music, consciousness, and action
appears to be intrinsic to who the participants are.

The participants' stories suggest that they are seekers asking quintessen-
tial questions about life and that U2's music is part of their quest. They describe the "democratic habits of the heart"—respect for others, self-respect,
willingness to accept responsibility for the common good, willingness to
welcome diversity and to approach others with openness—which they
attribute to the wider U2 community, of which they feel a part.[6] They
see the U2 culture and concert scene as portals for a natural and expected
engagement with social issues.

The theme of consciousness raising relates to the participants' epis-
temology and how U2's music is tied to their paths of knowledge. This
theme reveals that U2 supports them to think autonomously and reflexively
in ways that challenge habitual modes and reveal systems of oppression and
injustice. U2's music is part of what is playing the role of a master narrative in the participants' knowledge construction. Their epistemologies are
being formed through informal or covert learning. These forms of learning might include learning in social action that might not be recognized
immediately but which takes place during collective activity involving a
group of people who might share social background, a common history,
or interest; or when people become aware of the learning potential of their

activities and decide to learn from their experiences, through assimilative or incremental learning, propelled by an integrating circumstance that is usually the culmination of a relatively long-staged process—conscious and/ or unconscious—of searching and exploring for something that is missing in one's life; or through ideology critique and conscientization—the critically reflective dimension to learning—which happens through the process by which people learn to recognize how uncritically accepted and unjust dominant ideologies are embedded in everyday life or when people are aware of themselves within their social context and capable of acting to change it; or through epochal transformation in habits of mind, which could be the result of a disorienting dilemma or event that triggers a sudden, dramatic, and reorienting insight. Transformative learning theory suggests that once a personal transformation has taken place, people seldom return to their old perspectives.

The theme of developing, expressing, and reinforcing values illuminates how U2's music, integrity, and humanitarian efforts affect how participants determine for themselves that which is moral, aesthetic, and worthy of choice. My findings describe a connection between U2's music and axiology—the branch of philosophy dealing with values—whereby the participants perceive their axiological schemas in the music and in the integrity they see in the band members that amplifies the participants' voices, reinforces their value systems, and supports them to live authentically.

For the participants, U2's music speaks the language of theologian Martin Buber: "Relation is reciprocity . . . inscrutably involved; we live in the currents of universal reciprocity."[7] Through U2, they are supported to embrace values and make life choices that run counter to a consumer culture that suggests that we are individual self-seekers, rather than having a moral obligation to serve others and work for justice.

The music may not give only, or even mostly, new information or values messages to the participants; it does give a sense of belonging, a renewed commitment to social action for the common good. Adult educator Stephen D. Brookfield writes, "We need others to serve as critical mirrors who highlight our assumptions for us and reflect them back to us. . . . We also need our critical friends to provide emotional sustenance, to bring us 'reports from the front' of their own critical journeys."[8] U2 and the U2 community can be such critical friends.

The theme of enhancing connections shows how U2's music supports the participants to access modes of perception beyond the linear-rational and move beyond the self toward an enhanced connection with others that links personal development with social change. "Others" include those whose experiences may seem alien and incomprehensible as well as the Spirit, or that which is transcendent. These enhanced connections in turn enhance the participants' sense of agency, empowerment, responsibility, reciprocity, and mutuality.

U2's music seems to express and maybe even answer a deep spiritual longing, countering what seems to be a common condition in the modern world of spiritual vacancy or "soul loss"—what contemporary North American Hispanic communities call *susto*. My findings suggest there is something raw and accessible about the spiritual element of U2's music; it transcends religious categories or denominations and is evident in the way that the music transmits joy, evokes a natural euphoria, and moves the listener to fully engage with life. The participants describe U2's music as being and speaking deep truth, and they suggest that the spiritual element of the music and of themselves is inseparable from the spiritual element of justice work and the need for justice in the world. Their stories tell of U2 concerts as "church the way it should be," crafted for the audience and band to cocreate a spiritual experience that builds an energetic field beyond the physical world into the realm of transcendent, uplifting diversity. U2's music is calming not in an escapist way but in an engage-the-world-from-a-place-of-inner-peace way.

For the participants, U2 brought catharsis and hope in the face of crisis. Their stories highlight a unifying element in the music, such as what it provided for concertgoers after the attacks of September 11, 2001. By generating a sense of communion and building cross-cultural bridges, the U2 culture fills the roles of a community as outlined by West African elder Malidoma Somé: a healthy sense of belonging; an outlet for natural abilities; and a recognition that the needs of the one are the needs of the many, not the needs of the one over the needs of the many.[9] The unity at U2 concerts could be a model for unity in daily life.

The participants say that seeing U2 and others in the U2 community working for progressive issues reassures their own direction. Such a feeling echoes systems thinker Sally Goerner's sense that no one has to tackle the rethinking of society alone, because millions of people are already working on it one spot at a time.[10] U2's music, concerts, and community play the role of a critical friend who challenges feelings of helplessness and hopelessness in the face of the need for change and highlights the need for coalition building.

Finally, the theme of synthesizing ways of meaningful being and action reveals that the participants have constructed a foundation for their progressive awareness built with essential themes that they perceive in U2's music. Their foundations form a base that nourishes their state of being and balances their state of doing. The core themes of U2's music build this foundation, and these themes distill to a metatheme that addresses politics in the widest, nonpartisan sense: the politics of being human. Becoming more fully human is a key component of an evolution toward a culture of peace, and despite all the suffering, violence, and problems in the world, we are moving in this direction.

Love is a central theme of U2's music, not romantic love but love in accordance with what feminist poet Audre Lorde envisions as the erotic: the source of energy and ground of all being from which to pursue genuine change in world.[11] This love resonates with feminist scholar Carol Christ's description of love as the deep connection to other people and all beings in the web of life that rises from our deepest knowledge and which is a well of replenishing and provocative force.[12] It fits with critical pedagogue Paulo Freire's view that "no matter where the oppressed are found, the act of love is commitment to their cause—the cause of liberation."[13]

For the participants, the subjectivity of U2's music leaves it open to interpretation by listeners. U2's lyrics can be interpreted in multiple and equally valid ways, indicating that the human condition may be understood as a constant effort to negotiate contested meanings. U2's music supports the idea that inner development and outward-oriented action and personal and social change are all interconnected and are critical for improving the world. This is consistent with the Buddha's central doctrine of causality, *paticca samuppada*: one's personal awakening is integral to the awakening of one's community, and both play an integral role in the awakening of one's country and the world. These developments do not occur sequentially, in a linear fashion, but synchronously, each abetting and reinforcing the other.

The participants' stories suggest that music changes the world because it changes people and that being a better human being—a mandate or effect of U2's music—is in itself a way to change the world. U2's music prompts changes in perspective that cue changes in being, which is an illustration of transformative learning in action and supports the inextricability of individual and social change. Opportunities for committed action are found through U2, and U2 concerts are themselves a site for action.

Implications for Radical Education and Action for Social Change

For the participants, U2's music reflects and reinforces what are the best, commonly held threads of theories and approaches in the areas of radical education and action for social change. U2's music is rich with potential for transformative learning through challenging taken-for-granted assumptions, creating spaces for open dialogue, and developing critical perspectives; it can promote a culture of peace by integrating and valuing complexity and intricacy, relationship, and interconnection and by articulating a need for fundamental changes in values, attitudes, and behaviors for critiquing oppressive structures and developing alternatives to cultures of war characterized by violence, authoritarian decision making, exploitation, and the image of the Other as enemy; and it is useful for Freire's pedagogy of the oppressed by heightening empathy for and identification with the Other and challenging the "education for social control" model known as the "banking approach."

My findings show that U2's music has a powerful effect for loosening the grip of ego. Habits of mind and points of view that are often emotionally charged and strongly defended when tied up in a sense of self can begin to change when one's ego is less controlling of one's self and one's self-interests. Loosening ego attachment is also needed for *connected knowing*: using the tools of empathy, imagination, and storytelling to enter another's frame of mind when disagreement seems to prevail.[14]

U2's music seems to also offer an egalitarian model for relationships and places an emphasis on thinking for oneself, searching, seeking, challenging the status quo, and questioning. In its call to think for oneself, U2's music supports problem-posing education; *mindful learning*, the continuous creation of new categories, openness to new information, and awareness of more than one perspective, and *autonomous thinking*, the ability of a learner to negotiate one's own purposes, values, feelings, and meanings rather than act on those of others. The potential for using music as a tool in formal educational settings is largely unexplored despite the prominence of popular music as a cultural form and the sociopolitical dimensions of music such as U2's. No curriculum or learning process, no matter how passive, is entirely devoid of spaces for alternative forms of learning that question, contest, or subvert dominant values, norms, and modes. I see a need to explore the educative potential of popular music as a site for resistance and to identify spaces and strategies for using it as a tool for cultural empowerment in and beyond the prevailing educational system. This is a possible application of my findings, as is developing music-dense centers for grassroots civic learning in the mold of the Highlander Center—one of the few activist educational institutions in the United States to recognize music's value for social movements. Centers such as this may offer more democratic access to learning and help to develop a more alert citizenry, as many in our society are cut off from the authorized sites of higher education.[15]

Educational methods have tended to focus on the head and ignore the rest of our being, but from a spiritual perspective, learning does not just involve the intellect. Instead, it includes every aspect of our being—the physical, emotional, aesthetic, and spiritual—and is often accompanied by a sense of awe and wonder. Transformative learning theory suggests that the arts offer alternatives to making meaning by rational forms only and are central to self-knowledge and learning through soul. My findings strongly suggest that U2's music and concerts have great potential for bringing the spiritual dimension back to the educational sphere.

Paradigmatic shifts in societies can be difficult because people are generally entrenched in their organizing systems of belief. But as one's foundation of progressive awareness develops and is buttressed, one can consistently act in the world to effect paradigmatic changes that seem intangible but have deep-reaching implications for changes in systems. As my study found that U2's music helped reinforce the participants' connection to progressive awareness, I suggest that the U2 culture can help leverage systems changes.

As music is used worldwide, particularly in the developing worlds and in indigenous communities, for peace building, reconciliation, and trauma healing, my findings suggest that with its strong connection to the theme of peace, U2's music can help support a culture of peace in mainstream Western society by promoting generative, as opposed to combative and reactionary, discourse.[16] Social movements have traditionally had an active and outward-directed focus, while the New Age movement, which posits a peaceful, inevitable transition to a new kind of future with a different type of consciousness, has been largely a movement with an inner focus. A great strength of transformative learning and the culture of peace is that they combine these elements, and my findings speak to a similar nexus of inner/outer and personal/social change supported through U2's music.

Writings about U2 often describe the band members as prophets and shamans; to the participants, the musicians are more like spiritual brokers or conduits for their audience. U2 may contribute to reintegrating the language of spirit into political and civic life by helping to expand the role of the artist in our society beyond that of mere entertainer, thus reintegrating the language of spirit into civic life.

A culture in touch with its spiritual connection is a culture poised to evolve; in this respect, I contend that our culture is stagnant. My findings suggest that we can use U2's music as a spiritual technology to develop our spiritual capacities, and the ritual quality of U2's concerts and community can evoke our emotional self and transpersonal experiences, provide healing and the reaffirmation of each individual's life purpose, and enable people to live and act with authenticity. By creating rituals tailored to solving specific social issues and by actively involving people in seeking solutions based in ritual, we can achieve a deeper solution than through words and rhetoric alone. Malidoma Patrice Somé suggests that breaking circular arguments through the power of ritual is an area where indigenous people can help the West.[17] Perhaps there is an opening here for U2 concerts as rituals of today to forward the cause of social change? And on the personal level, perhaps U2's music can be used for maintenance rituals to keep one in normal running condition, providing a self-care tune-up at the level of the spirit, helping activists and change agents engage their work from a place of strength instead of reactionary depletion. The resonant leadership concept of the cycle of stress and renewal offers a similar strategy for using U2's music.[18]

When considering a society's youth, activist and music industry insider Daniel Goldberg appropriated the phrase *teen spirit* as the central concept for his book *How the Left Lost Teen Spirit* to refer to the energy that a political movement needs. This energy is needed to both mobilize young people and reach older people who are affected by the language of popular culture but make political decisions based on emotional and spiritual reasons rather than purely intellectual ones.[19] Teen spirit is a metaphor for the political energy of new generations. We need a jolt of it in radical education and action for social change; we need to enlist young people in these areas, and music can give us ideal inroads to Generation Next.

Adolescence was the time in the participants' lives when they had their first and most vivid experiences at the intersection of music, sociopolitical thought, and action and their emerging identity. U2's music was a primary mode of meaning making for them from youth onward over more traditional sources, such as school, parents, and church. We can leverage the strong influence that popular music has on youth by using it to expose them to messages and values that pose alternatives to the dominant discourse and to encourage autonomous thinking. We can look for ways to use music with youth to help them negotiate the developmental tasks of adolescence such that their potential for progressive awareness is nurtured. Educators of youth can use music as an effective strategy for prompting co-ownership of the learning process. Perhaps most important, we can capitalize on young people's affinity for popular music by letting it help us speak to them in their language, on their terms, to effectively engage them in radical education and social movement organizing.

American political culture desperately needs to build bridges with young people. Popular music is needed in politics if inroads to youth are to be forged because, as Goldberg points out, for many young people, their music is interwoven with their politics. Music can offer a vital point of entry for political and social engagement, but alone it doesn't make the change—music plus change skills are needed. Popular music is a largely untapped resource in education and training for developing the transforming skills that learners require to participate actively and effectively in processes of social change. We can harness music such as U2's to engage youth and teach them the skills they need to be part of the change process.

A Foundation at the Crossroads

Because it was limited to six research participants, my small, deep study may be used only as an introduction to how U2's music fits into the lives of a small group of listeners who see U2's music as having an impact on their progressive awareness. My work provides a foundation for wider theoretical reflection and further research in this rich area of inquiry that can affect the arenas of radical education and action for social change.

U2's music is not a panacea. The participants' stories have shown it to be one avenue for generating dialogue, encouraging action for social change, and shifting ways of thinking and being in the world. I anticipate a time when we will witness a great rebirth of stimulating sociopolitical debate and a wave of return to engaged civic life via forms of popular culture, and I think my research opens space for me, the participants, and you to take further action toward this end. I hope that this chapter will spark more questions than answers—questions that keep us discussing the civics of popular music. I hope to see you down at the crossroads of music and change.

Notes

1. Ron Sakolsky, "Hangin' Out on the Corner of Music and Resistance," in *Rebel Musics: Human Rights, Resistant Sounds, and the Politics of Music Making*, ed. Daniel Fischlin and Ajay Heble, (Montreal, Canada: Black Rose Books, 2003), 44–67.

2. Norman D. Livergood, *Progressive Awareness: Critical Thinking, Self-Awareness and Critical Consciousness* (Tempe, AZ: Dandelion Books, 2005).

3. For my full report, see R. E. Seiler, "Potent Crossroads: An Inquiry at the Intersection of U2's Music and the Progressive Awareness of Their Listeners," doctoral dissertation, 2010, UMI No. 3407385.

4. Leslie Rebecca Bloom, "Stories of One's Own: Nonunitary Subjectivity in Narrative Representation," in *Qualitative Research in Practice*, ed. Sharan B. Merriam (San Francisco: Jossey-Bass, 2002), 289–309.

5. Jennifer Clements, "Organic Inquiry: Research in Partnership with Spirit," draft manuscript, 2002.

6. Jack Mezirow, "Learning to Think like an Adult: Core Concepts of Transformation Theory," in *Learning as Transformation: Critical Perspectives on a Theory in Progress*, ed. Jack Mezirow and associates (San Francisco: Jossey-Bass, 2000), 3–34.

7. Bruce Wilshire, *The Moral Collapse of the University: Professionalism, Purity, and Alienation* (New York: State University of New York Press, 1990), 187.

8. Stephen D. Brookfield, "Transformative Learning as an Ideology Critique," in Mezirow, *Learning as Transformation*, 146.

9. Malidoma Patrice Somé, *The Healing Wisdom of Africa: Finding Life Purpose through Nature, Ritual, and Community* (New York: Penguin Putnam, 1998), 91.

10. Sally Goerner, *After the Clockwork Universe: The Emerging Science and Culture of Integral Society* (Charlotte, NC: Baker & Taylor, 2001), 8.

11. Audre Lorde, "Uses of the Erotic: The Erotic as Power," *Weaving the Visions: Patterns in Feminist Spirituality*, ed. Judith Plaskow and Carol Christ (San Francisco: HarperCollins, 1989), 208–13.

12. Carol Christ, *Rebirth of the Goddess* (New York: Routledge, 1997), 107.

13. Paulo Freire, *Pedagogy of the Oppressed* (New York: Continuum, 2006), 89.

14. Mary Field Belenky and Ann V. Stanton, "Inequality, Development, and Connected Knowing," in Mezirow, *Learning as Transformation*, 71–102.

15. Ron Eyerman and Andrew Jamison, *Music and Social Movements: Mobilizing Traditions in the Twentieth Century* (Cambridge, England: Cambridge University Press, 1998), 3.

16. Anne Goodman, "Transformative Learning and Cultures of Peace," in *Expanding the Boundaries of Transformative Learning: Essays on Theory and Praxis*, ed. Edmund V. O'Sullivan, Amish Morrell, and Mary Ann O'Connor (New York: Palgrave, 2002), 193.

17. Somé, *Healing Wisdom of Africa*, 161.

18. Richard Boyatzis and Annie McKee, *Resonant Leadership: Renewing Yourself and Connecting with Others through Mindfulness, Hope, and Compassion* (Boston: Harvard Business School Press, 2005).

19. Daniel Goldberg, *How the Left Lost Teen Spirit* (New York: RDV Books, 2005), 15.

The Authentic Self in Paul Ricoeur and U2

4

JEFFREY F. KEUSS AND SARA KOENIG

I N "WAKE UP DEAD MAN," on U2's album *Pop*, the song's protagonist, as voiced by Bono, laments the loss of understanding of who he is in the world. Mirroring the lamentation of the psalmist in Psalm 44, the protagonist speaks of three major struggles: first, isolation ("I'm alone in this world"); second, living in relation to his own mortality (the consistent refrain "wake up dead man"); and third, the continued striving to make sense of his life amid the cultural swirl of "rhythms that's confusing you . . . the sound of blades in rotation . . . the traffic and circulation," as opposed to "the story / the one about eternity / and the way it's all going to be." The conversation partner and confessor for U2's lament is Jesus, someone who the protagonist realizes is "looking out for us" and who is one with the "father," who "made the world in seven / he's in charge of heaven."

From U2's first album, *Boy,* to its most recent, *No Line on the Horizon,* songs such as "Wake Up Dead Man" are key to understanding U2's musical canon as containing a deep and abiding search for what it means to be human in a dehumanizing age—what we are calling the search for the authentic self. To explore this notion in U2's songs, we consider philosopher Paul Ricoeur's vision of authentic personhood, as outlined in two of his most seminal works, *Oneself as Another* and *Figuring the Sacred*, in which he reassesses the human subject as a hermeneutic movement—that is, the authentic self is not a fixed or static given that awaits one to passively receive it but is a task that is to be performed. Furthermore, as seen in both U2's canon and Ricoeur's philosophy, we do not perform the task of "authentic personhood" to garner or seal absolution ("be good and then you will be with God"), but rather, our identity as authentic persons is an indicative first and an imperative second ("You are chosen by God, therefore go and feed the sheep"). As U2 has affirmed throughout its canon, humans are created to be transcendent—in the language of the Christian tradition, made in the image of God—and, as such, find their vocation in returning to the Transcendent and calling out beyond their isolation and imminent failures to work toward a deep and abiding community.

Yet if humans are created for such soaring heights, why the malaise, despair, unresolved sorrow, and lamenting that define human existence? We suggest that both Ricoeur and U2 would say that the definition of an authentic personhood is ultimately not the modern, post-Enlightenment conception of the self as a singular, isolated, self-sufficient, self-sustaining reality; instead, they would say that the best self is one who is there with and for others. When U2 and Ricoeur are examined together, there arises a deep commitment to a humanism that is often absent from the philosophical discourses of the academy and the songs that fill many of our iPods.

Identity as Composite and Multivaliant

As Ricoeur masterfully explained in his book *Oneself as Another*,[1] selfhood or "who we are" is ultimately a composite of who we are over time and who we are in the moment—not merely as physical beings but, more importantly, as responsible, ethical beings in and for the world. Ricoeur believes that one of the problems with our understanding of the self is that we do not sufficiently understand the distinction between the self (in Latin, the *ipse*) and the same (in Latin, the *idem*) but instead frequently collapse them. In other words, we assume that being an authentic self is to remain the same over time, to not change. Admittedly, that is one element to being an authentic person: to remain consistent. Ricoeur refers to this as one's character, "the set of distinctive marks which permit the reidentification of the person as being the same" or "the set of lasting dispositions by which a person is recognized."[2]

But another way to be an authentic self is to keep promises or, as Ricoeur puts it, "keeping one's word in faithfulness to the word that has been given."[3] Here is where "self" and "same" diverge, for to keep a promise is not to remain the same through time but to defy the changes wrought by time. Ricoeur explains, "Keeping one's promise . . . does indeed appear to stand as a challenge to time, a denial of change: even if my desire were to change, even if I were to change my opinion or my inclination, 'I will hold firm.'"[4]

Ricoeur seeks to hold the ideas of sameness and selfhood (*idem/ipse*) in tension with each other to mediate between them. That is, for Ricoeur, an authentic self is one who both remains the same over time (*idem*) and is faithful to promises, maintaining her or his selfhood (*ipse*) in spite of change. If Ricoeur is careful to maintain the distinction between them, he is careful not to polarize them, and what mediates these two poles for Ricoeur is a "narrative identity." When Ricoeur puts sameness and selfhood in a necessary relationship, a tension and beauty emerge; U2 employs a similar dialectical strategy for making meaning for oneself with lyrical counterpointing. From the Latin *punctus contra punctum* (note against note), counterpointing happens when a composer draws together different, seemingly counter notes to actually create depth of meaning. One song that illustrates this lyrically from the U2 canon is "Hawkmoon 269," from *Rattle and Hum*, in which Bono strings together Beat poet Polaroid snapshots of seemingly random similes in an attempt to show the extent to which his lover's love is the organizing narrative for his identity: "Like heat needs the sun / Like honey on her tongue / Like the muzzle of a gun / Like oxygen . . . Like a needle needs a vein / Like someone to blame / Like a thought unchained / Like a runaway train." Without the constant refrain of "I need your love," the simile snapshots of the song would be chaotic and meaningless. Yet with the presence of and desire for love, they all make sense in relation to one another and further amplify the nature of the protagonist's love for another. Within any narrative, the disparate elements of a given character (her or his experiences, diversity, growth, etc.) become unified by the plot of the narrative. Ricoeur explains, "The narrative constructs the identity of the character, what can be called his or her narrative identity, in constructing that of the story told. It is the identity of the story that makes the identity of the character."[5] As seen in "Hawkmoon 269," to reduce the tension of the seemingly disparate and random elements that constitute the search for purpose in one's life can limit or even deaden the breadth, depth, and height of that which we were created for. It is one thing to say, "I need your love"; it is quite another to admit that what constitutes this love is far from certain or reasonable. Akin to Ricoeur's *idem/ipse* dialectic, within the lyrics of "Hawkmoon 269," it is the tension rather than the resolution where meaning is found and forged.

But a narrative composed of tensions also has some limitations. In a narrative, there is a sense of beginning and ending more so than in life: we humans cannot remember our birth or even our early childhood, and our death is recounted only by those who live after us.[6] Ricoeur refers to

Alasdair MacIntyre's idea of "the narrative unity of life" from *After Virtue*, which assumes that life must be gathered into a whole for it to be a good life. As MacIntyre notes, the narrativity of life becomes a quest that is conclusively more than a literary device; it is life itself:

> The unity of human life is the unity of a narrative quest. Quests sometimes fail, are frustrated, abandoned, or dissipated into distractions; and human lives may in all these ways also fail. But the only criteria for success or failure in a human life as a whole are the criteria of success or failure in a narrated or to-be-narrated quest. . . . It is in the course of the quest and only through encountering and coping with the various particular harms, dangers, temptations, and distractions which provide any quest with its episodes and incidents that the goal of the quest is finally to be understood.[7]

In this way, MacIntyre reminds us that the human life is one framed by unity and not discord. But this is a narrative unity rather than merely a reflection on the data points that populate our days. What seems random and haphazard is often the attempt to plot the meaning and context of our lives on a canvas that is too small. For our lives to take the direction toward that for which we are created, we need to embrace the reality of fiction in our existence; much of what is truly real and enduring requires an imaginative leap as much as a critical and reasoned reflection.

One of U2's recent songs exemplifying this call to take an imaginative leap of expansive trust and faith is "Stand Up Comedy" from *No Line on the Horizon*. Bono notes that while winning the "DNA lottery may have left [us] smart," it doesn't necessarily affirm our ultimate purpose. This lyrical riff on the "DNA lottery" is a fun spin on the current New Atheism and the so-called Intelligent Design debates. Bono undercuts all the rhetoric by acknowledging that even though we have "won" the planet's "DNA lottery"—whether by chance or by design—it doesn't get us to the heart of the matter. Bono sings that we "can stand up for hope, faith and love" as the grand Christian virtues but not just as objective intellectual assertions. As Bono continues the verse, he decries choosing knowledge and willpower over faith when he sings, "While I'm getting over certainty / Stop helping God across the road like a little old lady." This double challenge—(1) dropping the search for certainty in favor of faith amid the Intelligent Design debates and (2) allowing God to, well, *be* God— becomes the liberating truth for the protagonist of the song. True, we can objectively affirm "hope, faith and love," but until we actually "stand up" and do something about it—faith in action—we remain in a "helter skelter" life.[8]

The Responsible Self as the Sonic Mystic

For Ricoeur, there is no shortcut to personhood; one must take the long route. As U2 put it in "I Still Haven't Found What I'm Looking For," "yes, I'm still running." The authentic person responds to the other and expresses one's response in ethical aims and moral norms, or as U2 put it in "Stand Up Comedy," "stand up for your love." Bono, in a 1981 interview for *Rolling Stone*, identified the goal of the band as moving beyond punk and reestablishing rock and roll as a vehicle for people to think about their actions in relation to one another:

> The idea of punk at first was, "Look, you're an individual, express yourself how you want, do what you want to do." . . . But that's not the way it came out in the end. The Sex Pistols were a con, a box of tricks sold by Malcolm McLaren. Kids were sold the imagery of violence, which turned into the reality of violence, and it's that negative side that I worry about. People like Bruce Springsteen carry hope. Like the Who—"Won't Get Fooled Again." I mean, there is a song of endurance, and that's the attitude of great bands. We want our audience to think about their actions and where they are going, to realize the pressures that are on them, but at the same time, not to give up.[9]

As Bono stated, U2 desired to move beyond the idea of being an individual to considering how one's actions affect and relate to others. To wake up from the distraction of the isolated self that the protagonist in "Wake Up Dead Man" warns us of ("Listen over the hum of the radio / Listen over the sound of blades in rotation / Listen through the traffic and circulation / Listen as hope and peace try to rhyme / Listen over marching bands playing out their time"), we must be willing to listen to the true music of our lives that is found in responsibility of and for others. This move from selfishness to otherness as essential to forming an authentic self is in keeping with Ricoeur's assertion that the self cannot be fully understood as an autonomous being, living in isolation or in a vacuum. Rather, the other helps define the self, especially in relationship to keeping one's promises, or "self-constancy," which Ricoeur defines as that manner of conducting himself or herself so that others can count on that person. Because someone is counting on me, I am accountable for my actions before another. The term *responsibility* unites both meanings: "counting on" and "being accountable for." It unites them, adding to them the idea of a response to the question "Where are you?" asked by another who needs me. This response is the following: "Here I am!" a response that is a statement of self-constancy.[10]

By responding "Here I am!" to the question from a specific other, a self becomes grounded and even free enough to act for the other. While all the differing ways that a person can act and live may become overwhelming, by answering the call of the other, the self can move into action. In this way, self-constancy (the way that a self acts so the other can count on her or him) is primary to what it means to be an authentic person. Responding to the call of the other requires a relinquishment of our isolation and self-essentialism and, as such, a certain permeability in relation to others where the firm boundary of what constitutes selfhood is let go of in favor of community. For U2, the enduring metaphor of music as identity allows both the constancy of identity and the absolute relinquishment of the self.

The Sonic Mystic in U2

In the U2 canon, one of the key metaphors for illustrating authentic personhood is music, or at its most primordial, sound itself—both as the shape of our actions in the world as in "Magnificent" ("I was born / I was born to sing for you / From the womb my first cry, it was a joyful noise"), and as our very destination, as in "Get On Your Boots" ("Let me in the sound / Let me in the sound / Let me in the sound, sound / Let me in the sound, sound / Meet me in the sound"). Sound is completely permeable and therefore not restricted by boundary such that we can join with others in singing the chorus of "40" at the end of a U2 concert, for example, and add our voice to those of others. Sound is also distinct: my sound may be identifiable as my own signature, something that makes me different from another. Yet, I have the choice of joining with another in such a way that my own voice blends in or stands out, and sound can support harmony or dissonance in a way that other types of words sometimes cannot. In this way, self as sound is an apt method for the personhood of authenticity called for in both U2 and Ricoeur, in particular the way that sound as wave moves into the world without a requirement for return—the song remains efficacious even without the echo or response.

Ricoeur presents identity as being forged in addition to self-constancy when the individual exhibits what he refers to as "self-apophasis": something that occurs where an individual recognizes her or his emptiness and failure in relation to the other and is therefore willing to release himself for the sake of love. This self-apophasis resonates with the mystical tradition of the Christian faith and, in particular, the threefold movement of the Christian life as purgation, illumination, and union.[11] Much of the U2 canon advocates for this method of achieving our true identity. As people "born of sound," we are called to be "sonic mystics" and are called to a movement of Ricoeur's self-apophasis of purgation, illumination, and union. While the U2 canon is rich with examples of this call to sonic mysticism, two songs in particular that illustrate this theology are "With or Without You" from *The Joshua Tree* and "Walk On" from *All That You Can't Leave Behind.*

Historically, for Christian pilgrims or disciples, the first level of the mystical movement toward ecstasy that one would pass through is called the *Purgatio*, or purgation, during which one struggles through prayer and ascetic practices to gain control of "the flesh," specifically over gluttony, lust, and the desire for possessions. The Purgative stage consists of active purgation, the conscientious seeking of release from that which clouds the *Imago Dei*—the Image of God—which is our true identity, and passive purgation, comprising events beyond our control, such as revelations of wonder, suffering, and crisis. During this first stage, one is to learn that any strength that one has to resist these fleshly desires comes directly from the Holy Spirit. As Bono seeks union with the lover who is the desire of "With or Without You," he acknowledges that this call of the other for union will require his death, whether he chooses union or isolation ("with or without you I can't live"). In "Walk On," Bono points to the fact that only in absolute self-apophasis can we become freed to become what we are: "Leave it behind / You've got to leave it behind / All that you fashion / All that you make / All that you build / All that you break / All that you measure / All that you steal / All this you can leave behind / All that you reason / All that you sense / All that you speak / All you dress up / All that you scheme."

In "Moment of Surrender," from *No Line on the Horizon*, the protagonist acknowledges this coupling of the active and passive purgation within himself as mirrored in the world around him as well: "I've been in every black hole / At the altar of the dark star / My body's now a begging bowl / That's begging to get back, begging to get back / To my heart / To the rhythm of my soul / To the rhythm of my unconsciousness / To the rhythm that yearns / To be released from control."

The willingness to relinquish control and see that our life is ultimately a begging bowl through actively and passively laying down all that you can't leave behind moves one to the end of the *Purgatio* stage. Traditionally, this first stage would last many years and bring one to the point of learning to trust peacefully in the Lord for all of one's needs.

Next, the *Illuminatio* commences, during which one learns the paths to holiness revealed in the Gospel and practices the acceptance of suffering.

Traditionally, Christian disciples would take in visitors and students during this stage and tend to the poor as much as their resources allowed, all the while following Christ's teachings in his Sermon on the Mount and continuing to live humbly in the Spirit of God.

The final stage is the *Unitio*, a period when the soul of the Christian disciples bonded with the Spirit of God in a union often described as the marriage depicted in the Song of Solomon. This bond is an ecstatic union marked by ineffable joy, exaltation, and proclamation. As Bono sings in "Breathe," "St. John Divine, on the line, my pulse is fine / But I'm running down the road like loose electricity / While the band in my head plays a striptease." Stripped bare and moving as "loose electricity," Bono evokes the author of the apocalyptic Book of Revelation that at once marks the end of all things and yet the beginning of all things. Freed from the baggage that couldn't previously be left behind, the authentic self of "Breathe" is caught up, as was St. John in his vision on the Isle of Patmos, in a union with the divine that moves him to prophetically call to all those who have ears to hear: "We are people borne of sound / The songs are in our eyes / Gonna wear them like a crown / Walk out, into the sunburst street / Sing your heart out, sing my heart out / I've found grace inside a sound / I found grace, it's all that I found / And I can breathe / Breathe now."

This movement into *Unitio* is at once a proclamation and something ineffable that moves us beyond language itself. One of the most famous ineffable screams in the U2 canon is found late in "With or Without You." Immediately following the acknowledgment of lament that "you give yourself away / and you give / and you give / and you give yourself away" to the point of extinction, Bono utters a wordless, ecstatic sound, announcing a mystical union that draws one in from a place outside of sound and creates a oneness with the sound itself.

Does this union mean a complete loss of identity? Such a move would then challenge our responsibility to and for the world: if the goal is to lose the self for the sake of the other, how do I therefore remain concerned and responsive to the other? This "other" who calls the self out and to whom the self is accountable is not just the human other. To be sure, an individual's relationship to other humans is highly important for Ricoeur, but for Ricoeur as with U2, the self also ought to be understood in relation to the divine other, to God. In *Oneself as Another*, Ricoeur sets aside most of his conversations about the human's relationship to God as beyond the scope of philosophy and in the domain of theology. For example, as Ricoeur discusses how self-esteem is connected with the esteem of the other as a self, he footnotes the biblical commandment "Love your neighbor as yourself" and references Franz Rosenzweig's *The Star of Redemption*.[12] Rosenzweig argues that the primary way to understand God is through the interpretive lens of the Song of Songs, where God is the lover and humans are God's beloved. In this way, any of God's commandments are best understood as coming from the place of love, and Ricoeur's reference of Rosenzweig demonstrates how God's first command to the humans is that they love God and then love their neighbors. In other words, to love the divine other (God) is primary and from it flows the capacity to love the human other.

As with many rock bands, the ubiquity of love as a central theme for the U2 canon goes without saying. However, U2 should not be merely categorized as yet another post–New Romanticism rock band from the 1980s, coming into its own alongside acts such as Madonna, Debbie Gibson, and Culture Club. There is a distinctiveness to the type of love that U2 invokes: it is a love beyond fancy or immediacy of attraction. In "Windows in the Sky," Bono outlines the contours of what this love entails and provokes: "The shackles are undone / The bullets quit the gun / The heat that's in the sun / Will keep us when there's none / The rule has been disproved / The stone it has been moved / The grave is now a groove / All debts are removed." This is a love that does something to the protagonist, something that should be evident to observing him, as Bono sings in the chorus: "Oh can't you see what love has done? / Oh can't you see what love has done? / Oh can't you see what love has done? / What it's done to me?" It is important to note that the union that makes this love possible—a love that overturns systems of oppression, removes debts, and calls enemies into fellowship—is found in communion with the lover and is evident in the world through actions of justice and care.

For Ricoeur, the relationship of the self to the other is best expressed in ethics, which he distinguishes from morality. Ricoeur describes ethics as "the aim of an accomplished life," whereas morality is "the articulation of this aim in norms characterized by the claim to universality and by an effect of constraint."[13] Ethics, for Ricoeur, are superior to morals, because morality is just the self doing what it thinks it is supposed to do, while ethics are actions that take into account the other. Ricoeur defines the singular ethical aim as "aiming at the 'good life' with and for others, in just institutions."[14] And similar to the way that Ricoeur places conversations about God in the domain of theology, he keeps love off the list of motivators for ethical behavior. U2, however, makes explicit that what drives that aim for a "good life with and for others" is love. This is the call that Bono has taken to the world in his work as an activist when he challenges those who adhere to faith systems and moral codes but do not act on them. As Bono explained to Jann Wenner in his 2005 interview for *Rolling Stone,*

> I'm wary of faith outside of actions. I'm wary of religiosity that ignores the wider world. In 2001, only seven percent of evangelicals polled felt it incumbent upon themselves to respond to the AIDS emergency. This appalled me. I asked for meetings with as many church leaders as would have them with me. I used my background in the Scriptures to speak to them about the so-called leprosy of our age and how I felt Christ would respond to it. And they had better get to it quickly, or they would be very much on the other side of what God was doing in the world. Amazingly, they did respond. I couldn't believe it. It almost ruined it for me—'cause I love giving out about the church and Christianity.[15]

If we see this ability to live in love for others in the activism of Bono, we also find it in the lyrics of the U2 canon, especially in several songs from *No Line on the Horizon.* In "White as Snow," love is described as something complex and beyond human love: "Once I knew there was a love divine / then came a time I thought it knew me not." But the doubts about this love are countered by the lyrics in "Moment of Surrender," which proclaim, "It's not if I believe in love, but if love believes in me." Indeed, this love is not simply romantic nor up to the individual self to generate and make happen. Instead, the love that impels us to see ourselves with clear eyes, to recognize the sacredness in the face of the other, and to act ethically is a "love you can't defeat" ("Breathe"). This is the love that alters the lover, a love that "can leave such a mark," but also restores ("can heal such a scar") and enables us to join in working with and for the other, because "only love unites our hearts" ("Magnificent").

Notes

1. In the winter of 1986, Ricoeur explored the hermeneutics of the self in his Gifford Lectures at the University of Edinburgh and subsequently expanded his ideas into this book. He also abridged them—in his preface to *Oneself as Another,* Ricoeur explains two reasons why the book excludes the final two Gifford Lectures: "The Self in the Mirror of the Scriptures" and "The Mandated Self." The first is that he wanted to bracket out the convictions that tie him to biblical faith, lest his philosophy be seen as a "crypto-theology." Related to the first is the second: he defends biblical faith from becoming a "crypto-philosophy" and, in particular, hopes that biblical faith will not replace the *cogito* from being the ultimate foundation. Paul Ricoeur, *Oneself As Another* (Chicago: University of Chicago Press, 1992), 24–25. We note how where *Oneself* leaves out the question of the human relationship to God, it appears in Ricoeur's other work, as well as in

the lyrics of U2. The title of the work highlights the important themes discussed within, beginning with the idea of the self.

2. Dispositions are related to two notions: (1) habit, as being formed and acquired, and (2) the "set of acquired identifications by which the other enters into the composition of the same." Ricoeur, *Oneself as Another*, 121. Ricoeur also admits that his own understanding of character has evolved. He explains, "In the days when I was writing *The Voluntary and the Involuntary*, I placed character under the heading of 'absolute involuntary.' . . . I assigned it . . . to that level of existence which we cannot change but to which we must consent" (119).

3. Ricoeur, *Oneself as Another*, 123.

4. Ricoeur, *Oneself as Another*, 124

5. Ricoeur, *Oneself as Another*, 148.

6. Ricoeur, *Oneself as Another*, 160.

7. Alasdair MacIntyre, "The Virtues, the Unity of a Human Life, and the Concept of a Tradition," in *Why Narrative? Readings in Narrative Theology*, ed. Stanley Hauerwas and L. Gregory Jones (Grand Rapids, MI: Eerdmans, 1989), 104.

8. See Jeffrey F. Keuss, "The Comedy of *No Line on the Horizon*: A Theological Reading of U2's Latest Album," *The Other Journal: Journal of Theology and Culture*, no. 15 (March 2009), http://theotherjournal.com/article.php?id=689.

9. *Rolling Stone*, "U2: Here Comes the Next Big Thing," February 19, 1981, http://www.atu2.com/news/u2-here-comes-the-next-big-thing.html.

10. Ricoeur, *Oneself as Another*, 165.

11. These movements of self-apophasis are akin to the mystical union with the divine where the movement of the subject in relation to the divine as the threefold movements of purgation, illumination, and union. Key figures who articulated these movements include John Cassian (360–435) in his two major works, *The Institutes*, which deals with the external organization of monastic communities, and *The Conferences*, which deals with "the training of the inner man and the perfection of the heart." These stages are later articulated by St. John of the Cross (1542–1591), a Carmelite monk and author of *The Spiritual Canticles* and *The Dark Night of the Soul*.

12. "Is this the secret of the commandment 'Love thy neighbor as thyself'? This commandment would seem to belong to ethics . . . more than to morality, if one could, following Franz Rosenzweig in *The Star of Redemption* . . . maintain that the commandment 'Love me' addressed by the lover to the loved one in the spirit of the Song of Songs is earlier and superior to all laws." Ricoeur, *Oneself as Another*, footnote 32, 194.

13. Ricoeur, *Oneself as Another*, 170.

14. Ricoeur, *Oneself as Another*, 172. He discusses each one of these clauses in further detail.

15. *Rolling Stone*, "Bono: The *Rolling Stone* Interview," November 3, 2005, http://www.rollingstone.com/music/news/bono-the-rolling-stone-interview-20051103.

DON'T EXPECT, SUGGEST II

Vocal Layering as Deconstruction and Reinvention in U2　　　**5**

CHRISTOPHER ENDRINAL

BY 1990, U2 HAD PROVED BEYOND any doubt that it was an international superstar. With combined worldwide sales of *The Joshua Tree* and *Rattle and Hum* albums—released in 1987 and 1988, respectively—eclipsing twenty million, it would have been easy for the band to comfortably rest on the laurels of its massively successful recordings or even ride off into the proverbial sunset. However, the band did the exact opposite: its challenged its own success and reinvented its sound on a series of albums in the 1990s. *Achtung Baby* (1991), *Zooropa* (1993), and *Pop* (1997) served as reactions to the iconic status that the band had attained thanks to *The Joshua Tree* and *Rattle and Hum*.

Several elements have composed the core of U2's unique sonic signature throughout its career, including Adam Clayton's subtle yet forceful bass lines, the syncopated driving percussion of Larry Mullen Jr., and the Edge's trademark guitar echo and delay. Often overlooked, however, as an essential component of U2's sound, which became prevalent in the 1990s, is the vocal layering technique that the band employed on that decade's three studio albums.

Here I analyze pitch, rhythm, texture, timbre, and lyrics to identify, illustrate, and examine U2's use of two specific types of vocal layering on these albums. The first is a layering technique in which the same lyrics and melody are sung and/or spoken in different registers. The second type consists of two or more distinct sets of lyrics that often are sung and/or spoken simultaneously, with each layer having its own musical characteristics. It should be noted that *vocal layering* does not refer merely to harmonic lines layered with the main vocal melody. While harmonies do serve to stratify the vocal part and add richness and fullness to a musical texture, many times they are simply cosmetic additions, superfluous add-ons that have little or no bearing on the song's deeper-level meanings. Harmonies in most cases are secondary to the melody in terms of importance within the song's overall texture. This secondary importance is conveyed through differences in levels, vocal quality and timbre, duration and quantity, lyrical content, or any combination of these elements. Regarding the differences in levels, the main vocal line is usually mixed the loudest and thus is the most aurally prominent. Frequently, the harmony lines are sung with a different timbre from the main vocal line or are sung by a different vocalist entirely, further distinguishing them from the melody. Many harmonies often are used sparingly and are only a few beats or measures in duration, usually at key moments in the song, such as the end of a transition as a lead-in to the chorus. Finally, harmonies function primarily as shadows to the melody and therefore usually do not have an independent set of lyrics. My analysis here concerns U2's incorporation of vocal layers that are equally as significant as the primary vocal melody; it also examines the effects that these different layers have on a song's meaning and interpretation, as well as how the various layers signify major personality shifts for the band.

Multiregister Layering

Rock musicians commonly multitrack the lead vocals. That is, they often record several versions of the same vocal line and use two or more versions concurrently in the final mix of the song. Because each of these renderings has slight variations from the others (e.g., intonation, timing, phrasing, breath placement), this simple technique subtly gives more heft and depth to the vocal track, thickening its texture and sometimes giving the illusion of more than just one vocalist singing. U2's "Angel of Harlem" from *Rattle and Hum*, for example, provides a model instance of this basic type of vocal layering. In the verses, Bono's vocals are single tracked: only one layer of vocals is present. The vocal line in the chorus, however, is double tracked. Beginning on the lyrics "Soul love," a second vocal layer enters, singing the same pitches, rhythms, and lyrics, giving the vocal part more substance for the chorus section. Each layer is distinguished from the other by slight differences in breath placement, phrasing, intonation, and vibrato. The position of the layers within the stereo field is also a distinctive feature of each track. The main vocal track is mixed in the center of the stereo field, equally distributed between the left and right channels, while the doubling track is mixed to the right of center. A stereo waveform of the song reveals this placement.

As figure 5.1 illustrates, the sound density of the right channel (lower graph) is slightly thicker than that of the left channel (upper graph), reflecting the presence of the second vocal layer that doubles the main vocals. In addition to using this doubling technique, U2 uses a different type of vocal multitracking, which I call *multiregister layering*. Instead of merely recording the same vocal line several times, Bono records several versions of the line in different registers or even spoken versions, often adding electronic effects to one or more of them, thereby changing the quality and timbre of his voice in those layers. The final mix of the song incorporates two or more of these unique renderings. As a result, the vocal track has noticeably different strata, with the main melody line layered with at least one other version. U2 is fortunate to have a front man with Bono's wide vocal range. His ability to sing well in low, middle, and high registers gives the band even more creative flexibility with the vocals. Layering the main vocal line provides a similar effect to the echo/delay on the lead guitar: two or more versions of the melody presented simultaneously create a sense of sonic space. This is especially true when a song uses several vocal lines that are in different tessitura, or pitches.

The second track from *Achtung Baby*, "Even Better Than the Real Thing," uses the multiregister layering technique throughout the entire song. There are three layers of vocals: One layer hovers around the pitch A3 while the other two layers sing the same melody and lyrics an octave above, around A4. In the verses, transitions, and interverse, the chest voice delivery of the lower layer and one of the high-register layers obfuscates the presence of the third layer, which is distinguished from the other two by an airy falsetto quality.[1] This third layer is more easily audible, however, in the chorus sections. This is due perhaps to the different instrumentation in that section or simply to the fact that that layer is mixed at a higher level in the chorus from that of the verse. It is not immediately clear which layer

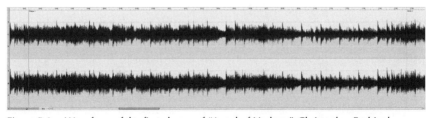

Figure 5.1.   Waveform of the first chorus of "Angel of Harlem." *Christopher Endrinal*

is the principal layer, although a case could be made for the low-register voice as the primary vocal line because it is arguably the most aurally prominent of the three within the texture. By using three vocal layers, U2 asks the listener which voice is the real Bono: the midrange baritone, the high tenor, or the light falsetto? Which Bono is "the real thing"?

The sound crafted for *The Joshua Tree* was rock based, with the guitar/bass/drums setup serving as the core of the band's musical identity. U2's mid-1980s rock sound incorporated spacious, atmospheric timbres with messages of hope, faith, and love. *Achtung Baby*, however, signaled a radical departure for the band: those messages were now cloaked in irony and masked by alternate personas. The band's sound was shaped as much by electronic distortion and signal processing as by the Edge's signature echo and delay. Which sound, then, is the "real" U2? The use of multiple vocal layers challenges the listener's (pre)conceptions of what U2 "should" sound like. Although this shift in sound clearly was symbolic of the band's embrace of technology, it served as the thematic foundation of a dark irony on which the band based the album and subsequent concert tour. U2 claimed that technology, which the band used to alter its sound, was altering the way the world was perceived, so much so that reality, as presented over the airwaves, was becoming increasingly more skewed and therefore more difficult to trust. "Even Better Than the Real Thing" not only asks the listener which Bono is the real Bono or which U2 is the real U2 but also urges the listener to contemplate the world as it is being presented by the mass media. In effect, the band is asking, "Is the digital world really better than the real world?"

In February 1992, U2 embarked on the Zoo TV tour, an ambitious, over-the-top sensory barrage intended to promote the *Achtung Baby* album. This concert tour, along with the *Zooropa* album—which was recorded, mixed, mastered, and released in the midst of the tour in 1993—further reflected U2's departure from its earlier sound, with electronic effects and techno influences becoming the focus, along with lyrical themes depicting life as a rock star and the increased multimedia onslaught of everyday life. One of the ideas developed on tour was the character of MacPhisto, whom Bono described as "a sort of old English Devil, a pop star long past his prime returning regularly from sessions on The Strip in Vegas and regaling anyone who would listen to him at cocktail hour with stories from the good old, bad old days."[2]

Bono describes "Daddy's Gonna Pay for Your Crashed Car," from *Zooropa*, as a song about "a woman who's protected from the consequences of her own actions by an indulgent sugar daddy."[3] This begs the question, just who is this sugar daddy? Bono continues: "Is it God or is it the Devil? Who's going to get you out of this mess? It's a song about being strung out. You can be strung out on a lot of things, not just [drugs]. The thing you need is the thing you're a slave to."[4] In this case, perhaps the sugar daddy about whom Bono sings is the fame and fortune associated with being a rock star, and perhaps the mess to which Bono refers—the thing to which U2 is a slave—is the self-perpetuating cycle of fame and fortune: wealth and celebrity fueling a desire for even more.

I suggest that "Daddy's Gonna Pay for Your Crashed Car" represents U2's experience of the fame-and-fortune cycle, which is conveyed in part through the lyrics and by the use of the multiregister layering technique. These layers, however, are not present throughout the entire song, as in "Even Better Than the Real Thing." In figure 5.2, each layer is identified by a different style of text: Bono is in plain text; MacPhisto is in underlined text; and the portions of the song that are sung by both voices simultaneously are in bold.[5]

Figure 5.2.   Vocal layering in "Daddy's Gonna Pay for Your Crashed Car."

Verse 1	You're a precious stone, you're out on your own.
	You know everyone in the world, but you feel alone.
	Daddy won't let you weep, Daddy won't let you ache.
	Daddy gives you as much as you can take.
Chorus	A-ha, sha-la. A-ha, sha-la.
	Daddy's gonna pay for your crashed car.
Verse 2	<u>A little uptight, you're a baby's fist</u>
	<u>Butterfly kisses up and down your wrist.</u>
	When you see Daddy coming, you're licking your lips,
	Nails bitten down to the quick.
Chorus	A-ha, sha-la. A-ha, sha-la.
	Daddy's gonna pay for your crashed car.
	Daddy's gonna pay for your crashed car.
Verse 3	<u>You've got a head full of traffic, you're a siren's song.</u>
	<u>You cry for Mama, and Daddy's right along.</u>
	He gives you the keys to a flamin' car.
	Daddy's with you wherever you are.
	Daddy's a comfort, Daddy's your best friend.
	Daddy'll hold your hand right up to the end.
Chorus	<u>A-ha, sha-la. A-ha, sha-la.</u>
	Daddy's gonna pay for your crashed car.
	Daddy's gonna pay for your crashed car.
Coda	<u>Sunday, Monday, Tuesday, Wednesday,</u>
	<u>Thursday, Friday, Saturday's alright.</u>

Note. text = Bono; <u>text</u> = MacPhisto; **text** = both

Bono begins the song, but as it progresses, he is replaced by MacPhisto; the last time Bono sings by himself is at the beginning of the second chorus. This replacement signifies the band's transformation: the low-register Bono voice represents the older U2 sound and persona—atmospheric rock with a virtuous message—while the MacPhisto voice represents the new electronic U2 sound and the band's obsession with technology and fascination with life in the limelight.

The importance of vocal layering and how each register represents a different character is reinforced by Bono's character and wardrobe changes during live concert performances on the Zoo TV tour. As seen in the concert film *Zoo TV: Live from Sydney*, after the main set and as the encore begins with the drumbeat to "Daddy's Gonna Pay for Your Crashed Car," the camera cuts to Bono backstage getting into the MacPhisto character: white makeup, gold lamé suit, platform shoes, and devil horns. When the vocal part starts, he sings the entire song in his upper register, forgoing any singing in his lower tessitura. The physical transformation is complete, as represented by the costume change; all that remains is the vocal transformation. Bono, the character, no longer exists. The singer onstage is MacPhisto now, and so he must sing in the appropriate tessitura.

Much of the critical attention paid to U2 during the 1990s focused on *Achtung Baby* and rightfully so, as that album is a landmark of the band's career and announced its personal and musical philosophies for the decade. Comparatively little attention has been focused on the other two albums from that period. *Pop* in particular has received an inordinate amount of negative criticism, but it is arguably the most underrated album of U2's extensive catalog and deserves more scholarly and (positive) critical attention. On the much-maligned album, the band was committed to making "self-consciously kitsch" pop music that had distinct U2 elements, such as a driving syncopated percussion part, an active bass line, and a guitar solo saturated in echo. *Pop* shows that the band was still willing to take chances and push the experimental envelope even further than it had on its previous two releases while still retaining many of the characteristics that make up the "U2 sound."

"Discothèque," the lead single and first track from the *Pop* record, is the band's answer to all those who thought U2 had lost its way during the decade. Beginning in the first line of the lyrics and continuing throughout the entire song, Bono references an "it" but never directly defines what "it" is. He alludes to "bubble gum" and "lovey-dovey stuff" in the transitional section, perhaps referring to the "bubble-gum pop" music sensation that captivated audiences worldwide in the 1980s and 1990s, with the likes of New Kids on the Block, Britney Spears, and the Backstreet Boys, to name a few examples. He sings to the listener, "You know what it is but you still want some," which can be interpreted to mean that, despite any stigma related to liking such music, the listener actually wants more of it. In the coda, Bono acknowledges that "Discothèque" and the rest of the *Pop* record is U2's contribution to the "bubble gum." His high falsetto "haa's" in second part of the coda simulate a slow, deliberate laughing gesture, aimed perhaps both at the listener and at himself, because he knows that the band has captured the listener's attention. He is also laughing at himself and the band because he recognizes the irony that both "Discothèque" and *Pop* create. In the early stages of U2's career, the band had made a conscious effort not to be a part of mainstream pop music but to stand alone and make music on its own terms. On *Pop*, almost twenty years into the band's career, U2 is pushing its creative limits by trying to incorporate multiple elements of contemporary pop music—rock, electronica, techno, and dance—into its sound.

Perhaps the most important section of the song, from a lyrical perspective, is the coda. Niall Stokes describes "Discothèque" as "an earnest little riddle about love, disguised as trash . . . a song about the pleasures of the flesh and the heart's yearning."[6] This interpretation can be drawn directly from the line "Oh you know there's something more." The subject of inner desires and deep emotions had always been one of the key themes for U2. In the late 1990s, however, the band was masquerading these topics in the form of a "cheesy hybrid of metal and dance."[7] Nevertheless, I interpret the song differently. While the song certainly can be construed as being about love and desire, I interpret it as being about something much more specific to the band and its artistic endeavors. The song directly challenges the listener, aiming at the U2 fan, daring him or her to not enjoy the song and, on a larger scale, U2's electronic experiments of the mid- and late 1990s. With its catchy guitar hooks and infectious club-inspired beat, "the implicit message to humorless U2 fans [is], 'You didn't think you'd like this, now did [you]?'"[8]

One of the musical elements that encourages this interpretation is the song's use of vocal layering. "Discothèque" employs the multiregister layering technique in a similar manner as in "Even Better Than the Real Thing" and "Daddy's Gonna Pay for Your Crashed Car," including vocals in both high and low registers. However, the mix in "Discothèque" is different from that in the other two songs, with the emphasis alternating between the vocal layers. Much like the song's beginning, which seems to swirl between the left and right channels, the upper and lower voices seem to alternate prominence, as if they are fighting for the listener's attention. The main vocal line shifts between the upper and lower registers. In the verses, chorus, and interverse sections, the upper register seems to be the more prominent layer. An echo is added to the high layer in the first half of the first verse. Additionally, the lower register disappears in the chorus sections, leaving only the high register singing the lyrics. The low register is not without its own prominence, however. Beginning in the second part of the first verse, on the lyrics "You can push," the lower register gains more importance in the song's overall texture. This increase in prominence accompanies the percussion entrance, thereby lending the vocal layer even more significance. It is in the transitional prechorus sections, however, that the low-register voice can be perceived not just as an important element of the song's overall texture but also as the main vocal layer. Here, starting on the lyrics "You know you're chewing bubble gum," the low-register layer is mixed more loudly than earlier in the song, shifting the listener's attention to the lower octave. At this point, the vocal layers are equally prominent within the texture. As a result, the listener is presented with a kind of "aural illusion," which is the sonic equivalent of an optical illusion in which one picture can be viewed multiple ways. In the prechorus of "Discothèque," because of the equal prominence of the high- and low-register vocal layers, the listener must decide which is the main layer.

Multivoice Layering

U2's use of vocal layering not only contributes to a particular song's meaning and interpretation but also symbolizes major stylistic, musical, and ideological shifts for the band throughout the 1990s. Additionally, multiple strata of lyrics in a song allow for increased lyrical and musical latitude, affording Bono the opportunity to create different personas, like MacPhisto. These alternate personalities serve as a kind of a looking glass through which the band comments on, reflects on, and deconstructs society, success, stardom, and even its own music. U2 represents these alternate personas with different musical layers. For example, in "Until the End of the World," the fourth track from *Achtung Baby*, the vocal layer portrays the Judas character while the lead guitar represents Jesus. In terms of vocal layering, multiple personalities can be represented in one song by including various vocal layers, a layering technique I call *multivoice layering*, in which two or more layers of dissimilar vocals—different text, melody, and rhythm—are used, often concurrently, to create a dense, complex vocal texture.

Figure 5.3.   Verse 1 of "Last Night on Earth." *Christopher Endrinal*

On "Last Night on Earth," the sixth track on *Pop*, there are two characters, each represented by its own set of lyrics, grammatical construction, and vocal range. The verses and second half of the chorus are both sung by the narrator in third person, referencing the main character of the song with the pronoun "she." These sections are sung in a midrange register raging from Eb3 to F4. The first part of each chorus and the interverse contrast these sections both grammatically as well as musically: the voice shifts to first and second person, with a reference to "you," "we," and "me"; also, the register of the vocals is an octave higher, ranging from Eb4 to C5. This second character perhaps can be construed as a guardian angel figure, advising the female main character to let go of her worries and live in the moment. For her to achieve happiness, she must "give it away." Figures 5.3 and 5.4 illustrate the differences in each section.

The multivoice layering technique is most apparent in the interverse, where the two vocal layers are presented simultaneously. In this section, the first-person voice (sung presumably by the Edge) sings a choppy, disjunct melody in a soft, high falsetto voice while Bono's vocal layer sings in a low-register chest voice. Texturally, the two layers are mixed opposite of their lyrical content: the Edge's falsetto—which sings complete sentences—is mixed softly, almost as an unintelligible background element hovering over the rest of the song's texture. However, Bono's full-voice

Figure 5.4.   Chorus of "Last Night on Earth." *Christopher Endrinal*

layer is mixed more as a foreground component yet sings primarily incomplete thoughts and phrases. Figure 5.5 illustrates the lyrical and range differences between the two layers.

In "Last Night on Earth," the layering of the two vocal lines represents U2's commentary about the state of contemporary culture. The song can be interpreted as being about living life to the fullest, escaping the weight and pressures of modern society that result from matters such as the dizzying pace of technological advancement ("The more you have, the more it takes today") and the omnipresence of consumerism ("The more you take the less you feel"). By juxtaposing the two layers, U2 is acknowledging the fact that while modern life has many interesting and amazing aspects (e.g., the Internet, Hollywood, sports), these may just be rose-colored glasses through which to see the world, distracting people from the fact that real problems exist (e.g., environmental destruction, the AIDS epidemic, and religious persecution). The falsetto layer represents these distractions. Its soothing, understated timbre mellows the overall texture of the song, and its difficult-to-decipher lyrics force the listener to focus more attention on that particular layer, taking attention away from the low-voice layer that clearly sings the lyrics "Too many slipping away" and "The world turns and we get dizzy."

The *Zooropa* album also features the multivoice layering technique. In a rare lead vocal performance by the Edge, he drones a litany of "don'ts" over an intricate background in "Numb." Throughout the entire song, in fact, the Edge's vocals chant only one note: G2. Approximately 1:40 into the song, the texture dramatically changes. After seven verses of "don'ts"

Figure 5.5.   Interverse of "Last Night on Earth." *Christopher Endrinal*

that collectively last for well over one minute, Bono enters two octaves above with what Stokes calls a "soulful falsetto,"[9] providing a stunning (and necessary) contrast to the Edge's unwavering, literally monotonous delivery. Not coincidentally, this textural change occurs just after the Edge sings the lyrics "Just play another chord / If you feel you're getting bored." For the remainder of the song, roughly two and a half minutes, Bono intersperses his "fat lady voice" among the Edge's seemingly innumerable forbidden activities, singing mostly "I feel numb" but also crooning "Gimme some more" and "Too much is not enough." Figure 5.6 illustrates the registral and lyrical differences between the two parts.

"Numb" functions as a commentary about modern society as well as a reflection on life as a rock star. It achieves this simultaneity primarily through the layering of multiple voices. The cold and impersonal nature of technology is reflected by the Edge's single-note deadpan delivery. At the same time, it also captures a "jaded rock star frozen into physical and emotional immobility by the self-imposed strictures of his position [as a global icon]."[10] By *Zooropa*'s release in 1993, U2 had proudly staked its claim to the title of "biggest band in the world," and while this distinction certainly has its privileges, there are many drawbacks associated with constantly being in the limelight. As an international superstar, one's every word and move are documented and almost instantaneously broadcast to the waiting world. The Edge's unchanging intonation is symbolic of the band's lamenting its loss of privacy.

Figure 5.6.   Drone and Fat Lady voice in "Numb." *Christopher Endrinal*

"Numb" also addresses the irony of living in a rapidly developing, technology-based culture. The contrast in the vocal layers, particularly the distance between their respective ranges, symbolizes the central point of the song. Two octaves separate the Edge's monotonous drone from Bono's falsetto, yet the lyrics express an inability to feel. This two-octave space between the layers represents the detached, emotionless state referenced in the lyrics. Despite the busy, almost hectic, background—one that includes a constant sixteenth-note bass pulse, a distorted guitar, synthesizers, crowd noise, and various electronic noises and scratches—the distance between the two voices cannot adequately be filled. U2 is unable to reconcile the disconnect it feels in a connected, "plugged-in" society. Ironically, the presence of an infinite number of stimuli has anesthetized the band and left them cold and unfeeling.

Perhaps nowhere is the vocal layering technique more significant and more symbolic than on the *Achtung Baby* album, particularly on the first single released from that record, "The Fly." *Achtung Baby* contains a myriad of stylistic innovations, not least of which is the character known by the same name as the song's title, "the Fly": Bono's megalomaniacal alter ego in bug-eyed sunglasses and leather suit, created during the album's recording sessions and brought to life on the record and subsequent music videos and Zoo TV tour. Throughout the entire song, the vocal track consists of multiple voices, all sung by Bono. The verses are in a relatively low-register B3 to G4, especially compared to earlier U2 songs, such as "Pride (In the Name of Love)" and "I Still Haven't Found What I'm Looking For" (see figures 5.7–5.9).

Figure 5.7.   Verses 1 and 2 of "The Fly." *Christopher Endrinal*

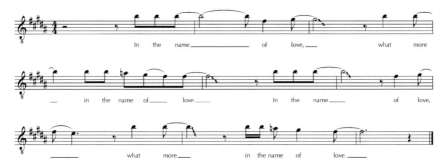

Figure 5.8.   Chorus of "Pride (In the Name of Love)." *Christopher Endrinal*

Layered with the main vocals in this song is a filtered vocal line that shadows Bono's "normal" voice. Each of the two voices is mixed slightly off center, with the Fly shaded to the right channel and the "real" Bono mixed slightly to the left. A waveform (figure 5.10) reveals this stereo mix, as the core levels of the left channel (the upper graph) are less dense than those of the right channel (the lower graph).

The electronic processing applied to the Fly's voice layer causes the layer to occupy a wider part of the audio spectrum, resulting in the thicker bands in the right channel. Clayton describes the Fly's voice as "over-driven, which suits this demented and almost psychotic delivery."[11] The processing lends a dark, subversive, scheming quality to the voice, reflective of the band's ironic and reactionary attitude toward the success and fame garnered up to this point in its career.

A third voice—the "Gospel Voice," labeled as such in the album's liner notes—enters in the chorus section, singing more than an octave above both Bono and the Fly. As can be seen in figure 5.11, every facet of this third voice is different from the other two voices heard in the verse:

Figure 5.9.   Verse 1 of "I Still Haven't Found What I'm Looking For." *Christopher Endrinal*

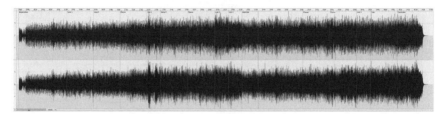

Figure 5.10.   Waveform of "The Fly." *Christopher Endrinal*

vocal quality (falsetto as opposed to "chest" voice), tessitura (B3–B4 vs. B2–G#3), rhythm (straight vs. syncopated), and articulation (lyrical and legato vs. speechlike and choppy).

The lyrics between the two layers are starkly different as well: Bono and the Fly combine their low register with lyrics of crawling and begging, while the Gospel Voice sings of love and shining stars in a bright upper register. Also new in the chorus is the placement of the Gospel Voice within the stereo field. Bono and the Fly are mixed slightly left and right of center, respectively, while the new Gospel Voice is mixed directly in the center, as if trying to separate the two alter egos. The addition of the Gospel Voice to the song's overall texture is an example of the multivoice layering technique. Here, multiple layers of dissimilar vocals—Bono, the Fly, and the Gospel Voice—are used concurrently to create a dense, complex vocal texture.

At first, the high-range delivery of the Gospel Voice could be seen as a tribute to the vocal acrobatics that Bono performed on previous albums. The concept of love—familial, brotherly, spiritual, and romantic alike—has been a central theme in U2's music throughout its entire career. Therefore,

Figure 5.11.   Chorus of "The Fly." *Christopher Endrinal*

it is not unexpected to hear Bono sing a high G#4 on the word "Love" at the beginning of the chorus. What is surprising, however, is the fact that he is doing so in a falsetto delivery. The use of "head voice" reveals that the Gospel Voice is not paying tribute to the band's earlier works, but rather it is satirizing them. Described by Bono as a "Fat Lady voice, a kind of campy falsetto,"[12] the Gospel Voice could be heard as a jab at earlier U2 songs that regularly employed Bono's upper range. This is particularly significant considering that "The Fly" was the first commercially released single from *Achtung Baby*. The song heralded a new direction for U2 and began the band's experimental, electronic-centered period that spanned the 1990s.

After an interlude in "The Fly" that features a piercing guitar solo by the Edge, a third chorus section begins. This chorus, however, is different from the previous two in that the Gospel Voice sings its lyrics without interruption, with no other vocal layers present. Could this be the homage to past U2 music that tried to make an appearance earlier in the song but was interrupted by Bono and the Fly? Could this be a sign that the band was just dabbling in a new style, a temporary foray into electronica? The end of the song—the last chorus section and subsequent coda—answers these questions with a resounding *no!* A false sense of hope is created by the lack of other vocal layers in the third chorus. This hope, however, is short-lived: it is immediately quelled by the reemergence of the Fly character in the last two song sections. In fact, the Fly and Bono not only interrupt the Gospel Voice but overtake the song completely in the coda, while the Gospel Voice disappears from the song's texture entirely after the last chorus. Ending the song with a Bono/Fly "duet" in the coda cements the band's move away from its atmospheric rock of the latter half of the 1980s and convincingly points the band in a new direction.

The falsetto delivery used in "The Fly" cleverly infuses the song with irony, a kind of "campiness" that the band had tried so desperately to avoid in the 1980s. Its anticamp mentality of that decade was one of the subjects the band was attacking in the 1990s, yet the camp aspect of "The Fly" would have been lost if not for the layering of the three voices. Layering afforded the listener an immediate side-by-side—or channel-by-channel—juxtaposition of the various vocal textures that Bono employs. Even the positioning of the voices in the song's mix reflects the band's new musical perspective: by placing the Fat Lady Voice in the middle and flanking it on either side with the other two voices, U2's assault came from all sides on its 1980s righteous, stadium-filling reputation, deconstructing both its music and its image simultaneously. All three vocal layers combine to not only attack and deconstruct the band's carefully crafted reputation and sound but also redefine the band and its music for the last decade of the twentieth century.

The Joshua Tree's massive success actually led U2 to steer in a completely different creative direction. The band's dramatic shift in the 1990s served as a defense mechanism: the impossibly high bar that resulted from the immense popularity and critical acclaim of *The Joshua Tree* album led U2 to focus its creative energy toward crafting a new sound and image to avoid any artistic plateau or even decline. Part of this new sound is the regular incorporation of the multiregister layering and multivoice layering techniques. While U2 had used these techniques on albums before and after their third style period, the *Achtung Baby*, *Zooropa*, and *Pop* records feature vocal layering much more prominently and with greater frequency. Out of thirty-four songs that compose those three albums, eighteen (approximately 53 percent) employ vocal layering. In fact, there are more songs in this style period that use vocal layering than there are in the band's other three style periods combined.

That these three albums collectively represent more than half of U2's vocal-layering usage throughout its career reflects the importance of the technique as it relates to the band's artistic and sonic shifts in the 1990s. That decade saw vocal layering become a defining characteristic of the band's sound, in addition to the Edge's distinctive guitar echo and delay, the propulsive percussion of Larry Mullen Jr., and Adam Clayton's rich bass lines. It provided an avenue for Bono to create his Fly and MacPhisto personae, and it allowed the band to add even more complexity and richness to its already intricate and multilayered sonic signature.

Notes

1. The *interverse* is a new term for the section previously called the *bridge*. Because of the semantic implications of the word *bridge*, I redefined the section and called it an *interverse*. For a detailed definition, as well as examples of the various types of interverses, please see my dissertation, "Form and Style in the Music of U2," available online at http://etd.lib.fsu.edu/theses/available/etd-04122008-130601/.

2. Neil McCormick, ed., *U2 by U2* (London: HarperCollins, 2006), 248.

3. Niall Stokes, *U2: The Stories behind Every U2 Song* (London: Carlton Books, 2009), 114.

4. Stokes, *U2*, 114.

5. U2, *Zooropa*, CD (Island Records, 1993).

6. Stokes, *U2*, 121–22.

 7. Stokes, *U2*, 121–22.
 8. Stokes, *U2*, 121–22.
 9. Stokes, *U2*, 110.
10. Stokes, *U2*, 110.
11. McCormick, *U2 by U2*, 224.
12. McCormick, *U2 by U2*, 225.

"Bullet the Blue Sky" as an Evolving Performance

6

STEVE TAYLOR

> *U2 go for the heart. It's not just the aesthetics. It's the heart . . .*
> *without preaching.*

—GAVIN FRIDAY[1]

I N 2009, AN ADVERTISEMENT FOR U2'S NEW ALBUM *No Line on the Ho-rizon* appeared on YouTube. It opened with images of Bono writing lyrics, followed by Bono and the Edge jamming, and then the band performing live. A voiceover from Bono accompanied the images and of-fered insight into how he understands the creative process and the power and potential of music:

> When I write it's there. There's no staring at a blank page. A song can change your mood, the temperature of the room you're in. Songs are incredible. It's not like the movies where you see them once or twice or three times. They become part of your life. It's like, they're more like smells. Songs . . . [*chuckles*] . . . there's a few bad smells out there of ours. But when we get it right, there's a scent. *Songs can change the world* [em-phasis added].[2]

For Bono, the creative process seems to have a power and a potential that can be accessed by the writer ("it's there . . . no staring at a blank page"); it also has the potential to "change your mood, the temperature of the room." Not all songs reach this creative potential, Bono admits; nevertheless, he has an optimistic belief that a song can change the world.

I would like to explore the world-changing influence of U2's music, but rather than simply echo Bono's bold, almost messianic, assertion that "songs can change the world," I am rearranging his declaration to ask this question: Can a world change a song? What happens to a song, written for a particular time and place, when a world changes? How might a song written in the 1980s in response to the United States' involvement in Central America connect with a new generation in a new millennium?

I address these questions by analyzing one particular song, "Bullet the Blue Sky," through an investigation of the methods that have allowed the live performance of the song to evolve. Then, drawing on theories pertaining to installation art, I suggest how for many who attend a U2 concert, there is a sense that U2 is able to reach "the heart . . . without preaching."

The Album Version: The Original of the Species

"Bullet the Blue Sky" is the fourth track on U2's 1987 album, *The Joshua Tree*. The album has been described as "U2's global coming of age."[3] While it went on to sell more than twenty-five million copies, win Album of the Year at the 1988 Grammy Awards, and put U2 on the cover of *Time* magazine, for music journalist Bill Flanagan, "the heart of the album is two songs that were not hit singles, but which have endured . . . as the centerpiece of countless U2 concerts— 'Running to Stand Still' and 'Bullet the Blue Sky.' . . . One is a whisper, the other an explosion, and together they demonstrated how deep U2 were prepared to go."[4]

The band described *The Joshua Tree* as an attempt to create "a 'cinematic record' where every song would conjure up a physical location."[5] Edge outlined this in more detail as the search for "music that can actually evoke a landscape and a place and really bring you there."[6] In other words, the aim was to write a highly contextualized album with every song defined by a specific, particular, and original context.

Bono described "Bullet the Blue Sky" as emerging from a 1986 visit to Nicaragua and El Salvador during a break from the Conspiracy of Hope tour. He wrote of the genesis of the song:

> I took a break in Los Angeles with Ali. I was interested in what was going on in Nicaragua and El Salvador, which was the big political issue of the time. There was a group called Sanctuary, supporting peasant farmers who were caught in the crossfire of what was essentially a civil war in El Salvador. There were guerillas and government troops torturing these people, covertly backed by US forces who feared the Nicaraguan socialist revolution would spread.[7]

It was this particularized context that would shape the song. Bono recalled, upon his return from El Salvador, "I described what I had been through, what I had seen, some of the stories of people I had met, and I said to Edge: 'Could you put that through your amplifier?' I even got pictures and stuck them on the wall [of the studio]."[8] The song began with a personal journey to a particular context—a civil war in Central America—and was created to describe that specific context. Furthermore, it is placed in an album that had the overall aim of attempting to conjure up specific physical locations. However, now, some thirty years later, that context is simply history. A song can change a world, but can a changing world change a song? Can the particular relate to the universal, and if so, what are the processes by which it might relate without losing its particularized authenticity?

Before I consider the evolution of performing "Bullet the Blue Sky" live, a further recollection of Bono's is relevant to my inquiry. In writing the song, Bono said that he was seeking "something biblical." He wrote of an "understanding of the scriptures [as] the psalms of David and the lyricism of the King James Bible" and "tried to bring that in, to give it a religiosity."[9]

Bono explained his understanding of "religiosity" years later in an introduction that he wrote for an edition of the Psalms:

> Man shouting at God. . . . Abandonment and displacement are the stuff of my favorite psalms . . . for me it's despair that the psalmist really reveals and the nature of his special relationship with God. Honesty, even to the point of anger. . . . Words and music did for me what solid, even rigorous, religious argument could never do—they introduced me to God, not belief in God, more an experiential sense of GOD.[10]

It is such themes—shouting at God in the face of abandonment, displacement, and despair; honesty even to the point of anger—that help to make sense of "Bullet the Blue Sky." Perhaps this is why Flanagan argued that with reference to the song, it "is as true in Iraq as it has been in Bosnia, Chechnya, Rwanda or Darfur since the music was first played."[11] Could it be that the particularity of one context can find resonance with the particularity of another? Could this happen in such a way that neither is obscured and both are humanized in the process?

"See the Sky Ripped Open": From Album to Live Performance

While not a hit single, "Bullet the Blue Sky" was to become a mainstay of U2's live concert performance. It was first played live on April 2, 1987, at the Arizona State University Activity Center, at the beginning of the Joshua Tree tour. For concert reviewer Pimm Jal de la Parra,

> "Bullet the Blue Sky" is visually stunning, with a dozen or so lighting operators up in the rigging circling angry red spotlights over the stage and the crowd. Criticizing American military intervention in El Salvador, the number captures the terror Bono felt when during his trip to the country, he witnessed the bombing of a small village in the farmlands. Bono holds a light on Edge during his soaring guitar solo.[12]

The song was last played live on December 9, 2006, at Aloha Stadium, Honolulu, as the Vertigo tour ended. Over those nineteen years, it was a mainstay of U2's live concert performances, having been played over 646 times.

To shift from album to concert requires one to pay attention not only to sound but also to the art forms of lighting, design, video, theater, and audience participation. Joe O'Herlihy, U2's sound director, describes the transition from song to live concert as a "very important point in the preparation." It requires "understanding what the band are trying to achieve from every song, and what the different arrangements and mixes do in relation to the character of each song."[13]

This idea, of a song becoming shaped and reshaped by the concert performance, is echoed by Matt McGee, who after viewing a number of consecutive concerts on the recent 360° tour, observed,

> The set lists were pretty similar, but *the show was completely different*. So much had changed in three weeks—the visuals, some transitions between songs, the band's actions/gestures on stage. . . . You might hear the same songs, but if you're paying attention to the entire performance, it might be completely new from one night to the next.[14]

One way to pay attention to live performance is to view commercially produced live concert video footage. This has a number of advantages. First, the band produces live concert videos to provide "live snapshots of every tour," suggesting that video can be used as an almost "emblematic summary."[15] Second, using commercially available live concert video ensures a high quality of sound and visual production.

One tool for handling the range of data generated by viewing a live concert video performance is a method called *narrative mapping*, which uses time as the framework by which to document unfolding events. For Stephen Mamber, it is a tool useful for dealing with complexity, ambiguity, density, and information overload that allows one to analyze unfolding events over time. This makes it extremely useful with regard to a live concert experience and for charting differences between evolving versions. Thus, narrative mapping is an appropriately helpful method for analyzing the live versions of a song like "Bullet the Blue Sky," especially given the way that U2's live concert performances have evolved in their digital complexity. If a live concert performance is a production that pays "immense attention to detail and a thoroughly articulated and realized artistic vision that has broad appeal,"[16] then narrative mapping allows us to pay attention to the detail of a song in a changing world and, in so doing, begin to appreciate U2's artistic vision.

I therefore apply narrative mapping to three commercially available concert films that include performances of "Bullet the Blue Sky": the 1987 concert at the Hippodrome in Paris;[17] the 2001 concert at Slane Castle, Dublin;[18] and the 2005 Vertigo tour concert filmed in Chicago.[19] Using the three films provides a space of eighteen years of development in three contexts—France, Ireland, and the United States. It also allows us to consider another dimension of particularity: how the prophetic anger generated from one context (Central America) might be channeled in the band members' own context (Dublin) and in the context being critiqued (the United States).[20]

"Bullet the Blue Sky": The Paris Version

Over seventy thousand people attended the Hippodrome in Paris on July 4, 1987. The Joshua Tree tour had entered its second leg, touring Europe. U2 was playing to sellout crowds in England, Ireland, Germany, Italy, Holland, and France, with the concert at the Hippodrome attracting what was then the largest attendance ever at a single rock performance in France's history.[21]

The stage design for the Joshua Tree tour was described by concert reviewer Pimm Jal de la Parra as "simple but effective, with . . . an unobstructed view of the stage for those at the side or the rear."[22] Set designer Willie Williams described a "focus drawn towards the group rather than towards the special effects . . . minimalism on a grand scale."[23] Furthermore, the "production gestures remained simple but had finally developed a distinctive style. . . . U2 finally had a show big enough to fill an arena on their own terms: arresting, unique, yet apparently effortless."[24]

At the Hippodrome, "Bullet the Blue Sky" began as the first song in the encore. The stage was dark. The drums began to pound, the guitar howled, and Bono introduced the song with a voiceover: "Sunny skies over Paris.

Sunny skies above London." The song, live, followed the pattern of the album: verse, chorus, verse, chorus, verse, verse, guitar solo, outro.

The guitar solo (at 3:35) consisted of Bono chasing the Edge with a large spotlight, "illuminating Edge's guitar solo with a hand-held lamp at point-blank range."[25] For Williams, the use of a spotlight was a deliberate part of the overall lighting plan. Developments in lighting technology had made computerized lighting commonplace. In response, the Joshua Tree tour used twenty-three human-operated follow spots, which "proved an extremely powerful source of energy."[26] The lighting served to underline the tensions in the song. First, the spotlight was turned on the Edge as he put Central America "through the amplifier." Then, as the song drew to its end, Bono continued to carry the spotlight, and he swung it, still on, back and forth over the floor at his feet. It all acted to emphasize the interplay between "sunny skies" and the darkness happening in Central America. As the song finished, the spotlight that Bono was holding was turned off; the stage returned to dark; and the opening piano chords of the next song in the evolving live performance, "Running to Stand Still," were played.

"And I Can See Those Fighter Planes": The Dublin Version

The Dublin concert was filmed at Slane Castle, Ireland, on September 1, 2001, as part of the second, European, leg of the Elevation tour. While the tour was designed to be an indoor arena affair, Slane Castle was the venue for an annual outdoor Irish musical festival. Hence, the "Elevation production, so intimate, so engaging and moving in its normal setting, [was] dwarfed by the enormity of Slane—the massive audience, the 'picnic in the park' experience."[27]

As at the Hippodrome, some fourteen years earlier, "Bullet the Blue Sky" was the first song in the encore. However, the song had evolved. It now included

> several new video sequences that were used to introduce "Bullet the Blue Sky," a veteran U2 song, but now entirely reinvented in the context of gun control. . . . Bono stalked the stage, scanning the audience with a hand-held lamp, though not the comforting light of the War tour—this was a sharp beam from a unit that even looked like a handgun.[28]

This evolution of the song brings into sharp focus the contextual question of how one might now play a song "reinvented in the context of gun control," in a space dwarfed by an Irish castle and just outside an Irish city.

At Slane Castle, the song started with a sound sample, a recorded chant by Irish singer Sinead O'Connor recorded especially for U2 by John Reynolds and described as "a new intro for *Bullet the Blue Sky* [that] will become a feature of the third leg of the Elevation Tour."[29] Alongside the keening Irish lilt from O'Connor, the song began with this visual of white words flashing on a black background:

At 0:15, the words "USA, UK, France, China, Russia";
At 0:38, the statement "The Five Biggest Arms Traders in the
    World"—
At 0:50, the words "USA, UK, France, China, Russia."

The pounding drums and howling guitar began at 1:00. The lighting by then technicolor, red to blue, flashed white in time to Edge's power cords. As in Paris, Bono carried a spotlight but this time used it in a very different way during the guitar solo.

At 3:09, Bono began to walk the ellipse. The ellipse was a heart-shaped walkway designed especially for the Elevation tour, an innovation that allowed "the band to get out into the audience and then return to the stage without having to stop and turn around. . . . The simple act of walking the stage would create drama, making the stage itself the key to the whole show."[30] This creation of drama was accentuated by a theatrical sample (Bono walked, covering his eyes, with his hand holding the microphone) and by the playing of a sequence of video images (a sampling of women and children, people in military uniforms, political leaders, the devastation of war), with Bono, his eyes covered, unwilling to look at the black-and-white images of the impact of war.

At 4:08, with the guitar solo still continuing, the stage lighting faded to dark, and the sampled video images ceased. The importance of the timing with regard to these video samples is underlined by Willie Williams's explanation that on the Elevation tour, only "a small portion of the show would use video as an effect, so we could be very precise in its execution."[31]

Then, at 4:34, after some twenty-six seconds of darkness, Bono began to use his handheld spotlight, pulsing the light in time to the drumbeat. At 5:23 he shined the spot to the sky and sang, "I can see those fighter planes." He then pointed to the audience, lighting it with the spotlight, then back to his face, lighting himself. Both he and the audience were thus caught in the glare of the spotlight. At 6:00 he added a chant that changed the original ending of the song. To the concluding line "Outside

America," he added "Outside France, UK, EU." The spotlight, as the only source of light, was still flashing, on the crowd and then onto himself, as Bono concluded, "IRA, British Army, Real IRA."

In sum, the live performances of "Bullet the Blue Sky" evolved. It now included an introductory song sample, video images, theatrical performance, lyrical changes, and the use of the handheld spotlight. The context was no longer El Salvador but Slane Castle, Ireland. The issue was no longer civil war but arms control. The song, lyrically and with the use of the spotlight, was no longer addressed to *them* in "America" but to *us* in "France, UK, EU, IRA, British Army, Real IRA." What was a psalm of lament in 1987 seemed, by 2001, to have become a psalm of confession, both personal and communal in nature. Us, all of us lit by the spotlight—Bono and the audience—lived in countries that traffic in bullets that rip open not only the blue skies of El Salvador but Ireland too.

"Outside, It's America": The Chicago Version

The evolving live performance of "Bullet the Blue Sky" and the most dramatic example of multiple sampling in which a world changes a song occurred during the Chicago concerts, filmed as part of the Vertigo tour on May 9 and 10, 2005. By now, American military intervention had ceased in Central America. However, the United States was now militarily involved in Iraq. How might this changing world change "Bullet the Blue Sky"?

The song was now, unlike at Paris and Dublin, no longer an encore but included in the main set list. In Chicago, it was preceded by "Sunday Bloody Sunday" and, as at Paris, followed by "Running to Stand Still." The stage was initially lit in red, white, and blue. The drums began to pound and the guitar howled.

This performance now included three song samples. The first song sample occurred at 1:55, when, after the second verse, Bono sang the opening lines from "When Johnny Comes Marching Home," a song from the American Civil War era that expressed the longing for the return of relatives and friends from the battlefield. This song sample was followed by a visual sample of the outline of a fighter jet, in blue lights, "flying" as the Edge launched into an extended guitar solo.

The evolving performance included not only video and sound sampling but also a sustained piece of theatrical sampling. Historically, U2's early concerts included a dimension of theatrical performance, but not until the Zoo TV tour was it so central to the concert experience. In this Chicago performance, the theatrical aspect was employed once again. Bono knelt (at 2:46) in center stage, placed a blindfold over his eyes, and crossed his hands above his head, referencing (sampling) the treatment of prisoners during the war in Iraq. Then at 3:20, Bono stood, blindfolded, and walked forward, hands outstretched, searching for the microphone stand.

A second song sample occurred at 4:05. Bono (still blindfolded) held his hands aloft and sang, "These are the hands that built America," a line from a song that U2 wrote for the movie *Gangs of New York*. This was followed by a third song sample (at 4:30), a repeat of the lines from "When Johnny Comes Marching Home." These samples—theatrical, musical, and visual—replaced the usual extended third and fourth verses and outro of "Bullet the Blue Sky" ("Across the field you see the sky ripped open / See the rain through a gaping wound / Pounding on the women and children / Who run / Into the arms / Of America").

It is impossible to fully appreciate the live performance without reminding oneself of the context of US military involvement in Iraq. The samples evoked a complex range of contexts and emotions: a desire for safe homecoming, the complications of dealing with prisoners of war, and audience complicity in these events. A psalm of anger in Paris that evolved into a psalm of confession in Dublin now sounded like a corporate psalm of personal petition for the safe homecoming of US personnel involved in Iraq.

This new meaning got reinforced by a verbal segue that Bono used to introduce the next song, "Running to Stand Still," which he dedicated to "all the brave men and women of United States." During the song, Bono repeatedly sang "alleluia" as "a prayer for anyone who has a sister or a brother overseas and they're in danger." It is a simple, but powerful way of inviting the audience to pray with him, singing "alleluia."

"At the Moment of Surrender": Drawing upon Installation Art

It was the total experience of a U2 set that counted.

—BILL GRAHAM[32]

Now that I have used narrative mapping to outline U2's use of sampling through the evolution of performing "Bullet the Blue Sky," one way to consider the data is through the lens of installation art. Nicolas De Oliveria, in writing on the contemporary challenges of viewing art, says, "We now live in a material environment where earlier twenieth century models of spectatorship, contemplation and experience are inadequate for understanding the conditions of cultural creation and reception."[33] Part of what has changed the conditions has come from new technologies, unknown in the 1980s, that now allow the use of song samples and the projection of visual images. With specific reference to installations, new technologies such as DVD, video, and sound sampling "have been instrumental in changing the role of the artist from that of a generator of original or primary materials, to that of editor of existing cultural objects to be inserted into new contexts."[34] Creativity is now as much in the remixing as in the making.

However, U2's live performances are not driven simply by their use of new technology. One way to consider how U2 is able to "go for the heart . . . without preaching" is to consider how the band's use of samples is employed in a way that seems to evoke "awakenings of communal memory."[35]

This notion of communal memory has a number of layers. The first layer is the individualized communal memory that is associated with a song. One way to fully appreciate this is to simply pay attention to the audience as it attends a U2 concert. A U2-released video of the audience in Glasgow during its most recent 360° tour shows concertgoers with eyes closed, hands clapped or raised, singing along to "With or Without You" with considerable emotional intensity.[36] Hearing a song played live can awaken a range of individual memories and result in a sense of shared communal memory. However, this phenomenon is not unique to U2—all songs have that potential.

What I am arguing for here is that when U2 employs all its forms of sampling, the band is awakening a second layer of communal memory. Its skill in using evocative samples in particularized contexts allow U2 to "go for the heart . . . without preaching." In a US concert, audiences know "When Johnny Comes Marching Home." In a Dublin concert, audiences connect with the Irish singer Sinead O'Connor. The use of samples, carefully considered, allow not just a communal sharing of individualized memory but a genuine communal awakening.

This process of sampling for communal awakening is helped by a dimension essential to effective live concert performances. De Oliveria describes the importance in art installations of "strategies of de-familiarization," the deliberate attempt in installations to create another world.[37] A rock concert incorporates many dimensions of "de-familiarization": the fan queue, the crowds, the crush of bodies, the lights going down, and the extreme sensory experience created by sound and lighting. With specific reference to U2, lighting director Bruce Ramus described his work as shifting people from their head to their bodies: "I take them out of their heads and into their bodies and hold them there for their concert."[38] It is when people are in their bodies that U2's samples are more likely to awaken communal memory and thus connect with "the heart . . . without preaching."

Defamiliarization has the potential to simply be a form of escapism, giving people a good experience, but it need not be. Again, installation art theory is a helpful conversation partner. For De Oliveria, a key dynamic of club culture as installation art is the creation of an experiential space that is introspective, immersive, and social,[39] which allows for a "viewing of the self contemplating the external world."[40] This surely is what is happening as communal memory is awakened in the evolving performances of "Bullet the Blue Sky." The self can lament at the external world at Paris; the self can confess at Slane Castle; and the self can both confess and petition in Chicago. U2's use of sampling crafts an experience that allows introspection with regard to how one should act in relation to the wider world.

A further element to consider is how U2's efforts act to humanize humanity. Because of how U2 employ its samples, war is no longer something that happens over there—on the news in El Salvador, on the television in Iraq. "Bullet the Blue Sky," lyrically and with the use of the spotlight, is no longer addressed to *them* in "America" but to *us* in "France, UK, EU, IRA, British Army, Real IRA." It is what we, *us*, all of those lit by the spotlight, have become implicated by and complicit with. War is what happens to "those brave men and women of United States," the "sister or a brother overseas." U2 invites you to take a psalm of petition for those you know personally and extend it for the prisoner of war, sampled so memorably by Bono's theatrical performance. Perhaps it is this ability to humanize communal memory that makes U2's show, in the words of Bruce Ramus, "feel like a great spiritual exchange between the tour and the audience."[41]

The outcome is that in a culture that "mourns the loss of public space," a live concert, particularly a U2 concert, is one of few "public space experiences" left in our culture.[42] This is especially evident in relation to the third leg of the Elevation tour, which was played soon after September 11 (and the Slane Castle concert). De la Parra noted, "Before the start of leg three, fans had speculated whether U2 would be playing *Bullet the Blue Sky* again in post-9/11 America."[43] In other words, to return to our initiating question: Can the world-changing events (of September 11) change a song?

While "Bullet the Blue Sky" did not appear in the first concert of the third US leg at South Bend, Indiana, after that, things returned to a more familiar order: "*Bullet* is back in the set, but the images of guns and war are no longer projected on the screens. Instead there are more abstract pictures, distortion and 'snow.'"[44] With specific reference to the notion of communal memory, de la Parra summarized the third leg of the tour this way: "What their audience seem to want right now is a sense of community, of togetherness, which is something the band have always been good at delivering—and has been at the core of the Elevation Tour since its conception."[45] With careful attention to sampling by using a new set of video images, the song changed once again, and a public space was again humanized.

U2 took incredible live performance risks on the third leg of the tour. It employed new samples—scrolling the names of those killed in September 11 on video screens and inviting New York firemen onstage—with the effect of again using communal memory for a humanizing effect. As the audience remembered and wept, the band allowed for, as Bono sought in the initial writing of "Bullet the Blue Sky," a "shouting at God . . . abandonment and displacement . . . honesty, even to the point of anger."[46]

Sampling, the collagelike reappropriation of already-existing elements, is U2's creative approach to using one of its signature songs to try to change a changing world. One website noted twenty-eight samples played over the years during live performances of "Bullet the Blue Sky."[47] Another concertgoer wrote of "being surprised at the number of covers and snippets of other groups' songs that the band played."[48] U2's ability and willingness to sample video images, songs, and theatrical poses are essential elements to the successful evolution of its performances and is the creative genius that allows for the band's continued reperformances to create communal memories, spiritual exchanges, and a going for the heart without preaching.

Notes

1. Gavin Friday, cited in Diana Scrimgeour, *U2 Show* (London: Orion, 2004), 294.

2. "U2 360° tour," YouTube video, http://www.youtube.com/watch ?v=FFXSliHDLrs (accessed December 2, 2009).

3. Willie Williams, "The Joshua Tree, Rattle and Hum, Love Town," in Scrimgeour, *U2 Show*, 54.

4. Bill Flanagan, *The Joshua Tree U2: 20th Anniversary*, liner notes (Universal Records, 2007), 3.

5. Edge, in U2 and Neil McCormick, *U2 by U2* (London: HarperCollins, 2006), 177.

6. U2, *The Joshua Tree*, Classic Albums Series 2, DVD, dir. Phil King and Nuala O'Connor (Eagle Rock Entertainment, 2000).

7. Bono, in U2 and McCormick, *U2 by U2*, 174, 177.

8. U2 and McCormick, *U2 by U2*, 179.

9. U2 and McCormick, *U2 by U2*, 179.

10. Bono, "Introduction to *The Book of Psalms*," in *The Book of Psalms* (New York: Grove/Atlantic, 1999), viii, ix.

11. Flanagan, *The Joshua Tree U2*, 4.

12. Pimm Jal de la Parra, *U2 Live: A Concert Documentary* (London: Omnibus Press, 2003), 79.

13. Joe O'Herlihy, "Sound," in Scrimgeour, *U2 Show*, 213.

14. Matt McGee, "Off the Record . . . ," para. 1 of 12, http://www.atu2.com/news/column-off-the-record-vol-9-382.html (accessed December 17, 2009).

15. Joe O'Herlihy, "Sound," in Scrimgeour, *U2 Show*, 214.

16. Pat Morrow, "Show Video Production," in Scrimgeour, *U2 Show*, 239.

17. U2, *The Joshua Tree: Live from Paris, Collectors Edition*, boxed-set DVD (Interscope, 2007).

18. *U2 Go Home! Live from Slane Castle*, DVD, dir. Enda Hughes and Hamish Hamilton (Island Records/Interscope, 2002).

19. *U2, Vertigo: Live from Chicago, 2005*, DVD, dir. Hamish Hamilton and Eric Forstadt (Island Records/Interscope, 2005).

20. Viewing other concerts is possible, as "Bullet the Blue Sky" appears on the following concert films: *Rattle and Hum, Zoo TV, PopMart, Elevation*.

21. de la Parra, *U2 Live*, 107.

22. de la Parra, *U2 Live*, 79, 80.

23. Williams, "The Joshua Tree, Rattle and Hum, Love Town," in Scrimgeour, *U2 Show*, 54.

24. Williams, "The Joshua Tree," in Scrimgeour, *U2 Show*, 54.

25. Williams, "The Joshua Tree," in Scrimgeour, *U2 Show*, 54.

26. Williams, "The Joshua Tree," in Scrimgeour, *U2 Show*, 54.

27. De la Parra is describing the first concert on August 25, 2001, not the second concert, from which the DVD is made, on September 1. Nevertheless, the comments on page 257 in regard to size are relevant.

28. Williams, "Elevation, Superbowl 2000–2002," in Scrimgeour, *U2 Show*, 154–55.

29. de la Parra, *U2 Live*, 256; de la Parra is describing the Earl's Court concerts of August 18, 19, 21, and 22, 2001.

30. Williams, "Elevation," in Scrimgeour, *U2 Show*, 154.

31. Williams, "Elevation," in Scrimgeour, *U2 Show*, 55.

32. Bill Graham, *U2: The Early Days, Another Time, Another Place* (London: Mandarin Paperbacks, 1983), 33.

33. Nicolas De Oliveria, Nicola Oxley, and Michael Petry, *Installation Art in the New Millennium: The Empire of the Senses* (London: Thames and Hudson, 2003), 6.

34. De Oliveria, Oxley, and Petry, *Installation Art*, 21–22.

35. De Oliveria, Oxley, and Petry, *Installation Art*, 7.

36. U2, "Glasgow—'With or Without You,'" YouTube video, http://www .youtube.com/watch?v=sx0Nb7he9y0 (accessed October 23, 2009).

37. De Oliveria, Oxley, and Petry, *Installation Art*, 7.

38. Bruce Ramus, conversation at the curtain-raiser, Wellington, New Zealand, 2008.

39. De Oliveria, Oxley, and Petry, *Installation Art*, 51.

40. De Oliveria, Oxley, and Petry, *Installation Art*, 53.

41. Bruce Ramus, "Lighting," in Scrimgeour, *U2 Show*, 238.

42. De Oliveria, Oxley, and Petry, *Installation Art*, 29.

43. de la Parra, *U2 Live*, 259.

44. de la Parra, *U2 Live*, 259.

45. de la Parra, *U2 Live*, 258.

46. Bono, "Introduction."

47. "Bullet the Blue Sky (Lyrics)," U2Gigs.com, http://www.u2gigs.com/ Bullet_The_Blue_Sky-s19.html (accessed September 30, 2009).

48. Charles Thomas, "U2 Concert Review: Paris France (4 July, 1987), the Hippodrome," U2Tours.com, http://www.u2tours.com/displayfan.src ?ID=19870704&XID=1013&Return= (accessed December 2, 2009).

U2: An Elevated Brand   7

MICHELE O'BRIEN

ORMED IN DUBLIN IN 1976, U2 HAS BEEN a dominant force in popular music over the last three decades. The band's youthful energy
and unique sound kicked open the door of the 1980s with its début
album, *Boy*. Fast-forward to present day and the band has sold more than
140 million records worldwide; it has a host of awards under its belt, including twenty-two Grammys; and its 360° tour was the highest-earning
rock tour of all time. Producing good music and giving great concert
experiences are not the only reasons for U2's continued success. A band
of its stature did not climb to the top on its sound alone. U2 made careful
decisions that would secure the band's integrity and ensure its longevity. Over the years, in partnership with band manager Paul McGuinness,
U2 has crafted some of the best marketing and promotional activities to
launch albums and connect with its audience using new forms of media. It
recognized the importance of creating a fan base on a worldwide scale; it
embraced the power of visual cues; and it has preserved the band's DNA
even while reinventing the U2 identity at times in its history. In many
ways, U2 has operated as a clever business carefully managing "brand U2."

The world's favorite brands, such as Coca-Cola, Nike, Apple, and even
Guinness, have been measured according to different criteria: the strongest,
the most popular, the most loved, even the coolest. But by using seven attributes that the advertising industry considers evidence of good brand behavior, I contend that U2's advertising and marketing prowess has placed
them at the level of other world-renowned brands: U2 is flexible; it has a
consistent vision; its brand is memorable; it is innovative; it acts ethically;
it has an army of brand ambassadors; and it acts like a market leader. In

the following pages, I expand on these seven attributes as they pertain to brand U2 to present what makes this iconic Irish band an elevated brand.

U2 Is Flexible

Longevity of a brand can either help or harm it. Many of us can think back and remember brands that we embraced in years past, but where are they now? Brands that trade solely on their age and past credibility will not survive in a changing marketplace. But elevated brands listen to their consumers and adapt to the current market context, reinventing themselves when necessary.

The music industry has always been challenged when it comes to developing a band's longevity and instead takes a more "flavor of the month" approach to its business. There has been a recent trend of classic rock bands of the 1960s and 1970s riding the comeback wave and trying to compete with bands thirty years younger. Very few, if any, of these aging bands are producing music that is better than or even of comparable quality to the music they made in their past.

This is not the case for U2, who have earned twenty-two Grammys, the most ever awarded in history. U2 started racking up accolades in 1987, when it was awarded Album of the Year for *The Joshua Tree*; it repeated the honor nearly two decades later in 2005 for *How to Dismantle an Atomic Bomb*. The band also received critical praise and industry acknowledgment for its most recent body of work, *No Line on the Horizon,* its twelfth studio album. U2 was not only in the running for Best Rock Album in the 2010 Grammy Awards but also received two additional nominations for its hit single "I'll Go Crazy If I Don't Go Crazy Tonight," in the Best Rock Song and Best Rock Performance categories, though the band went home empty handed.

U2's consistency in delivering a good product has resulted in its financial success, and it is counted as one of the most commercially successful bands in popular music history. U2 has sold over 140 million albums worldwide, not counting sales of *No Line on the Horizon*, which sold nearly half a million copies in the United States in its first week alone in March 2009, making it the band's second-best US début ever.[1] It is fair to say album sales could have been higher if not for the inadvertent digital download available a week before its scheduled release.

U2 is known to be at its best playing in front of an audience, so it is no wonder that its concerts continue to sell out, sometimes just minutes after tickets go on sale. Over three million people attended the Vertigo tour of 2005, making it highest-grossing tour of the year.[2] In 2009, U2 sold out forty-four shows for its 360° tour. The ongoing success of the tour prompted U2 to add additional dates and venues to take it well into 2010. In an interview with the *Financial Times*, Paul McGuinness calculated that the 2009 and 2010 tours "should gross about $750 million including merchandise sales, smashing the $398 million record set by U2's Vertigo tour in 2005 and 2006."[3]

Just as time is not static, neither is an elevated brand nor its consumer. U2 has always worked against stagnation, which is perhaps why the band has attempted to reinvent itself from time to time and has had occasional missteps when doing so. Following the vertigo-inducing success of *The Joshua Tree*, critics and fans alike criticized the follow-up as being pretentious—specifically, *Rattle and Hum*, an album and a film: the expression of U2's exploration of America and its musical roots. Reported to be the brainchild of Paul McGuinness, who has a cinematography background, *Rattle and Hum* started as a low-budget documentary for U2 fans but exploded into a Paramount Pictures release with ticket sales peaking on opening day. The album, too, is without any great acclaim, although Paul McGuinness said that selling twenty-five million copies is a failure he can live with. Edge once remarked, "Rather than using *The Joshua Tree* as a springboard to something even greater, we made a movie and almost ran out of road."[4]

To mark the end of U2's journey through Americana, Bono announced that they would need to "dream it all up again." U2 moved into the 1990s influenced by the dance culture that was taking over Europe. While *Achtung Baby* arguably stands out as one of the band's finest albums, there is heated debate over *Zooropa* and *Pop*, the two experimental albums that followed. The heavy dance-influenced tracks on *Pop* could have alienated fans of U2's traditional rock sounds, but most fans accepted this detour and even embraced the buried hits on the two albums, which topped the US charts and many others worldwide.

U2 is always striving for ways to make its music and live performances as engaging and accessible as possible for its fans, and it avoids trading on past success alone. While some of the band's attempts at reinvention have polarized fans rather than unravel its core fan base, U2 has held on to the common threads of honesty and passion that run throughout its body of work.

U2 Has a Consistent Vision

The strongest brands are ones that sometimes have the simplest visions. This is not to say that is why they are successful—their strength and commitment to uphold their vision are what set them apart. The Chanel brand, for example, has been a leading force in the fashion industry since the start of the twentieth century, designing no-nonsense clothing not dictated by trends. The brand's unwavering commitment to adhere to Coco Chanel's original vision has no doubt aided the brand's success and longevity.

"Vision over visibility," a phrase that has been a mantra of sorts for Bono since the 1980s, in conversations, in his poetry, and as a title of a self-portrait he painted, has recently found its place in the U2 song "Moment of Surrender."[5] The phrase could also be used as a way to summarize the collective drive that all four band members and manager Paul McGuinness have possessed since U2's inception.

U2's earliest vision was to play music that people could feel. Bono has used the words "atmosphere," "bigger," and "grand" to describe the unique sound that U2 sought for itself in the early days, avoiding the classic rock-and-roll formula adopted by many bands.[6] Bono has referenced the Edge's musical genius on numerous occasions and stated in an interview with *Rolling Stone* in 2009 that the Edge's lack of dependence on blues scales is what sets him apart.[7] There is no doubt that the Edge's mastery of delays, overdubs, and other guitar effects are a driving force behind the sound that is so unique to U2.

In 1984, when the band was piecing together what would later become *The Unforgettable Fire*, Bono remembers the group's realization that without a doubt it was on the path to being the next big thing. Standard popularity, however, was never an end goal for the band. "We felt we had more dimension than just being the next anything, we had something unique to offer. The innovation was what would suffer if we went down the standard rock route. We were looking for another feeling."[8]

Over the years, U2 has extended its vision of creating an atmosphere in its music to the way that it stages memorable live shows. In recent years, the band has embraced the latest technology to engage its audience in a way that often makes attendees feel as though they are the fifth member of the band. In all areas of how U2 connects with fans, the U2 vision is palatable. It's not just about making good music; it's about making people feel something. It is about building an atmosphere but not in a Starbucks sort of way. It's about connecting with the fan in a highly emotive way at every touch point, from its official fan communications, such as the early *U2 Magazine* and the later *Propaganda*, to U2.com and its record-setting world tours. It's about delivering the feeling that U2 itself consistently provokes.

U2's Brand Is Memorable

U2's musical vision was to not sound like any other band. However, an elevated brand is not just one that stands out from the crowd; it needs to be distinct and memorable. For U2, the distinctiveness of its brand comes from its unique sound, from its fan loyalty, and from the way that the band represents itself visually throughout all communication opportunities.

Elevated brands have a unique product attribute, and for U2, the band delivers a very recognizable sound, with each song offering its own unique layers. Whether it is the pioneering riffs streaming from the Edge's guitar, the signature drumbeats of Larry Mullen Jr., the driving bass lines of Adam Clayton, or the belting trademark voice of Bono, the music of U2 is distinct, but it doesn't stop there. The band strives for memorable ways to present its unique product to its fans.

Just as companies launch new products, U2 uses best-in-class marketing strategies to launch new albums in memorable ways. In 2004, U2 surprised American fans with an unexpected performance in the Fulton Ferry State Park, under the Brooklyn Bridge, playing songs from *How to Dismantle an Atomic Bomb* a day before the album's US release. However, the band's marketing endeavors don't always come off as intended. To announce the PopMart tour, U2 arranged a press conference and miniperformance at a Manhattan Kmart, but some fans and critics thought the self-mockery went a bit too far. The stunt clocked in at no. 10 on the "15 Worst Ever Music Ideas" list, at the music and entertainment website Spinner.com, which called it a "crass spectacle."[9]

U2 returned to its roots as stadium rockers in the 1990s but infused its shows with the latest technology to take stadium rock to a whole new level. Starting with the Zoo TV tour, which supported *Achtung Baby* in 1992 and eventually *Zooropa* in 1993, the band focused on delivering memorable ways for fans to experience U2's music live. The multimedia Zoo TV tour used over thirty-six television screens to broadcast the pop culture themes of the *Achtung Baby* and *Zooropa* albums.[10] Images and messages flashed across screens, serving as a visual buffet that allowed the audience to decide which pieces of communication to digest. The 1997 *Pop* album was brought to life as a "sci-fi disco supermarket," as described on U2.com, and it allowed the band to mock itself and the entertainment industry, in ironic contrast to the band's earnest sincerity of the 1980s. The tour was trashy and kitschy and came complete with a forty-foot-tall motorized lemon from which the band emerged.

U2 has a historical reputation for connecting with its audiences at live gigs in an intimate way, despite the size of the venue. The Elevation tour, which supported *All That You Can't Leave Behind*, and the Vertigo tour, for *How to Dismantle an Atomic Bomb*, allowed the band to boil down the theatrics and design sets that matched the traditional sound and style of these two albums but not without innovative twists. Both tours featured a stage design similar to a circular catwalk that jutted out from the front of the stage, giving Bono and the band extended access to the audience.

The band truly outdid themselves on the 360° tour with a spaceship-like set design. Measuring 165 feet high at its tallest point, "the Claw" is the largest concert stage constructed to date. Despite its size, it still provided a level of intimacy by sitting near the center of stadiums and allowing fans to surround the stage, offering them a 360-degree view. Music critic Neil McCormick described U2's live performances as "making the epic intimate and the intimate epic."[11]

The power of good design should not be underestimated. The logos alone for the distinguished brands Nike and Apple stir certain, special feelings within consumers. Steve Averill has been involved in visualizing U2 since 1977, including the design of its first poster. Averill named the band "U2" when its original name, the Hype, was decided to be too punk, and Averill has acted as the band's art director, designing merchandise, album, and DVD art over the years. Around 1991, Averill enlisted designer Shaun McGrath to codesign the album artwork for *Achtung Baby* and the accompanying Zoo TV tour material.[12] Since 2000, U2 has had the support of Dublin-based agency four5one, where Averill resided as creative director until 2010 and McGrath remains as a senior designer. The book *Stealing Hearts from a Travelling Show: The Graphic Design of U2* chronicles Averill and McGrath's work for the band in its first twenty-five years. Averill's consistent hand in U2's visual landscape has added a tangible layer to brand U2, marrying strong graphic imagery to the stories of U2's music and the mood of each album. Averill and later McGrath have managed to capture each phase of the band in a visually stimulating and memorable way.

Photographer Anton Corbijn, one of the world's most influential portrait photographers in the music industry, is another name synonymous with the visual outputs of U2. Corbijn has been capturing and shaping U2's public image since 1982, with shots that featured on the album sleeve for *War*.[13] From the serious shots of *The Joshua Tree* album to the more lighthearted images from *Achtung Baby*, Corbijn's photography of U2 has peppered its albums, magazine covers and features, and various books over the years. Corbijn's iconic U2 photography has been recently resurrected and presented in a new light by four5one in the remastered albums for *The Joshua Tree* in 2008 and *The Unforgettable Fire* in 2009.

As an elevated brand, U2 does a great job of being distinct and memorable not only in the music it produces but how it performs this music live. U2 has always understood the importance of good design and how it can be a tool used to reflect the band's personality and what it stands for across all communication platforms. Like other elevated brands, U2 uses clever marketing strategies to build momentum for a new album, and it has used design as a vehicle to promote new sounds and new phases in its career.

U2 Is Innovative

It is essential for brands to remain agile so they can adapt to emerging technologies and be innovative in finding new ways to engage their audiences. U2 is a pioneer at meshing music with pop culture and new technologies. As U2 is committed to bringing fans the best way to experience its music, the band consistently searches for ways to use the latest technology for communication and performance.

While some brands regard the Internet as a threat to the livelihood of the recording industry, U2 has found a way to adapt its business model to embrace this medium. The U2 fanzine *Propaganda* existed from 1986 to 2000, bringing fans closer to their favorite band through a print magazine. U2 was one of the first bands to realize the power of the Internet, and it transferred all this inside information to U2.com as a more accessible way for fans to stay connected. The award-winning website features an extensive catalog of U2 lyrics, music videos, up-to-date news, tour information, and merchandise, and its design changes to reflect the look of U2's most recently released album.

In 2004, U2 recognized the impact that the Apple iPod would have on the world, and it made a smart decision to trade brands with Apple by creating the first ever special edition iPod. Timed to the release of *How to Dismantle an Atomic Bomb* and in support of the Vertigo tour, the U2 special edition iPod featured engraved signatures of the band members on its back. Apple iTunes also unveiled *The Complete U2*, the world's first digital box set comprising every U2 album at the time, as well as a selection of unreleased demos and live recordings, totaling more than four hundred songs in all.

U2's second attempt at the big screen was more successful in 2008, when it broke ground again with the release of *U2 3D*, a live-action film that employed the greatest number of three-dimensional cameras ever used for a single project. The film was codirected by Catherine Owens, the creative mind behind the screen visuals used in three of the band's world tours.[14] Featuring seven hundred hours of live concert footage filmed across seven Latin American shows during the Vertigo tour in 2006, *U2 3D* went on to win several awards.[15]

U2's latest digital endeavor is with Research in Motion, whose Black-Berry Smartphones are a major sponsor of the 360° tour. The "U2 Mobile Album" application lets fans interact with the new album on their Black-Berry and follow the band and the tour more closely, including linking up with other U2 fans during concerts. The launch of the app was a bit late though and hit the market six months after *No Line on the Horizon* was released and two months after the tour had begun. There was also a missed opportunity for more involvement with BlackBerry at the actual concert venues that would have helped tie the partnership together. The app itself is a bit deceiving in that only snippets of songs, not full-length tracks, are available. Failing to execute the app on time and to its fullest potential was a shortcoming of U2's latest digital venture with Research in Motion, but it indicates U2's willingness to experiment with the most current consumer technology.

U2 Acts Ethically

Elevated brands adopt their own set of values and have beneficial influences on the world, and their consumers are inclined to celebrate brands they trust to act ethically. U2 has offered its support to charities and environmental initiatives and has been an activist itself for furthering the good of humankind. One of U2's biggest and most evident charitable acts was its participation in Live Aid in July 1985. The event was a massive undertaking led by the efforts of fellow Irishman Bob Geldof, who had previously received U2's support along with a host of other Irish and British acts in the recording of the charity song "Do They Know It's Christmas?" Live Aid was the catalyst that not only sparked the band's success around the globe but also kick-started its desire to help raise awareness of global issues.

Over the years, the band members have individually lent their support to charities and affiliations, most notably Bono's work for DATA and ONE. In 2006, the Edge spearheaded an organization called Music Rising, which raises money to buy new instruments and equipment for New Orleans musicians affected by Hurricane Katrina in 2005. U2 and Green Day made a dual effort in recording the 1970s punk rock song "The Saints Are Coming" as a single for the charity.

U2 has also used its popularity to leverage support for the human rights group Amnesty International, and on a more public scale, it was a major player in the celebrity-driven Live 8 concert in July 2005. The initiative managed to persuade world leaders to agree to increase financial aid for troubled African nations, cancel debt for eighteen countries, and provide more access to drugs and care for AIDS orphans.[16]

U2 often invites its fans to join them in its fight for global causes. During the Vertigo and 360° tours, the band showed its continued support for Nobel Peace Prize laureate Aung San Suu Kyi, the democratically elected leader of Burma who had been under house arrest for nearly twenty years until her release in November 2010. At shows on the 2009 and 2010 legs of the 360° tour, Bono asked fans to don a mask of her face during "Walk On," a song written for her and played each night in her honor.

Whether U2 is focusing on preserving the environment, fighting for human rights, or aiding in positive change for disadvantaged communities, the band has always placed an importance on the mind and the heart of the world, as all good brands do. "Hearts + Minds" is an area of U2.com designated to the key campaigning groups that are lit by U2's globally conscious spotlight. The website reminds fans that "the music of U2 has always been about heart and mind, body and soul."[17] This public acknowledgment reaffirms U2's ability to promote its own set of values and have a positive influence on the world.

U2 Has an Army of Brand Ambassadors

Elevated brands have an army of supporters behind them, and U2 is no different. U2 fans have a high amount of brand loyalty and are often dubbed the most passionate fans in the world. This could be a result of U2's early decision to make building a loyal fan base a priority. U2 began fostering a dialogue with fans and building a community among them as early as 1981, with the birth of *U2 Magazine*. In its second issue, fans got a behind-the-scenes glimpse of the filming of the "October" music video, and by issue 9 in 1983, an entire section of the publication was designated to U2 pen pals and trade listings. The simplistic fanzine eventually evolved into a glossy, four-color magazine called *Propaganda,* which debuted in 1986.

By 2000, the band severed the paper trail and launched its official website U2.com, where the band's loyalty program has truly come into fruition. Not only is it a virtual community for U2 fans to interact with one another, but the website also offers paying subscribers first dibs on presale tickets and the opportunity to hear new songs and watch new music videos first. Footage shot by the band during studio recordings and by the crew while on tour is also available to subscribers.

Leading up to the Vertigo tour of 2005, subscribers were granted pre-sale access to tickets, but scalpers logged on to the site in droves, blocking many longtime fans from securing seats. Drummer Larry Mullen Jr. was quick to respond to fans. He made a public apology on behalf of the band by issuing a letter on U2.com promising that it was trying to find a fairer way to distribute tickets to its loyal fan base. This incident helped inspire the presale ticketing coordinated on U2.com for the 360° tour, where fans were granted access to the presale in order of how long they had been a U2.com subscriber. This tiered system rewards longtime fans with the first period of access to the presale tickets.

Elevated brands employ clever relationship management programs for loyal consumers, and U2 has demonstrated its status as an elevated brand in this regard by offering a reward that in turn allows fans to further support U2. This is a win–win equation where both the fan and the brand benefit from loyalty-based offerings.

U2 Acts Like a Market Leader

An elevated brand is a global brand as well. Coca-Cola is perhaps the best-known product in the world, and similarly, U2 is one of the most popular bands in the world. A behavior adopted by global brands at the top of their industry is that they act as market leader, often outspoken in their field about issues that affect their industry on a worldwide scale.

New technology threatens the music industry as much as it offers opportunity, and today's bands are trying to find ways to work with the Internet instead of being confined by it. Radiohead cut out the middleman record label and self-released its 2008 album *In Rainbows* as a digital download on its official website, asking customers to pay whatever they wanted to or not pay at all. Only Radiohead knows the exact figure of albums sold and the average price that was paid, although some initial reports showed three million album sales at an average price of $8 per copy.

Radiohead's experiment revealed that music piracy is a new-age epidemic. Even though the masses could have downloaded the album for free from a legitimate site controlled by the band, many people still chose to download it illegally. Forbes.com reported that it was illegally downloaded over 240,000 times from peer-to-peer BitTorrent networks such as Limewire on the first day of its release.[18] After the first month, it was reported that 38 percent of people that downloaded the album from the legitimate site paid something for it. To some industry experts, this shows that people still feel music warrants a cost. Jim Larrison, the general manager of Adify, an online advertising firm, said of Radiohead's gimmick that, "This is a true win for the music industry as it shows there is still perceived value in the digital form of entertainment. Of course, it does suggest that the marketplace is continuing to migrate and the music industry needs to shift with consumer behavior."[19]

Bono and Paul McGuinness have been equally candid in their opinions on the Internet's effect on the music industry and the illegal music downloading that runs rampant in cyberspace. They have often argued that while music piracy affects everyone in the music business, it should be most worrisome for bands of the next generation, who will suffer the loss of a true revenue stream from album sales.

In January 2010, Bono exercised his journalistic skills by writing a *New York Times* article listing his top ten ideas that could help better the world over the next ten years. Second on Bono's list is a word of caution for intellectual property developers:

> A decade's worth of music file-sharing and swiping has made clear that the people it hurts are the creators—in this case, the young, fledgling songwriters who can't live off ticket and T-shirt sales like the least sympathetic among us—and the people this reverse Robin Hooding benefits are rich service providers, whose swollen profits perfectly mirror the lost receipts of the music business.[20]

Bono was not just issuing a rallying call for the United States to help defend the creative community; he was also looking for solutions to help the music industry evolve in a technology-driven world. For instance, Vevo is a recently launched online service where professionally developed music videos and original content by artists are hosted on Google's YouTube, and it creates a way for artists to monetize their online content. So far, three of the top four major record labels are on board, including Universal Music, home to U2. Unveiled in December 2009, Bono enthusiastically introduced Vevo at the launch party, attended by many of the film and music industry's top stars: "Friends, we are gathered here today to mourn the loss of a great old cash cow that was the music business. But friends, we're also here to celebrate new shoots, new life, and the birth of a new model for our industry."[21]

U2 also struck its own deal with YouTube in the creation of the official U2 channel. On October 25, 2009, the band's show at the Rose Bowl was streamed live over the Internet, a first for YouTube, who had not yet broadcast a concert in its entirety. That night in California, over ninety-five thousand fans saw the show live, but a further ten million were able to watch it in the comfort of their own home.

In January 2008, Paul McGuinness addressed a crowd of music industry professionals in Cannes at the music business conference MIDEM. In his now much publicized speech, McGuinness pointed the finger at the Internet service providers' role in how music is illegally consumed over their networks. "The partnership between music and technology needs to be fair and reasonable. ISPs, Telcos and tech companies have enjoyed a bonanza in the last few years off the back of recorded music content. It is time for them to share that with artists and content owners."[22]

Television manufacturers and the movie industry are similarly concerned with the replacement of their mediums, given that movies and television shows are also illegally downloaded from the Internet. Market leader Samsung is leading the way with new innovations that the home PC can't touch yet. The company unveiled a range of home entertainment products, from televisions to Blu-ray players that incorporate three-dimensional technology, at the annual Consumer Electronics Show in January 2010. At a Samsung press conference, Jeffrey Katzenberg said that he hoped this new advancement in home entertainment will help reduce piracy.[23] It should help, at least temporarily, as three-dimensional viewing is not available via the Internet.

Elevated brands lead their market in the way of new technology and industry innovations. U2, like Samsung, has found ways to counteract the problems that the Internet has brought to light over the last decade in its industry. As market leaders, both brands are seizing technology and using it to their advantage.

Brand Elevation

U2 easily belongs among the ranks of the world's most favored brands, such as Coca-Cola, Nike, Apple, and Guinness, who have all elevated themselves above their competitors. U2 and manager Paul McGuinness decided early on that it would be wrong to get the music part right and the business part wrong. They have made careful decisions throughout their career to remain true to their vision, uphold the brand's integrity, and consistently support it through visual cues.

U2 has delivered on its promise to bring atmosphere to its music and provide memorable ways for its fans to experience it. The band has remained flexible, changing with the current landscape to reflect the mood of today's culture using new media channels. Very few brands have embraced technology so wholeheartedly. As the Internet threatens to take hold of the music industry, U2 is finding ways to adapt and even leverage the World Wide Web to its advantage by opening the band up to new audiences.

U2 seems satisfied with the feeling of never feeling satisfied. With the second decade of the twenty-first century ahead of us, U2 is poised to continue producing the best music possible and delivering the best live experiences possible for fans. Because of this, U2 has an army of brand ambassadors proudly wearing its T-shirts, buying its albums, attending its concerts, and supporting its causes. U2 has had a few missteps in its career, but within the big picture, it has emerged relatively unscathed and continues to have a stronghold on its core fan base. U2 has clearly become one of the most shining examples of what it means to be an elevated brand.

Notes

1. *Rolling Stone*, "Rock and Roll Daily," http://www.rollingstone.com/rockdaily/index.php/2009/03/11/on-the-charts-u2s-no-line-on-the-horizon-is-number-one-in-2009s-biggest-week/ (accessed May 17, 2011).

2. U2.com, "The Essentials," http://www.u2.com/essentials (accessed May 17, 2011).

3. Andrew Edgecliffe-Johnson, "Lunch with the FT: Paul McGuinness," *Financial Times*, December 4, 2009.

4. U2, *U2 by U2* (UK: HarperCollins, 2002), 207.

5. Brian Hiatt, "U2 Hymns for the Future," *Rolling Stone*, March 19, 2009, 50.

6. Terry Mattingly, "U2: Rockers Finally Speak Out about Their Rumored Faith," *CCM*, August 1982, http://www.ccmmagazine.com/news/stories/11534377/ (accessed May 17, 2011).

7. Hiatt, "U2 Hymns," 90.

8. U2, *U2 by U2*, 147.

9. Spinner.com, "15 Worst Music Ideas Ever," http://spinner.aol.com/photogalleries/15-worst-music-ideas-ever-u2-popmart-kmart (accessed May 17, 2011).

10. Olaf Tyaransen, "Closer to the Edge (Pt. 1)," *Hot Press*, December 4, 2002, http://www.hotpress.com/archive/2627068.html (accessed May 17, 2011).

11. Neil McCormick, "Boy to Man: How U2's Experiences of Growing Up in 1960s and 1970s Dublin Shaped the Band," (paper presented at "The Hype and the Feedback" U2 academic conference, Durham, North Carolina, October 2–4, 2009).

12. Lisa Godson, *Stealing Hearts from a Travelling Show: The Graphic Design of U2* (Dublin, Ireland: four5one, 2002), 37.

13. Anton Corbijn, "Photography—U2," http://www.corbijn.co.uk/ (accessed May 17, 2011).

14. Stuart Clark, "U2 Plan 3-D Concert Film," *Hot Press*, November 29, 2006, 12.

15. The Internet Movie Database, "U2 3D," http://www.imdb.com/title/tt0892375/ (accessed May 17, 2011).

16. Look to the Stars, "Live 8," http://www.looktothestars.org/charity/10-live-8 (accessed May 17, 2011).

17. U2.com, "Hearts + Minds," http://www.u2.com/heartsandminds/ (accessed May 17, 2011).

18. Andy Greenberg, "Free? Steal It Anyway," Forbes.com, October 16, 2007, http://www.forbes.com/2007/10/16/radiohead-download-piracy-tech-internet-cx_ag_1016techradiohead.html (accessed May 17, 2011).

19. Louis Hau, "Mixed Rainbow for Radiohead," Forbes.com, November 5, 2007.

20. Bono, "Ten for the Next Ten," *New York Times*, January 3, 2010, op-ed section.

21. Ryan Lawler, "Bono: Vevo Is Rebirth of Music Industry," Newteevee.com, http://newteevee.com/2009/12/08/bono-vevo-is-rebirth-of-music-industry/ (accessed May 17, 2011).

22. *Billboard*, "McGuinness Speech in Full," Billboard.biz, http://www.billboard.biz/bbbiz/content_display/industry/e3i062b16e707aa99916c212e660cbffd3e (accessed May 17, 2011).

23. Charlie Sorrel, "Samsung's Impossibly Thin 3D TV Tempts Hollywood Producer," *Wired*, January 6, 2010, http://www.wired.com/gadgetlab/2010/01/samsungs-impossibly-thin-3d-tv-tempts-hollywood-producer/ (accessed May 17, 2011).

Nothing Succeeds Like Failure   8
U2 and the Politics of Irony

KEVIN J. H. DETTMAR

THE CHALLENGE OF IRONY IN THE PUBLIC SPHERE—its spectacular availability, even vulnerability, to misinterpretation—has been virtually ignored by cultural critics. Irony, according to traditional literary critical tenets, is a formal feature of texts; it can be evaluated, so the thinking goes, according to purely internal criteria, without recourse to the actual processing done by real audiences. And if somehow the design of the artist and the design perceived by her or his audience happen to differ? Production trumps consumption. Wayne Booth's seminal study *The Rhetoric of Irony* (1974), for instance—a text that grew out of work begun in his encyclopedic *The Rhetoric of Fiction* (1961)—presents a thorough and complex account of how irony works; it's largely unconcerned, however, with what it means that irony often doesn't work. Irony, when it succeeds, teaches ethical lessons at a profound level that no other rhetorical form can touch; as Booth acknowledges, irony "risks disaster more aggressively than any other device. But if it succeeds, it will succeed more strongly than any literal statement can do."[1]

When it breaks down, however—and critics like Booth are conspicuously silent about what it means when irony goes wrong—it threatens simply to confirm us in our prejudices; this is a risk, as we'll see in the cases of U2, that some committed artists are finally unwilling to take.

For U2 inherited the crisis of representation that was set in motion during the modernist period; it accepted, without I think fully having thought through, modernism's "poetics of impersonality."[2] In its early 1990s albums *Achtung Baby* and *Zooropa*, the band adopted an obviously ironic stance toward its own musical legacy and the trappings of rock stardom, but it ultimately failed in its attempt to mount a politically efficacious critique, falling back, after three albums, into a kind of adult contemporary complacency (beginning with 2000's *All That You Can't Leave Behind*). In U2's failure, I believe, we see posed in stark form the larger question of the possible political efficacy of irony produced on a massive scale for a mass audience.

The two bands that dominated commercially viable "alternative" or "college" rock throughout the 1980s—REM, from Athens, Georgia, and U2, Dublin's favorite sons—faced a crisis of reinvention in the 1990s. In different though related ways, they had come to represent sincerity and engagement, especially in the persons of their lead singers and lyricists, Michael Stipe and Bono. Both bands attempted to remake themselves through a form of ironic refashioning. This ironic turn is complicated somewhat in the case of U2, whose Christian faith comprises an important part of its authority in matters of conscience. "Mock the devil, and he will flee from thee," a somewhat loose translation of James 4:7, became the group's credo during the making of *Achtung Baby*—not quite "evil, be thou my good," but you can imagine that it made Christian fans uncomfortable when Bono came out for the encore wearing a gold lamé suit, platform shoes, and devil's horns.

I begin, briefly, with U2's moment of transition: on New Year's Eve, 1989, the band left the concert stage in its hometown, Dublin, with lead singer Bono making this somewhat cryptic remark: "We won't see you for a while, we have got to go away and dream it all up again."[3] The gesture was widely interpreted at the time as the band's farewell, like Ziggy Stardust's announcement of "the last show that we'll ever play" on July 3, 1973, at London's Hammersmith Odeon, a moment famously captured in D. A. Pennebaker's film.[4] And in the same way that Bowie's words were true—it was Ziggy's last performance, as Bowie then retired that character from active duty, but by no means was it Bowie's last show—so too, the painfully earnest U2 that had dominated the alternative rock scene of the 1980s would never again be seen in quite the same guise.

Now, let's wind the tape back just a bit, to understand how things came to pass. In 1987, U2 was on top of the world. Its fifth studio album, *The Joshua Tree*, was the biggest-selling and most critically acclaimed album yet to emerge from alternative or college rock; if we were to imagine an index that multiplied sales success by critical success, *The Joshua Tree* would dwarf anything produced between *Sgt. Pepper* and *Nevermind*. As early, even prematurely, as March 1985, *Rolling Stone* magazine featured the band on its cover, naming U2 "Our Choice: Band of the Eighties";

one can only imagine how demoralizing this must have been for any band venturing to make music during the next five years. The album brought both the band's music and Bono's unique style of imagistically charged political songwriting to a new level; U2 immediately became the band to beat—and, consequently, the band to beat up on. The album topped the charts across the world in its first week of release; the first single, "With or Without You," was U2's first number one in the United States, and the second single, "I Still Haven't Found What I'm Looking For," also went to top of the pops, as well as becoming a staple of church youth groups throughout the English-speaking world. The four made the cover of *Time* magazine, only the third group ever to do so: the first two were the Beatles and the Who. Clearly, U2 had arrived.

Having finally figured out how to write pop hits—although earlier album cuts, such as "Pride (In the Name of Love)" and "Sunday Bloody Sunday," among others, certainly showed the band's ability to write catchy pop anthems many years earlier—the band began experimenting with longer-form, free-form pieces like "Bullet the Blue Sky," a song exploring the underbelly of American culture, with a sonic superstructure in every way suited to Bono's lyric about American intervention in Central America. As Eamon Dunphy wrote in his "definitive biography of U2" published upon the release of *The Joshua Tree*, "'Bullet' provides a clue to where U2 might head now that their ability to top the hit parade is no longer the issue."[5]

Dunphy must have pinched himself when he learned the title of the band's next project, the 1988 concert film and double album *Rattle and Hum*—the title taken from the lyric of "Bullet the Blue Sky." Another Dublin journalist, John Waters, was more prescient than he could have known when he wrote, in June 1987, that U2 had "done pretty much everything backwards. They have gone from writing music which was like nothing anybody had ever heard previously to music which hinted at the best of everything that had gone before."[6] Continuing in reverse, U2's next album more than "hinted at" the popular music tradition of which it was the inheritor; the album was an exercise in the musical roots to which, having caught the spirit of rock and roll by listening to punks in the late 1970s and early 1980s, the members of U2 had never been systematically exposed. The success of *The Joshua Tree* bought U2 a great deal of creative freedom; "*The Joshua Tree* did more than make U2 famous," Dunphy writes. "It set them free."[7] And the band took advantage of this freedom by indulging Bono's long-held desire to explore the nature of American music and culture.

The resulting album and tour film was an ambitious combination of live performances of some of U2's greatest hits to date ("I Still Haven't Found What I'm Looking For," "Pride," "Bullet the Blue Sky"), a handful of new songs ("Desire," "Silver and Gold," "All I Want Is You," "When Love Comes to Town," "Angel of Harlem"), and perhaps most provocatively, a whole slew of covers.

Great expectations notwithstanding, *Rattle and Hum* ranks up there with the great miscues in rock history. The band threw itself "into the arms of America" (the phrase that closes "Bullet the Blue Sky"); America threw it right back, rejecting the perceived musical imperialism of an Irish pop group that ought to have known better. Waters writes of the contradiction inherent in "U2, natives of a country colonized for generations, going to America, the great modern military and economic colonizer, and conquering it through the medium of a music which is itself colonized."[8] The gesture was understood by fans and critics, however, not as the ingenious double reverse that Waters describes, but as unabashed and—worse—unsuccessful audacity.

In a book of interviews with Michka Assayas, Bono presents the band's conception of the project:

> That was an amazing thing that happened. I realized the force of the media at the end of *The Joshua Tree*. We had a big record, and the natural thing to do would be to just make a live album at that point of the tour, cash in and go on holidays. But we decided: "Oh no, we can't do that." So we wrote songs to put on this. We'd have new songs. We'd make a film about our journey through America. We'd make it much more interesting: we'd make a double album, put it out at half price, and rather than being a band who thought they were the center of the world, we would put these musicians that we were fans of at the center of our world, and in the artwork, with pictures of Johnny Cash. We wrote songs—not all great songs—but we would sort of declare ourselves as the fans that we are. And this *Rattle and Hum* thing came out. But the opposite came back at us. It was like: "Oh, this is egomania, they think they are now one of the Pantheon of these great artists, and they feel they can quote our music." I remember thinking, "This is exactly the opposite of what we are trying to do!" But we actually couldn't undo that. It was just a given that these so-called fans had now lost the run of themselves. "Egomaniac," "messianic." These were the kind of words that were being thrown at us.[9]

Seventeen years after *Rattle and Hum*, when this interview was being conducted, it was quite clear that these criticisms still bothered Bono. And surely, some of the charges do in retrospect seem to miss the mark: not the charge of egomania, perhaps, but as the more recent controversy surrounding Bob Dylan's recent album *Modern Times* has reminded us, musical imperialism and plundering can be a many-splendored thing.

One thing that Bono never talks about, however, is just how truly awful most of the album's covers really are. In the essay I referred to earlier, John Waters writes about U2 in 1987, before the *Rattle and Hum* debacle, "[It's] difficult to imagine anyone having the empathy or the moral authority to cover a U2 song";[10] yet, *Rattle and Hum*, paradoxically, is all about the band covering the songs of other artists and revealing precisely that it didn't have the moral authority to do so. Even more interesting—and one of the almost unbearably embarrassing moments in the film—is when U2 jams in a New York church with the Gospel Choir of Harlem, who the band has learned do a powerful a cappella version of "I Still Haven't Found What I'm Looking For." Just because one is Irish doesn't mean that one is immune from cultural insensitivity (recalling the infamous triad that John Lydon invokes in the title of his autobiography, *No Irish, No Blacks, No Dogs*). To watch Bono and the boys walk into that church and take the song back from the black gospel choir is one of the film's most cringeworthy moments.

In fact, the film and album open with an explicit act of musical reappropriation, of "taking back." The song on which this act is performed is "Helter Skelter"; arguably, if there is one song in all the history of rock and roll that should never be covered, for historical reasons if no other, this is the one. And if one were looking for evidence of the band's arrogance—well, one might productively argue that U2's believing that it can undo the evil of the Tate-LaBianca murders through this kind of musical exorcism is worse than just silly. While it would be a major detour here to articulate a careful set of criteria for the critical evaluation of covers, at a minimum, one expects of a cover that it reveal something new about the original song or its current performer: U2's cover of "Helter Skelter" does neither. Bono still smarts from having been called "messianic," but it might have been worse. Given that he was channeling Charles Manson, he might have been called "satanic."

Another of the album's covers fails much more dramatically in the film than in the studio version included on the album: U2's cover of Jimi Hendrix's cover of Bob Dylan's "All along the Watchtower." To begin with, "All along the Watchtower" is one of those rare examples of songs—Aretha Franklin's recording of Otis Redding's "Respect" might be another—for which the cover becomes definitive: Dylan's version on

John Wesley Harding is of interest now primarily as the raw material for Hendrix's epochal cover. (Indeed, Dylan subsequently called Hendrix's version "definitive" and began covering Hendrix's cover when he played the song live.) U2's cover is uninspired and uninspiring; in the film, the band plays the song at an impromptu free concert in San Francisco, and the decision to do it seems to be merely a gesture at the storied musical scene of that city during the Summer of Love. Unfortunately, it comes off as more exploitation than homage; as the band talks in its trailer, about to step out into the park to play, Bono seemingly as an afterthought sends a roadie out, to find someone who actually knows the lyrics to the song.

The album and film also contain a handful of new U2 songs, all of them quite evidently bearing the mark of the band's recent immersion in the culture of American popular music. Each is interesting for a variety of reasons; at least one of these, the faux-Stax soul number "Angel of Harlem," is embarrassing in almost exactly the same way as the band's collaboration with the Gospel Choir of Harlem. Harlem, let's just say, wasn't very good to U2. The biggest problem with these songs—"not all great songs," as Bono has admitted[11]—is that, to mix metaphors, their roots are but poorly digested.

Part of the problem with this work is clear in even just the first thirty seconds of the track "Desire." The song is undeniably catchy and has become an audience favorite at U2 shows. But "Desire" is an "original" song that sounds for all the world like a cover. Most everything on the track is somewhat shopworn: the song's Afro-Cuban clave rhythm, known colloquially in these parts as the Bo Diddley beat; the gratuitous reference to Brat Pack author Jay McInerney's 1984 debut novel, *Bright Lights, Big City*; and the twisted Bob Dylan quotation in the lyric—from "All along the Watchtower," no less—"with a red guitar on fire," with the Dylan ambience then echoed at the end of the song in a brief Dylanesque harp solo.

But enough about *Rattle and Hum*: enough kicking that particular dog while it's down. The larger point here is that it's something like shame—embarrassment over the band's public outing of its oversize ambition and desire for authentic American roots—that ultimately moved U2 into the most productive and challenging artistic decision it has made in its nearly thirty-five-year history: its decision to go ironic with the 1991 album *Achtung Baby*. W. H. Auden famously writes in his elegy for W. B. Yeats, "Mad Ireland hurt you into poetry"; in this case, it might be said, angry fans and critics hurt U2 into irony.

If covers from the early part of a band's career serve as illustrious coattails upon which to ride, those in midcareer can serve to fine-tune a band's image, shaming the critics—as does Elvis Costello on his album *The Kojak Variations*, for example—into upgrading the band's significance for the future by retracing the range of its roots. U2's project *Rattle and Hum* attempts to exploit this temporal logic: covers of a variety of rock standards combine with the writing and recording of U2's own style of "roots" music ("Angel of Harlem," "When Love Comes to Town"). The covers, though, are less roots than root rot. *Rattle and Hum* failed quite spectacularly and famously, and U2 went quickly from being the biggest band in the world to hanging its head in shame. Yet it was finally its shame or, rather, its deflection into self-protective irony that dictated a productive new direction for its work, motivating the triptych of 1990s albums in which U2 turned on itself and generating some of the decade's most ambitious and challenging mainstream rock.

In the interview cited earlier, Bono goes on to describe the move from *Rattle and Hum* to *Achtung Baby*:

> "Egomaniac," "messianic." These were the kind of words that were being thrown at us. So I just thought: "Right. If people want megalomania, let's give them megalomania! Let's really have some fun with this!" [*laughs*] Let's try to communicate with the people who don't like U2, because we're not real rock stars. I don't think it was cynical, it was more fun. And by the way, there's a part of me that would kind of like to be that rock star.[12]

Note that last sentence: "And by the way, there's a part of me that would kind of like to be that rock star." That might serve as a handy, functional definition of the difference between irony and satire: for irony is, as Gayatri Spivak has said of deconstruction, "the critique of that which one cannot not want."

Achtung Baby is the album on which U2 first started to puncture its earlier pretenses with a healthy dose of postmodern irony; even more interesting was the elaborate tour the band conducted between February 29, 1992, and December 10, 1993: 157 shows on six continents. Known as the Zoo TV tour, it not only brought U2's audiences face-to-face with the band's growing awareness of its outsized ambitions but, even more risky, confronted its audiences with their own complicity. The band turned its irony on itself and its fans, for of course without the assistance of the fans, there would be no "egomaniacal" and "messianic" rock stars called U2. The concert film recording of the show done in Sydney, Australia, proved this tour to be one of the most ambitious and most intelligent rock tours ever put together: certainly the most challenging for its audiences. Though I wasn't able to attend, I can still remember the reaction of one of my students at Clemson University when she came to class the day after the show in Columbia, South Carolina. At least half the show had completely baffled her; she literally had no idea what to make of it. But she loved it when the band played "One."

But I've gotten ahead of myself. A large part of the complexity and ingenuity of the Zoo TV project is demonstrable in just the first five minutes from the opening of the concert film *Zoo TV: Live from Sydney*, in 1993 before an arena crowd of sixty thousand fans. The music that's playing as the film starts, before U2's own theatrics begin, is a track called "Television: The Drug of the Nation," by the group the Disposable Heroes of Hiphoprisy, a song that decries the negative effects of our television addiction.

David Foster Wallace's much-discussed attack on ironic disengagement in his 1990 essay "E Unibus Pluram: Television and U.S. Fiction" makes a convenient starting point for a consideration of U2's large-scale multimedia Zoo TV performance, conceived of the following year. Even those not familiar with Wallace's essay are probably familiar with its contours; his almost single-minded focus on television as the cause of this turn to a kind of enervated, reflexive irony is distinctive, but the larger charge that our culture has developed a defensive armor of unthinking irony is familiar from many sources, including Jedediah Purdy's 1999 tract *For Common Things: Irony, Trust, and Commitment in America Today*.

In Wallace's analysis, television is the culprit: "Irony, poker-faced silence, and fear of ridicule," he writes, "are distinctive of those features of contemporary U.S. culture . . . that enjoy any significant relation to the television whose weird pretty hand has my generation by the throat. . . . Irony and ridicule are entertaining and effective, [but] at the same time they are agents of a great despair and stasis in U.S. culture."[13] I have no idea whether Bono, the primary creative force behind U2 (and originator of the Zoo TV concept), ever read Wallace's essay; but even if he hadn't, it's hard to imagine a more direct and sympathetic response to its charge that television was turning us into a mass of mindless drones.

Here is a quick play-by-play of what happens after the "mood music" from Hiphoprisy comes over the PA system: The huge crowd waits restlessly for the show to begin; as drummer Larry Mullen Jr. has described it, there were "three loud bursts of applause" every night at predictable intervals: "The first when the lights go down [which is, simultaneously, the moment when the huge Zoo TV screens go on], the second when people see the band, the third when they see Bono's silhouette."[14] The song "Television: The Drug of the Nation" castigates the audience for its television addiction, but the song is drowned out by the applause as the stadium's television monitors come to life: Ironic Moment 1.

What those monitors show, among other things, is footage from Leni Riefensthal's two iconic Nazi propaganda films, *Olympia* and *Triumph of the Will*. It's hard to know what the typical stadium rock concertgoer makes of these images, and they are of course just one component of the crazy visual salad being served up on the stage's multiple screens. When the film of the *Hitlerjungend* (Hitler Youth) drumming at a Nazi rally takes center stage, the stadium's sound system isolates the sound of his drum, and very quickly—in about three seconds, most nights—the Zoo TV audience are clapping along in time: Ironic Moment 2.

Though, again, it seems unlikely that many of the fans are aware of these ironies; certainly, a viewer of the concert film is or can be. Certainly the band was: Bono has acknowledged that an echo of Hitler's night rallies was part of the effect the band was aiming for. U2 is here attempting—in a manner perhaps not impressively sophisticated by high-art or literary standards but pretty ambitious for a stadium rock-and-roll show—to demonstrate the audience's own complicity in the nearly fascistic structure of rock stardom. "On one level, you can look at these concerts and go: God, this is like Hitler's night rallies," Bono has commented. "You know, Zoo TV was playing into that whole idea: the night rally."[15] When Bono finally appears on stage, raised on a hydraulic lift, he steps out goose-stepping, his hand rising in an involuntary "Heil Hitler" salute modeled on Peter Sellers's in *Dr. Strangelove*. The strains of Schiller's "Ode to Joy" at the conclusion of Beethoven's Ninth come in next, a nod toward the anthem of the European Union and Anthony Burgess's (and Stanley Kubrick's) *A Clockwork Orange*. Then the Nazi imagery gives way to "a cascade of symbols of Europe in the last fifty years,"[16] and as the television screens are seemingly shattered, the band quietly slips onto the stage under cover of dark, and a silhouetted Bono rises on a mechanical platform only to be knocked about by the concert's opening song, "Zoo Station."

"Zoo Station," which opens both the concert and the 1991 album *Achtung Baby* with which U2 began its own ironic undoing, is a remarkable document. In the lyrics, Bono's stage persona, a character he calls "the Fly," speaks of his willingness to let go the reins of authenticity and sincerity—to, as he sings in another song from the album, "slide down the surface of things":

> I'm ready
> I'm ready for the gridlock

> I'm ready . . . to take it to the street
> I'm ready for the shuffle
> Ready for the deal
> Ready to let go of the steering wheel
> I'm ready
> Ready for the crush.

The song takes its title from a station stop on the Berlin subway; the image of the chaotic zoo proved resonant for Bono, and he took to describing the world after the fall of the Berlin Wall as the "Zoo World Order." In fact—and this is one of those facts that's almost too good to be true—when U2 went to Berlin to meet up with Brian Eno to record *Achtung Baby*, "they arrived on the last flight to East Germany before East Germany ceased to exist."[17]

The shock for a concertgoer of Bono's staggering appearance at the concert's beginning is, I think, hard to re-create at this distance in time. The guise in which Bono takes the stage, the Fly, has become a familiar figure: this parody of an aging rock star has, "ironically," been domesticated and become iconic of rock stardom. Certainly Bono meant it to signify along multiple intertextual paths, as he explained to one interviewer: "The rock star I put together for myself was an identi-kit. I had Elvis Presley's leather jacket, Jim Morrison's leather pants, Lou Reed's fly shades, Jerry Lee Lewis's boots, Gene Vincent's limp. You want rock 'n' roll stuff? I'll give you some."[18] Up through its career-making album *The Joshua Tree* (1987), the band members never wore much more than jeans and T-shirts, the typical alternative rock uniform.

So Bono's look would have been jarring: he looks just like everything he'd always warned us against. And the sound? The new wave band Devo used the slogan "The Sound of Things Falling Apart": that's the same sound with which Zoo TV opens. "Zoo Station" comes crashing onstage with an ugly, muddy, industrial screech; in the era of digital audio, the redlined opening of "Zoo Station" (both on the studio album *Achtung Baby* and in the Zoo TV tour performance) punctures the fourth wall of the recording studio and seemingly punctures the last necessary remnant of analog sound technology as well: the speaker cone. (I know that when I first put the album on for a listen, I was convinced that I'd turned the amplifier up too high and blown out my speakers.) Above this cacophony, the Edge's guitar slowly begins to soar; he's playin' guitar like he was ringin' a bell, the shimmering guitar line "giving a shape and a significance to the immense panorama of futility and anarchy which is contemporary history" (that last phrase lifted from T. S. Eliot's review of Joyce's *Ulysses*).[19] That bright guitar line, I would point out, is much more pronounced in the live performance than on the studio recording: fans hearing the song in this context, apparently, have need of a bit more reassurance.

Once U2 has blown through its first two numbers, "Zoo Station" and "The Fly," Bono takes a commercial break, as the band puts aside its instruments and Bono picks up an instrument of his own: an enormous, outsized remote control. He proceeds to channel surf for a few moments, skipping past a cricket test match and pieces of news footage, before turning back to the crowd and taunting it: "But you didn't come all the way out here to watch TV—now DIDJA?!" The crowd cheers on cue, and the band tears into another new song, "Even Better Than the Real Thing"; but the real question, the real challenge, goes unanswered, because of course the sixty thousand fans in Sydney did in fact come to watch television: for all but the thousand or two closest to the stage, the only way anyone in that stadium was going to see a rock show that night was by watching it on TV, Zoo TV. Indeed, most of the audience sees Bono's taunt, "you didn't come all the way out here to watch TV," *on* a TV monitor. The entire show is quite self-consciously conceived of as a television show; U2 transforms the economic necessity of video in the age of MTV into a resource for its own "propaganda"—a term the band has transvalued by naming its fan club "Propaganda."

Not all of the concert is as dense and rich as these first few moments: but actually, much of it is, and a great deal more can be said about its manifold strategies. Briefly, though, here are a couple more examples of the show's complex ironic critique of contemporary consumer culture and its consumption of rock and roll and the figure of the rock star. One would be the band's performance of "Even Better Than the Real Thing," again from the 1991 album *Achtung Baby*, the album that inaugurated U2's three-album foray into the world of ironic self-critique. In the song's title alone, its intertextual nature should be clear. For a generation coming of age in the age of television, "the real thing" is, of course . . . Coke. The U2 song is a pretty familiar song of courting; his head colonized by the language of marketing, however, the lover is at a loss as to how to convey to his beloved the extraordinary nature of his affection, and his appeal is swallowed up in a mire of pop songs and commercial jingles. "You're the real thing," he intones in the chorus—"even better than the real thing." The difference between statement and restatement here is, as Jean Baudrillard might say, the difference between mimesis and hyperreality, the simulacrum: "You're the real thing" / You're "even better than the real thing."

The speaker finds himself caught in the trap of the already-said: Calling his beloved "the real thing" reduces her to a commodity, in particular a bottle of Coke; overcorrecting and calling her "even better than the real thing" makes her into a simulacrum. Among other intertexual echoes, the song leans on the iconic television ad jingle and on the 1968 Tammi Terrell and Marvin Gaye hit "Ain't Nothin' Like the Real Thing Baby"—as well, in a later verse, as the Sly and the Family Stone hit "I'm Gonna Take You Higher." The song describes a crisis of authentic speech and authentic emotion in an age of media saturation; it has always reminded me of the moment in Don DeLillo's *White Noise* when Jack Gladney, convinced that he is about to die, enters the bedrooms of his sleeping children and adjusts their blankets and teddy bears, feeling that his good-bye gesture has been co-opted by the imagery of television commercials.

To close this discussion of the Zoo TV tour, let's examine the moment at which U2's glib postmodern spectacle of consumption runs headlong into the crisis of ironic representation instantiated in high modernism. "Bullet the Blue Sky," a song criticizing US imperialism and military intervention in Central America, had been a concert staple and audience favorite since its appearance on *The Joshua Tree* album in 1987. The song is sardonic but not ironic: there's nothing implicit, in other words, about the song's critique. It was always played during the "greatest hits" portion of the Zoo TV shows, during which older, more sincere material was played as a unit, and seemingly the audience was supposed to suspend the ironic form of consumption that the first half of the show had so carefully taught it. (Though space prevents me from going into it here, I believe this is an important problem for the show, one that was never satisfactorily addressed: for irony has a momentum, and it's not entirely within an artist's power to dictate when material is to be consumed ironically, when not.)

When the Zoo TV tour came to Berlin, the show was played in the Olympic stadium that Hitler built, the same place where Riefensthal's *Olympia* was of course filmed; the band was back in the city where *Achtung Baby* was created, and given the overwhelming Nazi framework that the band had constructed for the show, anxieties were running a bit high. For the Zoo TV tour, the band had produced a video montage packed with suggestive imagery of different kinds to play behind the performance of "Bullet the Blue Sky," and at the point that Bono sings, "See them burnin' crosses, see the flames higher and higher," computer-generated imagery gradually morphed a KKK cross consumed by flames into a flaming swastika. The tattoos of Germany's Nazi past scar the Olympic stadium; swastikas originally cut into the concrete are by law plastered over and yet haunt the space. In that setting, U2 was ultimately unwilling to let its clever computer graphics play as background without commentary; as Bill Flanagan writes of the performance that night, "there is considerable tension in the pause before Bono says, in German, 'This will never happen again!'"[20]

Bono has just violated modernism's "poetics of impersonality," its insistence that the artist must show, never tell: Bono just "told," and according to Flanagan, the audience responds with relief and "an explosion of applause and cheering."[21] Bono knows the rules: he

> figures that saying those five words, spelling out U2's message, is completely contrary to the spirit of Zoo TV—where there is supposed to be no moralizing, where symbols are held up to raise questions and examine contradictions. But at the same time U2 is aware that some things are more important than art theories, and opposition to fascism is way up on that list. The band decided that if they were going to use the swastika—the most potent semiotic of all—they had to break character and be absolutely clear that they regarded this as evil. They wanted to offer the audience, especially the audience in places where neo-Nazis are rooting around, an opportunity to celebrate being opposed to fascism.[22]

The best rock and roll has always been animated by a healthy dose of irony: always standing somewhat apart from its own pretensions and its own more fatuous pronouncements. But the danger has always been that you are mistaken for that which you mock: that the Kinks were kinky, the Stooges were just stooges, that David Bowie, rather than Ziggy Stardust, was flirting with rock-and-roll suicide at the end of the tour, vowing never to perform again. There's an edgy energy to irony that no other trope can touch, but fans by and large don't pay $75 to be subjected to ironic critique at a stadium rock show: it's not an inherently ironic discursive situation.

In the end, Bono chooses not to remain "within or behind or beyond or above his handiwork, invisible, refined out of existence, indifferent, paring his fingernails," in Stephen Dedalus's famous phrase, but comes out from behind the curtain and shows his hand.[23] Some might consider this aesthetic bad faith; certainly I did when I first read about it. I guess today I'd prefer to think of Bono's gesture as a kind of ironic pedagogy, modeling a kind of ironic literacy.

Bono's abandonment of the modernist "poetics of impersonality" at the Berlin show perhaps foreshadows the band's ultimate unwillingness to stick with its ironic project after the heady days of the early 1990s. The entire Zoo TV project—judging from the rather vapid recent albums *All That You Can't Leave Behind*, *How to Dismantle an Atomic Bomb*, and *No Line on the Horizon,* as well as the set lists of the band's recent shows—is one that U2 has all but renounced. Bono sums it up this way: "Let me say the music was not ironic in that period—it was wrapped in irony. Actually, there was real blood going through those veins. Secondly, concerning the packaging, the presentation, I think even then it was ironic in a very idealistic way. . . . I don't think [Zoo TV] was a crisis of faith. . . . Just looking for a new way to express old idealism."[24] The paradox at the heart of this project, however, is that were it not for the inglorious failure of *Rattle and Hum,* it's unlikely the Zoo TV project would ever have happened.

Notes

1. Wayne C. Booth, *A Rhetoric of Irony* (Chicago: University of Chicago Press, 1974), 41–42.

2. I adopt the phrase from Maud Ellmann, *The Poetics of Impersonality: T. S. Eliot and Ezra Pound* (Cambridge, MA: Harvard University Press, 1987).

3. Bill Flanagan, *U2 at the End of the World* (New York: Delacorte/Bantam Doubleday, 1995), 4.

4. *Ziggy Stardust and the Spiders from Mars: The Motion Picture,* DVD, dir. D. A. Pennebaker (1973; New York: Virgin Records, 2003).

5. Eamon Dunphy, *Unforgettable Fire* (New York: Warner Books, 1988), 278.

6. Dunphy, *Unforgettable Fire,* 307.

7. Dunphy, *Unforgettable Fire,* 280.

8. Dunphy, *Unforgettable Fire,* 309.

9. Michka Assayas, *Bono: In Conversation with Michka Assayas* (New York: Berkeley/Penguin, 2006), 154–55.

10. Dunphy, *Unforgettable Fire,* 307.

11. Assayas, *Bono: In Conversation,* 155.

12. Assayas, *Bono: In Conversation,* 155.

13. David Foster Wallace, "E Unibus Pluram: Television and U.S. Fiction," *A Supposedly Fun Thing I'll Never Do Again: Essays and Arguments* (New York: Little, Brown, 1997), 49.

14. Flanagan, *U2 at the End of the World,* 121.

15. Assayas, *Bono: In Conversation,* 134.

16. Flanagan, *U2 at the End of the World,* 265.

17. Flanagan, *U2 at the End of the World,* 1.

18. Assayas, *Bono: In Conversation,* 46.

19. T. S. Eliot, "*Ulysses,* Order, and Myth" (1923), in *Selected Prose of T. S. Eliot,* ed. Frank Kermode (New York: Harcourt Brace Jovanovich/Farrar, Straus and Giroux, 1975), 177.

20. Flanagan, *U2 at the End of the World,* 266.

21. Flanagan, *U2 at the End of the World,* 266.

22. Flanagan, *U2 at the End of the World,* 266–67.

23. James Joyce, *A Portrait of the Artist as a Young Man* (1916; New York: Viking, 1968), 215.

24. Assayas, *Bono: In Conversation,* 297.

TAKE THIS SOUL III

Playing the Tart
Contexts and Intertexts for "Until the End of the World"

9

DANIEL T. KLINE

> *Open your hearts to the Holy Spirit*
> *For Christ's sake.*
> *We'll be back to you in a moment*
> *After this commercial break.*[1]

IF YOU HAD BEEN A PRE-*WAR* FAN, as I was, you probably knew U2 as a band of spiritual commitment as well as political critique, but when *Achtung Baby* was released in November 1991, more than a few of us were—how shall I say it?—befuddled. After all, we followed when Bono kneeled in "Gloria," waved the white flag of *War*, praised Martin Luther King Jr. in "Pride (In the Name of Love)," decried American imperialism in "Bullet the Blue Sky," and helped us find what we were looking for. What we purists didn't understand then was that *Achtung Baby* represented "the sound of four men chopping down the Joshua Tree," according to Bono,[2] and that Bono's shape-shifting marked a return to the Dadaist-inspired street theater of Lypton Village, the self-created community of the band's Dublin adolescence.[3] *Achtung Baby* was no aberration; it was a return.

But what the hell was up with Bono? Black leather, cigarillo and shades, and a smirk? Where was "Our Band for the 1980s," as *Rolling Stone* dubbed them? We wanted our Bono pure and mulleted, as God intended. When I asked a friend, a New Testament scholar, about the Zoo TV Atlanta show, she sighed and said, "They've lost their political content." Of course, U2's politics had not disappeared. It had been relocated. Sure, we'd heard the Point Depot show at the end of the 1988–1989 Lovetown tour, when Bono remarked, "I was explaining to people the other night, but I might've got it a bit wrong—this is just the end of something for U2. And that's why we're playing these concerts—and we're throwing a party for ourselves and you. It's no big deal, it's just—we have to go away and . . . and dream it all up again."[4] A rumor circulated that the band was breaking up, but we thought that Bono had simply seized on the symbolism of the moment, the start of a new decade, to indicate a new direction for the band. However, this was different. Something else was going on. It seemed that Bono and the band were systematically alienating their most devoted fans and betraying our idea of the band by becoming what they were: rock stars (gasp!). For some of us, Bono was no longer a visionary leader. He'd had betrayed us. Bono was a Judas.

Undoubtedly, Bono had been thinking about Judas for a while. "Pride" identified the nonviolence of Martin Luther King Jr. with Jesus, the "one man betrayed with a kiss," the Judas kiss. U2's "Until the End of the World" (UTEOTW), on *Achtung Baby* (1991), is one of its most popular and durable songs, played at 420 shows since 1992, the thirteenth-most-played song in the U2 catalog.[5] It is also perhaps one of the band's most important, to judge from the prominent place that it has occupied on special occasions, such as the Rock and Roll Hall of Fame induction ceremony in 2005. It is also one of U2's most provocative and dynamic compositions. Lyrically, UTEOTW tells the story of Judas and Jesus but extends the story beyond Jesus's crucifixion into the afterlife, from Judas's perspective. Sonically, the music both supports and plays against the literal sense of the lyrics, beginning with the distorted cry of a *muezzin* calling for prayer and concluding in glorious, ambiguous musical delirium.

Inspired by the New Testament story via Irish poet Brendan Kennelly's *The Book of Judas*, Bono's lyrics trace three key moments in Judas's relationship to Jesus: the Last Supper, the Garden of Gethsemane, and Judas in the afterworld. The first two verses are clear from their biblical import, and the third is generally seen as giving voice to Judas's guilty conscience and suicide. However, I argue that it envisions Judas's ultimate redemption. The song therefore reconsiders the traditional Christian view of Judas as an irredeemable traitor and illustrates a social ethic, consistent across U2's career, of rejecting scapegoating as a theological necessity and a political imperative.

My examination in the following pages moves from UTEOTW's source material to its performance contexts. I first examine Judas in the New Testament and Christian history and then turn to Brendan Kennelly's *The Book of Judas*. Next, I focus upon UTEOTW in its contemporaneous media contexts (Wim Wenders's film *Until the End of the World*, the U2 promotional video, and *Achtung Baby*) before examining the song's place in Zoo TV. Finally, I examine UTEOTW in performance since the Zoo TV tour before considering an interpretation of the song itself in light of French philosopher Jacques Derrida's notion of "pure forgiveness." Most telling is UTEOTW's position and function in live performances since *Achtung Baby*'s release in 1991, and I call the various performances "Is This Rock and Roll?" (Zoo TV and Zoomerang tours), "The Bullfight" (PopMart and Elevation tours), "The Conjuror" (Vertigo tour), and "Across the Great Divide" (360° tour).[6]

Judas in the New Testament and Christian History

> *The damned are burning with insight*
> *Into time and eternity, mystery and art*
> *And into the mind of God.*[7]

Western culture knows Judas as the ultimate betrayer, the one who sells out his lord and master. The story is familiar: Judas Iscariot, one of the twelve disciples, betrayed Jesus to the Romans at the Garden of Gethsemane for thirty pieces of silver, a bribe from the temple establishment. Money hungry and demon possessed, Judas identified Jesus by giving him a kiss, and Jesus was then beaten, tried, and crucified. Realizing his guilt, Judas returned the money and, in his remorse, hanged himself and was buried in a potter's field. After Jesus was resurrected, the remaining disciples chose Matthias as Judas's replacement.[8]

Although this composite account carries the authority of tradition, we should remember that the New Testament contains four different narratives concerning Jesus and Judas. The earliest Gospel, Mark, does not give Judas a motive. Mark simply states that Judas "went to the chief priests in order to betray him" (Mark 14:10), yet the Greek term *paradidomi* is better translated as "handed over." Matthew, composed later, has Judas ask the religious establishment, "What will you give me if I deliver him to you?" (Matthew 26:15), making greed the traitor's cause and thirty pieces of silver his reward. Luke asserts that "Satan entered in Judas" before he consulted the religious leaders (Luke 22:3), upping the metaphysical ante. Like always, John differs from the synoptic accounts (Matthew, Mark, Luke). The Johannine Jesus is a divine figure completely in control of his life and death, and John records no betrayal or kiss in the garden. Instead,

Jesus asks, "Whom do you seek? . . . I am he" (John 18:4–6) as he voluntarily gives himself over (John 13:27–28). Thus, the traditional story of Judas is a composite derived from the four canonical Gospels yet identical to none of them. Theology and doctrine are, in fact, second-order operations, overdetermined fictions that perform the cultural work necessary to sustain the communities and institutions that spawn them. This is the work of theory making: to eliminate inconsistencies and discontinuities in favor of a consistent conceptual system. But texts, like life, are seldom so tidy as to fit neatly into any theoretical model. The same is true with any understanding of Judas or Jesus.

Traditional Christian theology depicts Judas as the ultimate sinner whose avarice leads to his downfall but whose treachery allows God to bring redemption through Jesus's salvific death. To be a Christian is categorically not to resemble Judas. More important, a malevolent, unrepentant Judas is necessary to sustain traditional Christian theology. Yet some, rethinking Judas's position in the drama of salvation, have taken seriously the soteriological paradox: If God's divine plan required Jesus to die on the cross, then didn't Judas ultimately serve as an agent of divine necessity and act as God's own victim? Isn't then Judas salvation's scapegoat? Early Christian groups confronted the question almost from the very beginning. Irenaeus (ca. 180) describes a minority sect, the Cainites (named for the primal murderer Cain), who revered Judas because "he alone, knowing the truth as no others did, accomplished the mystery of the betrayal."[9] This may be the same group behind the recently translated *Gospel of Judas*, a controversial apocryphal gospel.[10] A Coptic text likely dating from the early fourth century, the *Gospel of Judas* depicts Judas as Jesus's lone faithful follower whose betrayal is in fact in obedience to Jesus's command.[11] Jesus says to Judas, "As for you, you will surpass them all. For you will sacrifice the human that bears me."[12] Simply put, Judas's paradoxical position in the Gospels has elicited speculation from the very beginning, while doctrine has attempted to contain the uncomfortable possibilities unleashed by Judas's story. Poised at the boundary between orthodoxy and heresy, Judas continually provokes more questions than answers. U2's UTEOTW likewise throws the traditional account into question.

Brendan Kennelly's *The Book of Judas*

> Liars die peacefully in bed.
> There's no end to style.
> Self-insult is as sharp as any.[13]

In *The Book of Judas*, Brendan Kennelly accepted the challenge to listen to the voice of Judas, a figure universally hated, through the ears of those conditioned to hate him. As the Edge told Bill Flanagan, Kennelly was "fascinated with the whole moral concept of 'Where would we be without Judas?'"[14] Kennelly daringly insists that this *judasvoice* can be a source of art and self-critique in which we confront our own casual infidelities and violent complicities. Kennelly states that at least four primary concerns motivated *The Book of Judas*. The first is to "to let the outcast scapegoat Judas . . . speak back."[15] The second is "to capture the relentless, pitiless anecdotalism of Irish life," the gossip and rumor mongering particular to Dublin.[16] The third is to lay bare a society where "we are compelled to half-do a lot of things, to half-live our lives, half-dream our dreams, half-love our loves."[17] The fourth is to consider the process of scapegoating and to ask to "what extent have we elected Judas to be our real redeemer from the consequences of what we have ourselves created but like to blame somebody else for, when 'things go wrong.'"[18] As a result, Kennelly follows the *judasvoice* as it reconfigures specific, local concerns with broader historical themes, and Kennelly's book blends personal, moral issues with problems of language and representation. It is easy to see how Kennelly's straightforward concern for infidelity and betrayal, parody and rumor, faith and fecklessness, and creativity and condemnation appealed to the band in the aftermath of *The Joshua Tree*'s bracing success and *Rattle and Hum*'s bloated frustration. The voice of the betrayer propels us to think differently, and it forces us to reexamine our own prejudices and certainties. The *judasvoice* creates a privileged space from which to scrutinize what we thought we knew.

In five hundred poems organized into twelve books over four hundred pages, Kennelly traces Judas's life as a disciple, reoccurring in different personae, revealing in ragged breaths the contours of treachery and unfaithfulness, and "creating a *lingua franca* of betrayal."[19] Aware of his historical reputation in "Zone," Judas complains about those who pursue him across history, "trying to prove / I changed forever the history of mankind," and he objects particularly to those who divide "me from my redeemer; but the bond / Between that man and me will go on and on / Despite church, state, stories of betrayal and murder."[20] In "Halcyon Days," Judas unsentimentally calls "the four gospels a darned good read / Though I don't come well out of the scene."[21] The four Gospel writers "give mesmerizing versions of the man [Jesus]," Judas says, "But not the man I know."[22] Judas talks with the disciples, especially Peter, and witnesses Jesus's miracles. Yet at the final Passover meal, Judas knowingly carries out the fatal act: "I stuck my tongue into the cup when / it was passing around the table and I knew / I drank a heart."[23] In perhaps the book's longest poem, "Kiss," the *judasvoice* traces the infamous kiss across time and space. At the moment of consummation, Judas breathes, "He seems relieved."[24] Who but Kennelly has considered Judas's mother, visiting his body as it hangs from the tree, the stench of sweat and blood clinging to Judas's clothes as he dies, or the sounds of his suicide?[25] Marriage, the keystone to *Achtung Baby*'s shadowy architecture, does not escape Judas's pitiless eye: "Marriages collapse because they're based on what's true / At the time."[26] Judas emerges from Kennelly's work as a dark star that illuminates the deepest unexamined recesses of the heart. Kennelly's *The Book of Judas* makes it difficult as well as hazardous to cleave Judas too cleanly from Jesus. For Kennelly, Judas leaves an indelible residue on all of us and all of history.

Although Bono calls it "an epic coincidence" that UTEOTW and *The Book of Judas* were written at the same time, it would not be unfair to say that Kennelly's *The Book of Judas* lays out the emotional coordinates for *Achtung Baby*, a conceptual map for Zoo TV, and a guide to reshaping U2's image in the 1990s.[27] "Service," an early poem in *The Book of Judas*, presents *Achtung Baby*'s motto, "The best way to serve the age is to betray it," and concludes, "If betrayal is a service, learn to betray / With the kind of style that impresses men / Until they dream of being me."[28] In fact, Bono noted that Kennelly's admonition became U2's "theme for the next couple of years, to do everything that U2 weren't supposed to do."[29] As Bono describes in his 2004 address to the University of Pennsylvania graduating class, "betraying the age means exposing its conceits, its foibles, its phony moral certitudes. It means telling the secrets of the age and facing harsher truths."[30] In practice, this meant revealing U2's own pretentions, resisting its audience's expectations, and exposing the cultural mechanisms and personal foibles that sustain hypocrisy, a turn that led to Bono's more active involvement in, rather than opposition to, political and social causes. Furthermore, this betrayal has to have "a kind of style" in Kennelly's words, a self-conscious affectation. Perhaps for the first time in its career, U2 had style during the *Achtung Baby* era in a way that struck many fans as more nightmare than dream. "No Symbol" finds Judas complaining about his audience, like a rock star or Hollywood celebrity, "Betray, if you will; or be betrayed. / Someone will pin words on what you are and did and said."[31] As if speaking directly to the dour U2 of the 1980s, Judas declares, "The first cliché is love."[32] Kennelly's *The Book of Judas* turned a mirror to U2's own pretenses and provided a way out through excess.

Kennelly's *The Book of Judas* also appears to have stretched Bono's understanding of the New Testament story of Judas. In 1991, the Irish newspaper *The Independent* invited Bono to review Kennelly's *The Book of Judas* and Kennelly to review *Achtung Baby*. With characteristic antitheses, Bono lauds Kennelly's work as "a poetry as base as heavy metal, as high as the Holy Spirit flies, comic and tragic, from litany to rant, roaring at times, soaring at other times. Like David in the Psalms, like Robert Johnson in the blues, the poet scratches out Screwtape letters to a God who may or may not have abandoned him."[33] Yet Bono claims Kennelly "remade Jesus in his own image and collated a very different book of evidence,"[34] strangely mistaking the writer for *The Book of Judas*'s narrative persona, a trap Bono himself attempted to elude with his different Zoo TV personae. Bono later recapitulates this rather simplistic reading by calling *The Book of Judas* "a series of poems about the betrayal of Christ."[35] The alteration is small but telling, for Bono subtly shifts the attention from the betrayer to the betrayed, from the *judasvoice* as the source of art to the redeemer as the source of salvation. Although he praises *The Book of Judas*, Bono himself senses this change in focus, for ultimately he says, "I hope I am not getting off the point, there is light here, bright white light, but if you do find Jesus, you know Judas is just 'round the corner and he knows."[36] Bono accepts that Judas and Jesus are never far apart. As a reader, Bono leans toward Jesus, but as a performer, he embraces Judas. Bono and the poet later collaborated on "God's Laughter," a Kennelly composition that appeared in 2003's *Voices and Poetry of Ireland*, in which Bono also curiously misreads a line.[37] This map of misreading reveals perhaps more than Bono realizes.

Wim Wenders's *Until the End of the World*, the U2 Video, and *Achtung Baby*

> *When you talk about me, remember this:*
> *I was chosen.*[38]

UTEOTW shares its name with German filmmaker Wim Wenders's apocalyptic meditation *Until the End of the World* (*Bi sans Ende der Welt*, 1991). Wenders directed the promotional video for U2's cover of Cole Porter's "Night and Day," its only single between 1988's *Rattle and Hum* and 1991's *Achtung Baby*, and U2 offered a slightly stripped-down mix of UTEOTW for Wenders's soundtrack. Wenders's cinematic mélange combines film noir, dystopian fantasy, and sci-fi into a road film that imagines a nuclear satellite whose uncontrolled reentry threatens to contaminate the earth. As crowds flee potential crash sites, Claire Tourneur picks up a mysterious hitchhiker, Sam Farber, who is being hunted for stealing secret technology, a goggle-like device that records sensory images for the blind. While on the run, Sam records his far-flung family to show to his sightless mother, Edith. His estranged father, Henry, who invented the device, later modifies it to record dreams after the mother's death. The characters ultimately find themselves at the father's secret lab in an Australian cave, where they meet Sam's mother and father, and their destinies play out against the apocalyptic backdrop.

Wenders's *Until the End of the World* ultimately stages the conflict between words and images in their ability to mediate reality while cautioning against technology's ability to replace direct experience and human memory. In a key scene, Claire uses the goggles to record Sam's sister, who sits in a room straight out of a Johannes Vermeer painting: the gold and blue of *The Milkmaid* and *Girl with a Pearl Earring*; the rich tapestry of *The Artist's Studio* and *A Lady at the Virginals with a Gentleman*; the influx of light through window panes at the left, the play of shadows upon the white wall, and a framed image to the right suggesting so many Vermeer interiors.[39] Like Vermeer's work, *Until the End of the World* concerns the very processes of perception, memory, and artistic creation. Edith finally experiences the Vermeer-like scene of her daughter, a simulacra, but is driven to despair and death, while Claire becomes lost in reliving her dreams and is finally set free only through the written word. Wenders's film straddles the permeable membrane between text and interpretation and sight and insight. Such themes were clearly on U2's mind as *Achtung Baby* and Zoo TV took shape, and Wenders's dream images in *Until the End of the World* provide a rough draft of the digital overload of the Zoo TV video screens and the UTEOTW video.[40] The film simultaneously inspires and subverts Bono's desire to "dream out loud."

Wenders's most immediate impact was on U2's promotional video for UTEOTW.[41] Featured as part of *Achtung Baby: The Videos, the Cameos, and a Whole Lot of Interference from Zoo TV*, the UTEOTW video was never officially released, although its production implies that the band considered releasing the song as a single.[42] The UTEOTW video marks a stunning change in U2's sensibility and self-representation. First, its imagery is unlike anything that U2 had released previously. It's a fever dream, a hallucinatory journey through a psychic and sensory miasma of shimmering images reminiscent of, if not drawn from, the dream-recording device in Wenders's film. (It shares much with the postapocalyptic imagery of *Pop*'s

"Last Night on Earth.") Second, the UTEOTW promo video represented the band members in unfamiliar, even profane ways—at least in comparison to their 1980s personae. Adam and Larry become erotic icons—pale, bleached, static statuary open to our gaze. The Edge, wrapped in suffocating plastic, is a bloody, fleshy package more like freshly butchered meat than a human being. A dark lord, Bono beckons us to follow him into the darkness rather than the light. The video brilliantly recasts the band through the unexpected violence of the images themselves, particularly how they render the band members into artifice and commodity. U2 takes control of the very processes that turned them into clichés and negates their efficacy by literalizing their semiotic import. At the same time that the images subvert the band's iconic 1980s presentation, they make perfectly plain the stultifying effects of those same iconic representations. Semiotic violence yields artistic liberation.

U2's 1991 dark masterpiece *Achtung Baby* likewise subverted the band's image by channeling its personal and corporate crises through the music. The *Boy* of the 1980s had grown up and gotten sexy, nasty. Brian Eno famously remarked about *Achtung Baby* that the "buzzwords on this record were *trashy*, *throwaway*, *dark*, *sexy*, and *industrial* (all good) and *earnest*, *polite*, *sweet*, *righteous*, *rockist*, and *linear* (all bad). It was good if a song took you on a journey or made you think your hi-fi was broken, bad if it reminded you of recording studios or U2."[43] One thematic trajectory across *Achtung Baby* concerns the constant oscillation of things material and superficial against things spiritual and enduring, the appetites of the flesh pressing against the desire for God, Judas with Jesus. *Achtung Baby* itself announces the subversion of everything that we thought we knew about U2 from the first throbbing notes of "Zoo Station" and Bono's opening declaration, "I'm ready / Ready for the laughing gas." If this is fun, it's artificial, evanescent, noxious. The disorientation of "Zoo Station" leads into the clash of clichéd images in "Even Better Than the Real Thing," a play on the Coca-Cola slogan "Coke—the Real Thing."[44] In the commercialized, postmodern, post–Cold War world, relationships are little more than clichés and catchphrases, throwaway items like soft drinks to be consumed and then discarded. Investing emotionally in simulacra and consuming worthless commodities inevitably disappoints, however, and at the best of times, the lover and beloved may unite, but the union is orgasmic, fleeting. Suffering the love of the other is both a blessing and a curse. To receive forgiveness, we must sin; to be resurrected, we have to die; to be healed, we have to be crippled. "One" does not exist without the other, without the threat of separation; in the same way, there is no salvation without a Judas, no Jesus without a betrayal, no Lazarus without the worm of decay. The contraries are bound together: UTEOTW rises in an embrace of salvation and damnation, reaching across an impossible gulf for redemption. The clichés assert themselves again in "Who's Gonna Ride Your Wild Horses," while the infinite distance of intimacy leaves our beloved always "just out of reach." The hostile ambivalence of love, destroying the boundaries between self and other, must be breached, and differences must be restored lest the self and other fall into relentless identification; love without rules, without ethical boundaries, becomes brutality in "So Cruel."

The emotional rawness and the fragile hopefulness of the A-side gives way to the B-side, where the trickster Fly behind his mask speaks the truth about art in, I think, Bono's finest couplet: "Every artist is a cannibal, every poet is a thief / All kill their inspiration and sing about their grief." The Fly, a shining, falling star, takes the form of Lucifer, son of the morning, whose lie caused the universe to explode. Here, the Fly—the Lord of the Flies, Beelzebub, who will become Mr. MacPhisto—expresses the *judas-voice*: "Look, I gotta go, yeah I'm running outta change / There's a lot of things, if I could I'd rearrange." This fallen destitution is tempered by the love of the one who moves in "Mysterious Ways." Sometimes the difference between the *agape* and *eros* is knowable only in retrospect when we look back upon the love that held us, the distorted liquid images shimmering like a desert oasis. "Love calls us to the things of this world," as Richard Wilbur wrote. Although the great idealistic cause, "Tryin' to Throw Yours Arms Around the World," is bound to fail, it is something we must try. Returning to the beloved allows a momentary respite, a light bulb over a sickbed in "Ultraviolet (Light My Way)." Yet, when we're honest, we have to admit our own hypocrisy, our hypocritical nature, "To talk like this / And act like that" ("Acrobat"). Like Judas, we too often "take the money," the sure thing, when all we have ultimately is a blind leap of faith into darkness. "Love Is Blindness" whether we reach out to God or to a lover, and too often we would rather remain enveloped in the dark night of the soul than drag "the past out into the light" and reveal our complicity in our own suffering. Bono writes that during *Achtung Baby*, "I started to write about the hypocrisy of my own heart and the way I saw the relationships around me. . . . [UTEOTW] was a kind of vision, it was ecstatic in a religious way, a song about temptation. The temptation is not the obvious. The temptation is anything that will keep you from your destiny."[45] Ultimately then, *Achtung Baby* was as much a survival strategy as it was a conscious choice, the near-fatal crisis necessary to move the band forward.

"Is This Rock and Roll?":
UTEOTW, "The Fly," and Zoo TV

Pretend to be what they believe you are
You are what they believe they think
They want a guiding star you are that star
Want hope, be hope, exist to rise and sink
And listen to the wind that knocks the house.[46]

In support of *Achtung Baby*, the Zoo TV tour began with a leap day show in Lakeland, Florida, on February 29, 1992. Of the many subversive innovations unveiled with Zoo TV, the most fascinating was the metamorphosis of Bono's stage persona. The Fly character moves forward by stepping back, deconstructing Bono's image by piling on the stereotypes. Bono says that he created "an identikit rock star: 'I had Elvis Presley's leather jacket, Jim Morrison's leather pants, Lou Reed's fly shades, Jerry Lee Lewis's boots, Gene Vincent's limp.'"[47] Umberto Eco's famous essay "Casablanca, or, the Clichés Are Having a Ball," clues us into the motley Fly's significance:

> When all the archetypes burst in shamelessly, we reach Homeric depths. Two clichés make us laugh. A hundred clichés move us. For we sense dimly that the clichés are talking *among themselves*, and celebrating a reunion. Just as the height of pain may encounter sensual pleasure, and the height of perversion border on mystical energy, so too the height of banality allows us to catch a glimpse of the sublime.[48]

Banal and sublime, Judas and Jesus, Bono progressed through several characters during the Zoo TV and Zoomerang tours: the Fly, Mirror Ball Man, the Anti-smack Commando, and finally MacPhisto. The Fly is the recognizable, over-the-top rock star parody, and Bono clearly revels in playing the salty, sexy, swaggering, self-obsessed bad boy. Clad in a silver lamé suit, the Mirror Ball Man combines Las Vegas glitz and televangelist garishness when he appears at the encore during "Desire," "stealing hearts at a traveling show."[49] Often forgotten, however, is the Anti-smack Commando, a character Bono takes on during the solo in "Bullet the Blue Sky."[50] In the next number, "Running to Stand Still," the Anti-smack Commando mimics a junkie shooting up heroin as the song transitions sublimely into the beautiful opening arpeggio of "Where the Streets Have No Name." The line between heroin and heaven is narrow; the need for transcendence is great; and the Anti-smack Commando uncomfortably straddles that boundary between hell and hallelujah. For the first time in *Zoo TV: Sydney*, a recognizable Bono reemerges for "Streets" and the emotional high point of the show. Sans glasses, Bono sings directly to the crowd as images of the band during the *Joshua Tree* era play on the oversized screens. From there, the concert steamrolls through "Pride" before shifting gears into the encore, the show's final third.

The Mirror Ball Man did not have the impact on European audiences as he did in America, so Bono ultimately turned to MacPhisto during the 1993 Zoomerang tour. In *Zoo TV: Sydney*, U2 comes as close to its former nakedness only with "Streets" and "Pride," the official end of the concert, but the show takes another turn in the encore. The camera joins MacPhisto—Bono clad in red horns before a gaudy gold-framed mirror—as he puts on white pancake makeup, a gold lamé suit, and golden platform boots. Combining Mephistopheles and McDonald's, a wannabe who sold his soul to the devil and his body to commerce, MacPhisto represents the end of the rock star road, according to Bono: "a pop star long past his prime returning regularly from . . . Vegas and regaling anyone who would listen to him at cocktail hour with stories from the good old, bad old days."[51] During the 1993 Zoomerang shows, MacPhisto appears in his dressing room looking like a horror out of Weimar Germany's cabarets and launches into "Lemon," a song inspired by a film of Bono's mother as a young woman. Concealing Bono's emotional nakedness beneath MacPhisto's gauche posturing, the concert turns in upon itself again as MacPhisto removes the horns for "With or Without You." The band through Bono/MacPhisto acts out the love/hate paradox of rock stardom that *Achtung Baby* and Zoo TV undermines: Stars need the audience, and the fans trap the stars with impossible expectations. "And you give yourself away" is exactly what U2 is doing at that very moment in the show, and "Love Is Blindness" becomes both a benediction and a warning as Bono/MacPhisto brings a lone fan onstage for an intimate dance. The paradox, however, is never resolved, and as Bono/MacPhisto strolls offstage, he sings with the crowd "I Can't Help Falling in Love with You." "I can't live with or without you" is brilliantly poised on a knife's edge against "I can't help falling in love with you." The show's closing is more than irony, though it's hard to gauge whether the audience realizes it or not. It's a full-bore deconstruction of U2 and its relationship to the audience, going far beyond parody. Rather than simply reversing expectations or undermining its image, in Zoo TV U2 undercuts the basis upon which fandom exists while acting out the band's dependency on that audience. It's a beautifully brutal and effective evisceration.

During Zoo TV, UTEOTW quickly became a pivotal moment in the show. Beginning with apocalyptic images of destruction, UTEOTW hearkens back to the old U2's concern for nuclear holocaust. In *Zoo TV: Sydney*, the Fly launches the song by calling, "Hey, Judas, come on!" as the Edge's riff cascades across the audience. Drenched in sweat and black leather, the Fly takes on Judas's mantle by grotesquely pantomiming the application of lipstick into the camera, wetly kissing the lens, and then dry humping the apparatus. It's a direct "fuck you" challenge to the audience, daring it to see Bono as the earnest young man waving a white flag. The Fly drops himself into the audience at the line "going down on me," and then, snapping and snarling, his mouth a cauldron, the Fly finally sings:

> I reached out to the one I tried to destroy
> You, you said you would wait until the end of the world.

Buoyed by the crowd, he then turns, trembling like an ecstatic preacher, a perverse faith healer in black, and cries to the Edge, "Is this rock and roll?" before he approaches the guitarist in benediction and menace. Like magnets drawn to and repelled from one another, the Edge and Bono confront each other until the Fly lays his hand and the power of God on the guitarist, with a dramatic "Heal!" like televangelist Ernest Angley.[52] The magnetic poles suddenly shift, and laserlike the Edge leans into Bono and plants on his cheek the Judas kiss. Is this rock and roll, indeed? At an absolutely over-the-top rock show, the audience participates in a story of ultimate redemption and deliverance.

As the set list moves seamlessly from "One"/"Unchained Melody" to UTEOTW and then to "New Year's Day," the import of the sequence is clear: the betrayal and loving acceptance of "One" (and the promise of "Unchained Melody") opens to Judas's unfaithfulness and despair in UTEOTW, but the treachery and separation of UTEOTW give way to the crystalline clarity and hopefulness of "New Year's Day." Love in all its glorious, tragic complexity binds the songs together. *Zoo TV: Sydney* ultimately cements "One" and UTEOTW as an emotionally, theologically coherent unit. In a delightful little moment, when Bono delivers the line "Did you come here to play Jesus?" he gives a tiny wry smile and quips, "I did." In that definitive version of these three songs from *Zoo TV: Sydney*, it is difficult to see UTEOTW in anything but positive terms. Judas reaches to the one he tried to destroy, while "New Year's Day" ultimately asserts the hope for reunion after division.

UTEOTW during PopMart, Elevation, Vertigo, and 360

Out of the awful silences of the God of nothing
A voice, then voices: "Of course, you pig,
You dare not know it,
Judas is the ultimate poet."[53]

UTEOTW became a showpiece in subsequent tours, taking on new resonance during the PopMart, Elevation, Vertigo, and U2360° tours. The
song takes on its canonical performance shape near the end of the PopMart
tour in the *corrida*, or bullfight, between Bono and the Edge. In *PopMart
Mexico City* (1997), as the song begins, Bono waves his red guitar men-
acingly toward the Edge and then insolently lets it drop at the guitarist's
feet as both challenge and offering. The gift is a trap, and this submission,
a lure into battle. As the Edge approaches, Bono brings his forefingers to
the sides of his head and rushes the Edge like a bull charging the matador.
The tauromachy escalates during the closing guitar solo, with the matador
parrying the bull's thrusts until the Edge dispatches Bono, the bull still
kicking at the instrument of his downfall. In Mexico City, UTEOTW is
preceded by "Last Night on Earth" (written during the *Zooropa* sessions)
and is followed by "New Year's Day," continuing the themes of apocalypse and renewal, betrayal and redemption suggested during Zoo TV and
Zoomerang. During Zoo TV, Bono's oily alter ego, the Fly, receives the
Judas kiss from the Edge before ultimately morphing into the devilish and
decadent lounge lizard MacPhisto. Here, during PopMart, Bono enacts the
bull's sacrificial death at the matador's hands—the raw forces of muscular
nature subsumed by the lacing wounds of art—all for the benefit of the
Foro Sol stadium crowd.

   In support of the back-to-basics 2001 album *All That You Can't Leave
Behind*, the Elevation tour featured a stripped-down, heart-shaped stage
that emphasized audience intimacy over ironic distance. UTEOTW's staging during Elevation often reconfigures performance elements of the song's
previous incarnations.[54] In *Elevation 2001: Live from Boston*, UTEOTW
appears third in the list, preceded by "Beautiful Day" but followed by
"Stuck in a Moment You Can't Get Out Of" and "Kite" in a thematic
sequence that ends with "I Will Follow." Wearing a camera that records
the audience, Bono begins with "Jesus, this is Judas" as he walks out to the
B-stage from one side and Edge approaches from the other. Their confrontation begins with Bono taunting the Edge across the inner heart and

giving him the Judas kiss, prior to the crucial third verse of the song. As in Zoo TV, Bono leans into the audience at the crucial lines. Here, however, the roles are reconfigured as Bono reaches his hand out to heal the Edge, and their confrontation is the most extended of any of the official videos. Bono *literally* kicks the hell out of Edge's guitar as the song collapses in a haze of feedback.

During the Elevation tour, Bono often opened UTEOTW in the posture with which he concluded the song during Zoo TV. In *U2 Go Home: Live from Slane Castle*, the Ecstatic Preacher stands with hands overhead, pulsating with energy both divine and debased as he launches into the song. At Slane, Bono gives the Edge the Judas kiss after the second verse, before the "love, love, love" bridge, rather than Edge bestowing it at the end of the song, but like Zoo TV, Bono puts himself into the crowd as Judas reaches across time and space for Jesus. The *corrida* now has become a dramatic set piece, with Bono and Edge eyeing each other across the audience space, enacting a tension that feels as genuinely motivated by the immediate circumstance as it is an interpretation of the song's lyrics. As the song develops, Bono and the Edge go head-to-head during the final verse, agonistically acting out Judas's monologue at the end of time in the drama of confrontation and reconciliation. In context, UTEOTW is fifth in the set list, between "Beautiful Day" and "New Year's Day."

After dropping out of many Vertigo tour shows, UTEOTW began to reassert itself during the 360° tour, in part, at least, by the opportunities that the unique "claw" staging presented, especially with the two cantilevered catwalks linked to the outer ring. UTEOTW was first played eleven shows into the tour (Amsterdam, July 21, 2009), but it was included only fitfully in the first leg. It was always preceded by "One" but followed uncertainly by different songs, as if the band were searching for a provocative new sequence: "City of Blinding Lights" (Amsterdam, July 21, 2009), "The Unforgettable Fire" (Dublin, July 24, 2009), "Desire" (Gothenburg, July 31, 2009), and "Stay" (Zagreb, August 9, 2009). At Croke Park in Dublin (July 24, 2009), Edge and Bono flirt with the old bullfighting routine. Bono taunts the Edge as before, but as the Edge leans in to give Bono the Judas kiss, the guitarist pirouettes away at the last moment. The guitar player is now playing the tart.[55] During the tour's second leg, when the spectacular claw made its way to the United States, UTEOTW appeared more often. As the Edge and Bono learned how to take advantage of the new stage's possibilities, UTEOTW settled into a fairly stable series late in the leg ("Unknown Caller," UTEOTW, and "The Unforgettable Fire"), its resonance with "Unknown Caller" particularly provocative. The Rose

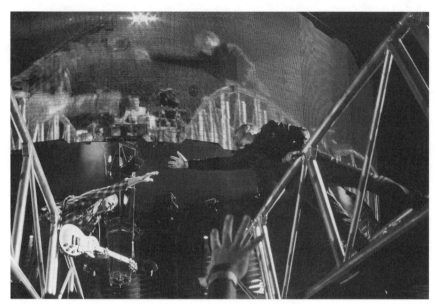

Figure 9.1.   Bono and Edge reach across a gulf but do not touch. *Ayaz Asif / u2photography* *.com*

Bowl show (October 25, 2009) streamed live on YouTube, shows the band settling into a new articulation of the song.[56] As in Zoo TV, the singer and guitarist approach each other from across the stage, this time from opposite catwalks, Bono singing the verses and reaching the stage-left cantilever as Edge prepares for the guitar solo. Edge then mounts the opposite cantilever as Bono sings the "love, love, love" bridge, and the two bridges arc toward each other as the song reaches its crescendo.

UTEOTW ends with Bono reaching but not quite touching the Edge, their performance reflecting the gulf between the song's protagonists and their movement toward reconciliation, just as the bridges part again (see figure 9.1). Although this new staging of UTEOTW appears to have developed only gradually during the 360° tour, the cantilevers allow the physical spaces of the stage to reproduce the psychological and spiritual dynamics of the song.

UTEOTW and True Forgiveness

> *I met an old goat who said Judas is well*
> *Heigh-Ho Judas is well*
> *And as long as that's true there's hope left in hell*
> *Heigh-Ho there's hope left in hell.*[57]

Stephen Catanzarite's reading of *Achtung Baby* generally stresses U2's theological conservatism, and he reads the album as an archetypal depiction of the Fall of Man and its consequences for humanity. "Each song on *Achtung Baby*," Catanzarite asserts, "provides a variation on that tune."[58] With Augustinian certainty, Catanzarite places Judas firmly and finally in hell. Although Catanzarite grants that UTEOTW's lyrics, particularly the third verse, ultimately are ambiguous, he contends that the dialogue between Judas and Jesus occurs in hell, after which "the door slams shut."[59] Rather than speculating about Judas's ultimate fate, we are better served contemplating our own "eternal trajectory" because, for Catanzarite, "our opinions on the fate of Judas beyond the grave simply do not matter very much, if at all."[60]

However, I believe it is exactly this question that U2 opens once again for examination. UTEOTW begins with an account of the Last Supper from Judas's perspective. In the intimacy of a "low lit room," Judas and the other disciples "ate the food' and "drank the wine" of the Passover meal, but Jesus's mind is elsewhere, focused on "the end of the world." UTEOTW continues the synoptic narrative from the Passover meal to Judas's account of the betrayal in the second verse: taking the money, tainting the drink, entering the garden, bestowing the kiss, and seeing Jesus's resignation. UTEOTW's final verse seems to confirm the traditional view that Judas kills himself in despair and ends up in hell. The song's *judasvoice* recalls, "In my dream, I was drowning in sorrows," but whence the dream? If the dream refers to Judas's physical life looking back from eternity, he has moved beyond that transient earthly moment to a transcendent spiritual perspective. If the dream refers to the current state of his soul, Judas seems not to be in hell but in a moment of spiritual transition. "Down the hold, just passing time" implies temporary storage. Like a cargo hold, the image links well to the notion of drowning after losing hope. The erotics of despair provide a comfortable respite from struggle as the hold fills, enclosing Judas and spilling over the brim of his deathly alcove. At exactly that moment of ultimate despair, with the surety that all is lost, an image appears before Judas's eyes that brings both joy and regret. In that moment of ultimate despair, Judas reaches out toward the one "he tried to destroy," with nothing more than the ringing echo of a promise in his dying ears: "You, you said you would wait till the end of the world." Judas sees Jesus before him and reaches for his hand. The question that any religious interpretation must answer is this: Does Jesus reach back?

A traditional understanding of Judas's crime would answer no: Judas is condemned and has damned himself for eternity. However, I answer yes.

Jesus reaches back for Judas. Bono provides the justification in the vocal bridge between verses 2 and 3: "Love, love, love." Throughout U2's career, Bono has consistently emphasized the power of love over law; indeed, "Love is a temple; love's a higher law," he sings in "One." Jesus's love is the opposite of calculation or exchange; forgiveness is not a tactic but a necessity so that Judas—even Judas—can be redeemed in what Derrida would call "pure forgiveness":

> I shall risk this proposition: each time forgiveness is at the service of a finality, be it noble and spiritual (atonement or redemption, reconciliation, salvation), each time that it aims to re-establish a normality (social, national, political, psychological) by a work of mourning, by some therapy or ecology of memory, then the "forgiveness" is not pure—nor is its concept.[61]

On the contrary, for Derrida, forgiveness "*should* remain exceptional and extraordinary, in the face of the impossible: as if it interrupted the ordinary course of historical temporality."[62] Forgiving Judas initiates exactly this historical interruption. Kennelly's *judasvoice* wheezes through hundreds of poems in dozens of masks, each marked by betrayal, awareness, and the inevitability of infidelity, much in the same way *Achtung Baby* examines love and betrayal as the flip sides of the same coin. Whether or not we designate forgiveness as spiritual or secular, we each must confront the limits of our own fidelity to those who are most important to us. It is a test few of us can pass unscathed. Derrida pushes the issue even further by declaring that forgiveness can start only from the concept of the unforgivable: "forgiveness forgives only the unforgivable. One cannot, or should not, forgive; there is only forgiveness, if there is any, where there is the unforgivable. That is to say that forgiveness must announce itself as impossibility itself. It can only be possible in doing the impossible."[63] True forgiveness must therefore forgive what is truly unforgiveable.

What is Judas's betrayal if it is not unforgivable? What is the love of God if it cannot forgive the unforgivable?

And as UTEOTW moves to its climax, the Edge's cascading guitar reaches toward transcendence. UTEOTW belongs to a special group of U2 songs, like "One Tree Hill" and "All I Want Is You," which reach an ecstatic state where Bono's voice—and language itself—fails and the Edge's guitar takes us somewhere else. Bono, that most loquacious spirit, is sometimes reduced to yelps and moans, but the music intervenes, like the Spirit, "with groanings too deep for words" (Romans 8:26). UTEOTW suggests the impossible: that even Judas is redeemed in a moment of fathomless mystery. Judas and Jesus can never be separated. The *judasvoice* reminds the redeemer that "you, you said you would wait until the end of the world."

I can't claim to know what theory of atonement Bono subscribes to, but in a number of UTEOTW performances over the years, he's sampled the Doors' "Break on Through," most recently during the second leg of the 360° tour. Bono looks back to but also looks beyond Jim Morrison's version of William Blake's excess or Arthur Rimbaud's dissipation. Bono's challenge is to break through the boundary between us and them, when we scapegoat others, like Judas, to serve our own purposes. Unlike Morrison and his drive toward death, U2 moves continually toward life, toward affirmation, toward an impossible love. In "Five to One" Morrison cried, "No one here gets out alive."[64] But as Bono told Michka Assayas, "*Everybody* gets out of here alive."[65] Even Judas.

Notes

1. Brendan Kennelly, "Open Your Hearts," in *The Book of Judas* (Newcastle upon Tyne, England: Bloodaxe Books, 1991), 68.

2. "*Achtung Baby* Scrapbook," in *The Best of Propaganda: Twenty Years of the Official U2 Magazine* (New York: Thunder's Mouth Press, 2003), 146–47. Like many Bonologia, this one can be found in multiple references.

3. Bono said, in the aftermath of his mother's death, "[I] found . . . fun and mischief again with my friends and the Village, as we used to call ourselves. We invented a Village, which was an alternative community, called Lypton Village." Michka Assayas, *Bono in Conversation* (New York: Penguin-Riverhead, 2005), 114. It was with Lypton Village that Paul Hewson initially became Bono.

4. Introduction to "Love Rescue Me," *Love: Live from Point Depot, the Complete U2* (Apple iTunes, November 23, 2004).

5. According to http://www.u2gigs.com/tourdb-stats.html (accessed February 13, 2010).

6. My account here is a representative rather than comprehensive review of the performance history of "Until the End of the World," and I draw primarily upon officially released concert footage.

7. Kennelly, "After Such Knowledge," *Book of Judas*, 89.

8. Although this composite account carries the authority of tradition, it is theologically freighted. William Klassen's *Judas: Betrayer or Friend of Jesus* (Minneapolis, MN: Augsburg-Fortress, 1996) details each of the four canonical Gospels' distinct representations as well as Judas's depiction in Judaic tradition. Kim Paffenroth's *Judas: Images of the Lost Disciple* (Louisville, KY: Westminster John Knox Press, 2001) presents an overview of different views of Judas throughout history.

9. Alexander Roberts, James Donaldson, and A. Cleveland Coxe, eds., *Against Heresies*, 1.31.1, in *Ante-Nicene Fathers*, vol. 1 (Buffalo, NY: Christian Literature,

1885), http://www.newadvent.org/fathers/0103131.htm (accessed February 2, 2010).

10. Joan Acocella, "Betrayal: Should We Hate Judas Iscariot?" *New Yorker*, August 3, 2009, http://www.newyorker.com/arts/critics/atlarge/2009/08/03/090803crat_atlarge_acocella?currentPage=all, reviews the recent Judasteria.

11. Scholars generally call the *Gospel of Judas* a "gnostic" text, though *gnosticism* is an eighteenth-century umbrella term for a diverse body of beliefs and practices. See Karen L. King, *What Is Gnosticism?* (Harvard, MA: Belknap Press, 2005). *Judas* has generated more controversy than consensus. At one end of the spectrum, Bart Ehrmann, in *The Lost Gospel of Judas Iscariot: A New Look at the Betrayer and Betrayed* (Oxford: Oxford University Press, 2006), and Elaine Pagels and Karen King, in *Reading Judas: The Gospel of Judas and the Shaping of Christianity* (New York: Viking Penguin, 2007), rethink early Christianity in light of a "positive" Judas, while James M. Robinson takes a more personal, skeptical view in *The Secrets of Judas: The Story of the Misunderstood Disciple and His Lost Gospel* (New York: HarperCollins, 2007). April D. DeConick criticizes the National Geographic Society's handling of the gospel in *The Thirteenth Apostle: What the Gospel of Judas Really Says* (New York: Continuum, 2007). The crux of the disagreement concerns the proper translation for the gnostic term *daemon* as *demon* (DeConick) or *spirit* (Marvin Meyer).

12. Karen L. King, "English Translation of the *Gospel of Judas*," in *Reading Judas: The Gospel of Judas and the Shaping of Christianity* (New York: Viking, 2007), 121.

13. Kennelly, "No End to Style," *Book of Judas*, 71.

14. Bill Flanagan, *U2: At the End of the World* (New York: Bantam-Doubleday, 1995), 52.

15. Brendan Kennelly, *The Book of Judas* (Newcastle upon Tyne, England: Bloodaxe Books, 1991), 10.

16. Kennelly, *Book of Judas*, 11.

17. Kennelly, *Book of Judas*, 11.

18. Kennelly, *Book of Judas*, 11.

19. Kennelly, "Dear Doll," *Book of Judas*, 249.

20. Kennelly, *Book of Judas*, 109.

21. Kennelly, *Book of Judas*, 19–20.

22. Kennelly, "Versions," *Book of Judas*, 62.

23. Kennelly, "Cup," *Book of Judas*, 117.

24. Kennelly, *Book of Judas*, 239. "Kiss" occupies pages 233–40.

25. Kennelly, "As You Might Expect" and "I Shall Not Forget," *Book of Judas*, 244–46; "Sounds," 251.

26. Kennelly, "Insincerity as a Detector of Human Worth," *Book of Judas*, 18.

27. Neil McCormick, ed., *U2 by U2* (New York: HarperCollins, 2006), 225.

28. Kennelly, "Service," *Book of Judas*, 17.

29. McCormick, *U2 by U2*, 225.

30. See "Because We Can, We Must," commencement address, University of Pennsylvania, May 17, 2004, http://www.upenn.edu/almanac/between/2004/commence-b.html.

31. Kennelly, *Book of Judas*, 169.

32. Kennelly, *Book of Judas*, 66.

33. *Propaganda* 18 (1993–1994) republished the reviews. Bono's review was reposted as "*The Book of Judas*—Reviewed by Bono, '91*,*" http://u2_interviews.tripod.com/id133.html (accessed February 13, 2010).

34. "*The Book of Judas*—Reviewed by Bono, '91.*"

35. McCormick, *U2 by U2*, 225.

36. "*The Book of Judas*—Reviewed by Bono, '91.*"

37. *Voices and Poetry of Ireland* (New York: HarperCollins, 2003), a book and three-CD collection. The text to "God's Laughter" is at http://www.u2wanderer.org/disco/lyrics.php?id=594 (accessed February 13, 2010). Bono reads *can* in the lines "Who, hearing words from his own mouth / and from others, *cannot* stop himself / laughing or freezing in terror."

38. Kennelly, "Am I There?" *Book of Judas*, 276.

39. The Vermeer Foundation website contains an easily accessible image archive of Vermeer's recognized works, http://www.vermeer-foundation.org/ (accessed February 13, 2010).

40. A minute-long snippet of the song appears approximately fourteen minutes into the film, and a mix slightly different from the album version rolls over the film's closing credits.

41. Wenders filmed the videos for "Stay (Faraway, So Close)" from *Zooropa* (1993), the later single "The Ground Beneath Her Feet," and directed *The Million Dollar Hotel* (2000) from Bono and Nicholas Klein's screenplay, while U2 provided "Stay (Faraway, So Close)" and "The Wanderer" for his 1993 film *In weiter Ferne, so nah!* (*Faraway, So Close!*) and "If God Will Send His Angels" for the American remake of Wenders's sublime *Wings of Desire*, the vastly inferior 1998 *City of Angels*.

42. *Achtung Baby: The Videos, The Cameos, and a Whole Lot of Interference from Zoo TV*, prod. Ned O'Hanlon (Island/Polygram, 1992).

43. Brian Eno, "Bringing Up Baby," *Rolling Stone* 618 (November 28, 1991), 48.

44. See the 1991 advertisement "Can't Beat the Real Thing," http://www.youtube.com/watch?v=GVag7D85b24 (accessed February 14, 2010). Coke first used "The Real Thing" slogan in 1969.

45. McCormick, *U2 by U2*, 226–27.

46. Kennelly, "Purified," *Book of Judas*, 333.

47. http://advancedtheory.blogspot.com/2005/06/bono-im-rock-star.html.

48. Marshall Blonsky, ed., *On Signs* (Baltimore: Johns Hopkins University Press, 1985), 38.

49. Available as a bonus track on the *Zoo TV: Live from Sydney* disc, where he sounds like a cross between a Texas evangelist and a bad Elvis imitator.

50. See the discussion, http://en.wikipedia.org/wiki?title=Talk:Zoo_TV _Tour#Personas (accessed February 25, 2010), about whether or not the Anti-smack Commando should be considered one of the "official" Zoo TV personas.

51. McCormick, *U2 by U2*, 248. *Time* magazine named MacPhisto a top-ten entertainment alter ego (July 10, 2009), http://www.time.com/time/specials/packages/article/0,28804,1909772_1909770 1909675,00.html.

52. Ernest Angley Ministries, http://www.ernestangley.org/index.php (accessed February 25, 2010).

53. Kennelly, "Send a Letter," *Book of Judas*, 349.

54. U2 released two DVDs for the Elevation tour: *Elevation 2001: Live from Boston* and *U2 Go Home: Live from Slane Castle*.

55. See the audience shot video on YouTube, http://www.youtube.com/watch?v=qFIdFUa_hUc& (accessed February 23, 2010).

56. U2's official YouTube channel for the Rose Bowl concert, http://www.youtube.com/user/U2official (accessed February 25, 2010).

57. Kennelly, "Heigh-Ho," *Book of Judas*, 241.

58. Stephen Catanzarite, *Achtung Baby: Meditations on Love in the Shadow of the Fall* (New York: Continuum, 2007), 3.

59. Catanzarite, *Achtung Baby*, 32.

60. Catanzarite, *Achtung Baby*, 33.

61. Jacques Derrida, *On Cosmopolitanism and Forgiveness*, trans. Mark Dooley and Michael Hughes (New York: Routledge, 2005), 31–32.

62. Derrida, *On Cosmopolitanism and Forgiveness*, 32.

63. Derrida, *On Cosmopolitanism and Forgiveness*, 32–33.

64. The Doors, *Waiting for the Sun* (Elektra Records, 1968).

65. Emphasis in the original. In context, Bono discusses with Assayas (*Bono in Conversation*, 77) Adam Clayton's absence from the November 26, 1993, show in Sydney, the only time that U2 has performed without a member. Question: "Were there moments when you thought it was putting the band in danger?" Answer: "Oh, yeah, for sure, I was always concerned. Everybody had to make it through this alive, to misquote Jim Morrison. Our motto was: *Everybody* gets out of here alive."

Where *Leitourgia* Has No Name   **10**
U2 Live

BETH MAYNARD

fter U2's concert in Poland in the summer of 2009, Gary Lightbody, the lead singer of Snow Patrol, wrote of the experience, "We were sharing something that simply never happens at rock shows anywhere. A collective emotional and spiritual surrender of epic proportions. This was majesty and tenderness married and that is a rare thing indeed. Last night was something I've never seen before and I can't quite fathom it. . . . It will sit alongside the greatest nights of my life."[1]

Seven years earlier, Steve Braden of the Jesuit magazine *America* described a U2 show at Notre Dame in similar terms:

> No longer a mere witness to a performance, I had been transported. . . . Images of star charts, candles entwined in barbed wire, symbolic doves of peace, suitcases decorated with a heart and other signs that point to spiritual realities flashed everywhere. While much of U2's stage show may be evangelical, the special effects were evidence of their sacramental imagination. . . . Just as pilgrims in medieval Europe would travel great distances to experience something transcendent, I felt a sense of solidarity among the fans milling about in the parking lot before and after the show. Some had traveled from other schools in Indiana; some were visiting from halfway across the country. . . . Several mentioned that the concert was a religious experience that would keep them aglow for days.[2]

Ordinary U2 fans as well often tend to gravitate to heightened, sacral language when describing seeing their favorite band live. "Three weeks from tonight, if all goes as planned, I'll be freeing my soul at the altar of U2 in Chicago's Soldier Field,"[3] wrote one young blogger. Another explained in her journal, "Going to a U2 concert borders on a spiritual experience because as enthralling and exhilarating as the show is, I know I at least felt cleansed afterwards."[4] An online review of the 360° tour claimed, "There is a transformative moment in every U2 concert that elevates it from the level of a mere performance to more of a spiritual journey."[5]

U2 itself and members of its artistic team also regularly acknowledge a numinous aspect to the live performances, often pointing to the centrality of the experience of working in front of an audience to the band's self-understanding and mission.[6] In an ABC news interview, Bono commented, "There's a thing where people tell me, even if they don't like our band, that if you go to a U2 show, and the band [comes] onstage, you will have an involuntary reaction—the hairs on the back of your neck just goes [sic] up. . . . What they don't know, is that that happens to us too . . . every night we walk out as a foursome. That happens."[7] Larry Mullen has spoken of U2's live concerts as "the sacred moment,"[8] and the Edge has attributed the uniqueness of U2 performances to the presence of "a special thing that goes on between the band and the audience."[9] Adam Clayton has referred to "a spiritual aspect to what's happening in the house,"[10] and show designer Willie Williams has said that a U2 show possesses "an alchemy that is greater than the sum of its parts."[11] Clearly it is not just U2's audience and reviewers who have observed the quality in U2 shows that people often, only half-joking, call "church."

As common as that metaphor is among U2 fans, however, "church" is in the long run a word chosen more for its emotional resonance than for its ability to provide accurate information about what goes on at a U2 concert. True, the term communicates a generic, popular-level evocation of having experienced something powerful and spiritual, but as soon as the conversation gets into specifics, "church"—a noun so broad that it can point to anything from a globally televised papal ceremony to an abandoned building to an impromptu gospel sing-along to four twentysomethings with Bibles in a Seoul living room—ceases to be helpful in offering any real insights as to what goes into creating the remarkable experiences that U2 generates with its audience. This chapter suggests that while it may indeed be useful to employ an essentially spiritual category in seeking to learn more about what underlies the particular impact of U2's live work, the term "church" is not the best choice. Instead, I propose we consider whether the more focused and technical category of *leitourgia* can effectively interpret and illuminate U2 shows.

The word *leitourgia* is a Greek composite word meaning a work (*ergon*) taken on as a public service by private citizens (*laos*). In classical Greek, it could apply to actions such as building a school or funding a community theatrical performance. If a *leitourgia* was a public service, then its leader, a *leitourgos*, was what contemporary language would term a "public servant," someone who acts to benefit the larger society. However, as the word developed in the ancient world, according to David Fagerberg's study *Theologia Prima*, it became more and more associated with "actions expressing [a] city's relations to the world of divine powers on which it acknowledged itself to be dependent."[12] *Leitourgia* in this sense involved a whole richly textured complex of public ceremonies and events, requiring the participation of community leaders alongside ordinary citizens, enacted with reference both to the secular public good and to the culture's sustaining and legitimating sacred myths.

Eventually, in the early centuries of Christianity, *leitourgia* came to mean public, structured gatherings aimed at responding to and affecting both political and spiritual realities, presided over by leaders who in a spirit of public servanthood facilitated everyone's participation in the process. Such gatherings included a ritual framework and a worshipful intent, but it is of great interest that despite the availability of many words describing cult behavior and devotion, what the nascent Christian movement gravitated toward to describe what they were doing was a term for actions with a public and political horizon. "When the early Christians chose the term *leitourgia* it signaled that they did not think themselves to be doing cult [i.e., a worship service], but they were doing the eschatological work of making Christ's kingdom present,"[13] embodying as a public service a glimpse of what they believed was God's promised future for all creation. I would argue the vision of that kind of gathering, which the early Christians understood not as private devotional events but as effective public *leitourgia*, resembles in important ways the vision of a U2 show. That is, the vision of both is to have a corporate work, presided over by leaders in a spirit of public servanthood that engages all who are present. Both gatherings attempt to process through a dialogue between political and spiritual realities until participants have tasted the hope that things can be different.

Despite the fact that a related noun, "liturgy," has evolved in English, I prefer to retain the original Greek word as a technical term to avoid associations that could undermine the usefulness of *leitourgia* as an analytical category for considering U2's work. When modern readers encounter the term "liturgy," it is unlikely that they associate it with public service, the anticipatory manifestation of a just society, or "the radical abolishment of cult."[14] In fact, it stands more of a chance of evoking an image very nearly opposite those things: arcane rituals conducted in private holy places by a spiritual elite to meet the religious needs of their institution's membership.

While such broad-brush characterizations are likely unfair to most congregations that describe themselves as featuring "liturgy," many writers would still argue that since the invention of the printing press, if not earlier, *leitourgia* per se has been increasingly hard to find in Christian meetings, having been widely replaced by more disembodied, privatistic pursuits, such as education, devotional reflection, and entertainment.[15] Thus, for the purposes of this chapter, just as with "church," I avoid "liturgy," as it could easily throw us off the scent.

As we examine U2 concerts as events similar with *leitourgia*, we should note that when theologians apply the term to a gathering, they assume that it is taking place within a context of theological assumptions that are basic elements of the Christian account of reality (among those would be the understanding of human nature as fallen; the incarnation of God in Christ and a resultant valuing of flesh and matter; the centrality of Jesus's death and resurrection; the present work of the Holy Spirit in community; the possibility of forgiveness and reconciliation after sin; and the promise of an ultimate embodied redemption). *Leitourgia* can also describe particular phenomenological distinctives that naturally flow from those assumptions. Since it has been comprehensively argued elsewhere that U2's art is grounded in a Christian worldview such that it shares most of the essential assumptions that undergird *leitourgia*,[16] I will not take time to restate those arguments. Instead, I focus on aspects of a U2 show that resonate with some of *leitourgia*'s more phenomenological characteristics. I do so while acknowledging that the appropriateness of using such a category as an analytical tool depends on the fact that while U2 rarely foregrounds Christian doctrine onstage, it does set its work within the framework of a Christian reading of the universe's story.

The first phenomenological characteristic that I consider is a unification of the spiritual and the material. The great Russian Orthodox theologian Alexander Schmemann, drawing on the foundational Christian theme of Incarnation, writes that despite the fact that *leitourgia* takes a ritual form, in principle it is "the end of cult, [the end] of the 'sacred' religious act isolated from and opposed to the 'profane' life of the community." [17] In *leitourgia* "the pseudo-Christian opposition of the 'spiritual' and the 'material,' the 'sacred' and the 'profane,' the 'religious' and the 'secular,' is denounced, abolished, and revealed as a monstrous lie about God and man and the world."[18]

While U2 became adept at presenting its own profane sides only after *Achtung Baby*, its overall work has never taken an isolationist stance or invited its audience to construe the world as involving a putative conflict between the "religious" and the "secular." As early as 1982, the Edge was able to tell an interviewer, "We really feel that the spiritual and secular, or whatever label you put on them, all belong to God."[19] U2 made a commitment as young men to write music that honestly reflected their spiritual preoccupations and biblical knowledge but to perform and sell it in public, secular spaces rather than in Christian environments. Over the years their output moved on to begin incorporating more political, sexual, and introspective themes, but the band never stopped seeing those themes through the lens of faith. In a 2005 *Rolling Stone* interview, Bono commented that, artistically, the important thing to him was not whether music was "running toward God or away from God" but that it "recognize the pivot, that God is at the center."[20] Structured around this pivot, then, U2's live performances include all registers of life onstage, not juxtaposing the sacred and the profane harshly as if to shock but simply refusing to admit there is opposition.

Examples of this principle are many, but a classic choice would be the Zoo TV iteration of "Mysterious Ways," with Morleigh Steinberg in belly dancer garb undulating closer and closer to the main stage as the song progresses, leaving herself always just out of reach of Bono's outstretched hand, until she finally yields up not an actual touch but a wisp of a scarlet veil that he grasps as she retreats. As we watch this tantalizing interaction, the song moves through its lyrical litany of "Move now, Spirit, teach me . . . heal me . . . take me." The whole scene is humanly fascinating and tastefully erotic, while just as much a restatement of the biblical concept that the Holy Spirit is as uncontrollable as the wind and leaves mysterious gifts during its visitations;[21] but there is also no cordoning of this topic, the so-called sacred topic, into a pious ghetto. With U2, as with Schmemann's description of *leitourgia*, the spiritual is not opposed to the material, but it is invited to inhabit it. Bono has described this conjunction as putting "one [hand] on the minus terminal, one hand on the plus, and [the energy] just goes through you."[22]

A second criterion can also be drawn from Schmemann: *Leitourgia*, he writes, is "an action by which a group of people become something corporately which they had not been as a mere collection of individuals."[23] Rooted in the notion of Christians as one body in their Lord, this phrase encompasses two features: a corporate aspect and an aspect of becoming or processing toward something else.

Inspired by artists such as the Clash and probably by its own youthful participation in the group-oriented charismatic movement, U2 had already embraced the ideal of creating a corporate experience in its live shows when band members were in their teens. A 1980 article in *Hot Press* praised their early concerts for evidencing "an intensity, a desire for communion that extends far beyond matey, laddish revelry."[24] In 1982, Bono assessed a particular Dublin gig as a triumph because of its "atmosphere of celebration, right from the front rows to the back. That kind of feeling between the band and the audience leaves me breathless."[25] One can tell from early recordings, however, that in that era, Bono was often striving to make a shared experience happen without quite having figured out how. Shows from the early 1980s frequently included moments of his simply screaming exhortations at the assembly, such as "tear the walls down" and "give it all," or artlessly praising audience members when they responded in unison, "Good! That's good!" Even his early daredevil exploits seem to have arisen in part from that instinct: when a reporter asked him what on earth he thought he was doing after a particularly harrowing climb up the lighting rig at the 1983 US Festival, his justification was simply to insist, "The entire crowd was united at that moment!"[26]

But in the intervening years since 1983, the band has developed much more subtle, skilled, and seasoned methods for uniting a crowd: eighty-thousand-person choral sing-alongs feature prominently, as does the long-standing tradition of closing concerts with the shared psalmody of "40," or more recently, of letting the crowd sing God's part in the karaoke of "Unknown Caller." U2's team-building techniques have also included call and response ("¡Hola!" from "Vertigo," "No more!" from "Sunday Bloody Sunday"), coached group gestures (a side-to-side wave in "Mysterious Ways," raised hands in too many songs to name, jumping in "Elevation"), and shared clapping rhythms (the rapid eighth notes during "New Year's Day," the alternating offbeat ostinato during "Bullet the Blue Sky"). Most characteristically, nearly all U2 shows incorporate repeated coaxing of the audience members to give themselves over to pure vocal sound, perhaps becoming a human backing instrument (the "Oh-oh oh-oh" in "Pride") or even taking ownership as a body of the climax of the song (the very different "Oh-oh oh-oh" in "With or Without You"). Through all of these methods, as their effects combine and build, a group of people is becoming something which it had not been as a mere collection of individuals.

And this experience is not just corporate; as Schmemann writes, it involves a structured process of becoming. In his book *For the Life of the World*, Schmemann describes *leitourgia* with images like "a journey or procession," "an entrance," "an ascending movement."[27] An event is not *leitourgia* without flow and a sense of shared development among all the participants, not just the leaders. On some U2 tours, such a process of moving the assembly from one state of being to another has been articulated with very deliberate intellectual sequencing. The Zooropa tour, for example, launched with a disorienting media onslaught ("The Fly"), moved through exaggerated revelry into a parched aftermath of seeking—perhaps in vain?—some way out ("Trying to Throw Your Arms around the World," "Satellite of Love," "Running to Stand Still"), brought out the broken-down devil MacPhisto for an object lesson in the wages of sin, and finally ushered the audience into a vulnerable, apophatic darkness ("Love Is Blindness"). The Elevation tour, unconscious though it may have been, had a set list that seemed loosely to echo the structure of a historic Christian Eucharist, moving from gathering ("Elevation" and "Beautiful Day") through instructional and intercessional material ("Stuck in a Moment," "Kite") to offering ("Bad" into "40") to communion ("Streets") to sending out ("Walk On").

However one assesses the specific intention in any tour's arc, at any rate, a U2 set list is never simply a mere series of songs; it processes and invites every audience member to process with it, through stages toward a goal. "I want an audience to feel washed after a U2 gig,"[28] said Bono in 1985. More recently, U2 biographer Neil McCormick described the sensation of riding through this group progression well: "A U2 show is a big love-in, with only a few carping critics holding out, scribbling in their notebooks and refusing to surrender. . . . But if you don't let yourself go, you are in danger of missing the whole point."[29]

We have observed thus far how U2 concerts create a context that exposes the lie of an opposition between the "sacred" and the "secular" and invite a collection of individuals into a shared process that unites them in movement toward a particular goal. What, then, is the goal that is in view? Theologian Peter Fink offers an answer drawing from the Christian understanding of the Last Things, or eschatology. Another characteristic of *leitourgia,* he proposes, is its ability to offer a foretaste of ultimate fulfillment in a form accessible to bodily, sensate nature. What *leitourgia* envisions is to "render what [God] promises perceptible to the senses."[30] While some U2 fans might wish to quibble about the need to involve a deity in the discussion, few would disagree that there is a promise, a vision of ultimate reconciliation, justice, and joy on the horizon at a U2 show. In fact, a half hour on the Internet will verify that if U2 audience members do not come away from a concert feeling that they have personally tasted and touched that promise, they will fill fan forums with complaints that the band was having an off night.

The summit of this "foretaste" phenomenon, at least for the past two decades, can only be performances of "Where the Streets Have No Name," which I have described elsewhere as an "eschatological barn-burner."[31] From its use in Zoo TV through the post–September 11 Elevation shows, "Streets" was almost invariably framed as an answer to an immediately preceding song (e.g., "Running to Stand Still," "Please," "Bad") that had led the audience into an experience of human sin and tragedy. In the face of that despair, the screens were lit by a subtle red dawn of hope that, as the noise of the crowd built, burst forth into a blinding, overwhelming white light of expectation, revelation, liberation. In more recent presentations, the band has elected to set up "Streets" by songs foregrounding the commitment to strive toward justice and equality ("Pride," "Walk On") and thus to frame it as an anticipatory celebration of that final achievement. But in either case, the power of "Where the Streets Have No Name" in a live show depends on it delivering an experiential sense of the presence of the hoped-for now.

U2 itself always sounds awed when it speaks about performing "Streets," as with these 2004 comments:

> [The band is] talking about a special place, a better place, and asking if the audience wants to go there with them. . . . We can be in the middle of the worst gig in our lives, but when we go into that song, everything changes. . . . The audience is on its feet, singing along with every word [note a hearkening back, here, to the goal of uniting the crowd as well]. It's like God suddenly walks through the room. It's the point where craft ends and spirit begins.[32]

Bono often reworks his texts over the years, and one of the Elevation tour–era changes to "Streets" inserted an allusion to an image of ultimate fulfillment from chapter 21 of Revelation, the Bible's final book: "I'll show you a place where there's no sorrow and no shame." In situ, this promise does not come off as a bait and switch: it's easy to be shown that place when, mysteriously, you discover that you're standing in it.

Theologically, it is "the manifestation of the new creation" that is in view here,[33] and this theme leads to another phenomenological characteristic of *leitourgia*: a sense of possibility that things can and will be put to rights and a call to participate in doing so. In a beloved maxim, theologian Aidan Kavanagh says that *leitourgia* boils down to "doing the world the way the world was meant to be done."[34] This image doubtless includes the notion of rendering a promised fulfillment perceptible to the senses, but it also evokes the ideal of justice: that within the corporate process of *leitourgia*, participants together enact in a ritual mode the righting of wrongs and the overturning of oppression. Liturgical theology suggests that as the assembly then disperses until its next gathering, participants should carry the experience with them, leading to changed behavior and a greater commitment to "the way the world was meant to be" outside the ritual context as well.

A dedication to bringing justice issues onstage with an eye to influencing its audience's commitments offstage has been part of U2's work from very early on. Perhaps its earliest conscious ritualizing of it might be the white flags of the War tour, flying to call forth an end to sectarian division in Ireland. Such symbols of putting the world to rights and opportunities to take action have abounded in U2's art ever since. For example, the Vertigo show illuminated darkened venues with the cell phone lights of people signing up for the ONE Campaign and the sight of their names scrolling minutes later across the screen. On the 360° tour, volunteers ringed the stage wearing the face of the imprisoned Burmese Nobel laureate Aung San Suu Kyi during "Walk On." An older example would be the band's PopMart performance of "Mothers of the Disappeared" in 1998 in Santiago, Chile, as elderly women whose children had been abducted and murdered by the Pinochet regime came one by one to the microphone on live Chilean television to name aloud their missing loved ones, the Edge repeating his simple rise-and-fall melodic gesture of grief over and over in the background.[35]

When this aspect of a U2 show is poorly integrated or overexplained verbally, it can tip over into didacticism; at their best, however, the symbolic acts carry a performative power that stays with listeners much longer than a lecture. There is no way ever to quantify how many audience members would cite something they saw or heard at a U2 show as a factor in their subsequent decisions to donate, lobby, volunteer, join Amnesty International, or explore a vocation in ministry or social work or development. However, the number is surely not negligible, and recent research has demonstrated that U2's efforts to "do the world the way the world was meant to be done" result in verifiable changes in at least some participants' attitudes and actions.[36] Adam Clayton has compared the process to having "open-heart surgery and . . . brain surgery at the same time."[37]

The last criterion that I consider returns us to Schmemann. In *leitourgia*, he says, a community is enabled to "offer to God the totality of all our lives, of ourselves, of the world in which we live . . . [in] a movement in which all joy and suffering, all beauty and all frustration, all hunger and all satisfaction, are referred to their ultimate End and become finally meaningful."[38] In a sense this remark only sums up many of the previous ones, but it does seem worth noting that for many people a U2 show provides a unique vehicle for them to experience what it is to offer up the uncensored totality of life as part of a structured group process, what one might appropriately even call a "ritual context." At times U2 itself encourages such an offering by deliberately referring to things that are likely to be preoccupations at the time; it seeks to motivate the audience to connect its own current experience with the process that the band has structured into the show—for example, regularly changing the lyrics of "Beautiful Day" to cite local landmarks or events, referring to American elections in November, including snippets of Michael Jackson's songs in the week following his death, and putting images of Princess Diana on the screen after hers. When U2 played a free show at the Brandenburg Gate to celebrate the anniversary of the fall of the Berlin Wall in 2009, the visuals projected across the monument for the song "One" invited the German audience to relive, over the song's four minutes, its nation's twentieth-century story of violence, division, isolation, and reunion.[39]

It is evident, then, that U2 plans quite consciously ahead of time for ways to turn each concert into a context for the particular community gathered in the venue that night to process its own joys and sufferings. But to its credit, U2 has also displayed a willingness to risk depending on people bringing something of their own to offer in the moment—and more than that, to risk relinquishing the spotlight to those people. The band has long had the habit of spontaneously inviting dancers, guitar players, and children onstage and encouraging them to play a role in the proceedings, whether by dancing for the crowd, participating in the performance of an unscheduled song, or leading a corporate call and response. At a Cologne, Germany, concert in 1997, a fan who came dressed in costume as the character MacPhisto was given the microphone to take over a brief section of "Bullet the Blue Sky." In 2001, guitarist Scott Perretta was welcomed onstage in Oakland, California, and without any prearrangement led the band in "A Sort of Homecoming," a track it had performed live only once since 1987. It is also not unusual for Bono to reach into the audience, accept a sign, flag, or other symbolic object that has been brought by fans, and incorporate it into the show. A noteworthy percentage of a U2 concert simply depends on audience participation, and as with *leitourgia*, if the people don't join in and contribute sincerely, the entire thing falls flat. Larry Mullen has claimed, accordingly, that the U2 band members are "a significant, but not too significant, part of our shows. The audience really carry us."[40]

The most developed instance of an audience using a U2 show as a channel to offer up its joy and loss would probably have to be the Elevation shows shortly after September 11, 2001. U2's manager Paul McGuinness has written, "An extraordinary loop of energy and emotion [passed] through the band and through the audience and through the material . . . and that became very explicit in the months after the twin towers. It was fascinating to watch it happen, night after night, to see songs suddenly transformed and bursting with new meanings,"[41] meanings that the audience had brought with them. U2 reworked its established set list in response, to highlight grief, healing, and comfort, inserting the terrorism lament "Please" and the poignant covers "What's Going On" and "When Will I See You Again," while deleting items like an edgy rap about John Lennon's murder and "The Fly." With characteristic visual intentionality, they scrolled the names of the dead and missing during "Walk On," a gesture about which Adam Clayton commented, "That was a powerful, cathartic moment . . . an audience has to really trust you to let you push certain buttons. And those audiences did; they trusted us and they went there with us."[42] At Madison Square Garden, surviving members of the New York Fire Department were allowed to take over the stage in an unplanned celebration of life, speaking about their departed colleagues and then jumping deliriously to "Out of Control."[43]

The Edge spoke later about that evening, "I don't think there was a dry eye in the house, including the band. . . . We were just happy to be there and try to be of service."[44] One rarely thinks of rock stars describing their posture during two hours headlining Madison Square Garden as having the privilege to "be of service," but the phrasing is characteristic of U2. Although ego is never absent from any human endeavor, the person presiding over the corporate process of *leitourgia* is not primarily motivated by the chance to claim a spot as an adored object of attention but by the commitment to facilitate the entire event for everyone. In numerous interviews, band members mentioned the deafening level of the crowd's singing in post–September 11 New York, and Bono commented on its meaning with a remark that perhaps reveals, just as much as the Edge's comment, how atypical U2's understanding of their onstage role is: "People are not screaming their lungs out for you . . . they're screaming for themselves."[45]

Liturgical theologian David Fagerberg has written elegantly of a similar role: "Like a needle pulling thread through fabric to stitch up a rent cloth, [the person presiding over *leitourgia*] moves in and out, in and out, between heaven and earth, between eternity and time, the sacred and the profane, plunging into one and then the other and drawing them together by the thread of his or her life," until all who are gathered have been taken to another place where they are able, as one body, to experience "the heart of the world above the altar, beating without sin's arrhythmia."[46]

If you were to look at my copy of Fagerberg's book, you would see that in the margin next to that last phrase of his is written "U2" and not just because of the almost eerie way it echoes the Vertigo tour's closing visuals, in which, as the band plays "Yahweh," a radiant beating heart soars heavenward to hover above its city in a final gesture of offering. "U2" is written next to that phrase because whatever else U2 is doing when it plays, it is seeking to stitch up what is rent, to marry the profane and the sacred in public, to render eschatological promise perceptible to the senses, to do the world the way the world was meant to be done, and to facilitate the offering up of all aspects of life in joy. In short, U2 is doing what we cannot help but call *leitourgia*—in an age where it is sorely needed but all too hard to find.

Notes

1. Gary Lightbody, "Something I've Never Seen Before," U2.com, August 7, 2009, http://www.u2.com/stream/article/display/id/5198.

2. Steve Braden, "U2's Hi-Tech Tent Revival," in *The U2 Reader: A Quarter Century of Commentary, Criticism, and Reviews*, ed. Hank Bordowitz (Milwaukee, WI: Hal Leonard, 2003), 175–78.

3. Nerdy Renegade News blog, August 23, 2009, http://nerdyrenegade .blogspot.com/2009/08/raising-dead-in-church-of-u2.html.

4. Kris and Judd blog, November 4, 2009, http://krisandjudd.blogspot .com/2009/11/u2-concert.html.

5. Doug Pullen, "Concert Review: U2's Message of Love Doesn't Grow Old," Pullen Blog, October 13, 2009, http://elpasotimes.typepad.com/pullen/ 2009/10/concert-review-u2s-message-of-love-doesnt-grow-old.html.

6. It is important to note up front that for all practical purposes and especially where its live work is concerned, "U2" is shorthand for an entire artistic team. Celebrity culture may tempt us to focus on the four official members of U2, but what the band's audience experiences under that rubric is actually the production of a large, dedicated collaborative. While the list may begin with familiar names, such as producers Brian Eno and Daniel Lanois, show designer Willie Williams, lighting director Bruce Ramos, audio director Joe O'Herlihy, visual curator Catherine Owens, and muse Gavin Friday, the official work on U2's stage productions, *U2 Show*, includes essays by sixty-four collaborators of the band.

7. Kate Snow, "One on One with U2: Reporter and Admitted Fan Hangs with the Band," *ABC News*, March 9, 2009, http://www.atu2.com/news/one -on-one-with-u2.html.

8. Tom Doyle, "Ten Years of Turmoil inside U2," *Q Magazine*, October 10, 2002, http://www.atu2.com/news/10-years-of-turmoil-inside-u2.html.

9. Ray Waddell, "The *Billboard* Q and A: U2's the Edge," *Billboard*, March 7, 2009, http://www.atu2.com/news/the-billboard-qa-u2s-the-edge.html.

10. Mark LePage, "Bass Notes: U2's Adam Clayton on Geography, Spirituality, and Rock 'n' Roll," the *Montreal Gazette*, May 26, 2001, http://www.atu2.com/news/bass-notes-u2s-adam-clayton-on-geography-spirituality-and-rock-n-roll.html.

11. Diana Scrimgeour, *U2 Show* (New York: Riverhead Books, 2004), 17.

12. David W. Fagerberg, *Theologia Prima: What Is Liturgical Theology?* (Chicago: Hillenbrand Books, 2004), 11.

13. Fagerberg, *Theologia Prima*, 83.

14. Fagerberg, *Theologia Prima*, 13.

15. Examples may be found in Fagerberg, *Theologia Prima*, 111, and in Aidan Kavanagh, *On Liturgical Theology* (Collegeville, MN: Liturgical Press, 1992), 124.

16. Among several works presenting a case for the Christian commitment underlying U2's work are Steve Stockman, *Walk On: The Spiritual Journey of U2* (Lake Mary, FL: Relevant Media Group, 2001); Robert Vagacs, *Religious Nuts, Political Fanatics: U2 in Theological Perspective* (Eugene, OR: Cascade Books, 2005); Christian Scharen, *One Step Closer: Why U2 Matters to Those Seeking God* (Grand Rapids, MI: Brazos Press, 2006); and Steven R. Harmon, "U2: Unexpected Prophets," in *Singing Our Lives: Christian Reflections* (Waco, TX: Center for Christian Ethics, Baylor University, 2006), 81–88.

17. Alexander Schmemann, *For the Life of the World* (Crestwood, NY: St. Vladimir's Seminary Press, 1973), 26.

18. Schmemann, *For the Life of the World*, 76.

19. Derek Poole, "U2: Gloria in Rock & Roll!" *Streams* (June 1982), 18-21.

20. Jann Wenner, "Bono: The *Rolling Stone* Interview," *Rolling Stone* 986 (November 3, 2005), 54.

21. Cf. John 3, I Corinthians 12.

22. Stuart Bailie, "Rock and Roll Should Be This Big," *NME*, June 13, 1992, http://www.atu2.com/news/rock-and-roll-should-be-this-big.html.

23. Schmemann, *For the Life of the World*, 25.

24. Bill Graham, "The Battle of Britain," in *The U2 File: A Hot Press U2 History,* ed. Niall Stokes (Dublin, Ireland: Hot Press, 1985), 38.

25. Niall Stokes, "U2: Poll Winners Speak Out," in Stokes, *The U2 File*, 78.

26. Audience recording of the MTV US Festival broadcast of May 30, 1983.

27. Schmemann, *For the Life of the World*, 26, 27, 42.

28. Steve Goddard, "U2: When Boys Go to War," *Buzz*, September 1, 1985, http://www.atu2.com/news/u2-when-boys-go-to-war.html.

29. Neil McCormick, "Secrets of Stadium Rock," UK Telegraph blog, August 17, 2009, http://blogs.telegraph.co.uk/culture/neilmccormick/100002560/u2-secrets-of-stadium-rock/.

30. Peter Fink, "Towards a Liturgical Theology," *Worship* 47, no. 10 (December 1973): 602 (quoted in Fagerberg, *Theologia Prima*, 125).

31. Beth Maynard, "A Brief History of U2 for Novices," in *Get Up Off Your Knees: Preaching the U2 Catalog*, ed., Raewynne Whiteley and Beth Maynard (Boston: Cowley Publications, 2004), 167-176.

32. Robert Hilburn, "The Songwriters: U2," *Los Angeles Times* (August 8, 2004). http://www.atu2.com/news/the-songwriters-u2-where-craft-ends-and-spirit-begins.html (accessed August 20, 2009).

33. Fagerberg, *Theologia Prima*, 17.

34. Personal conversation quoted in Fagerberg, *Theologia Prima*, 16.

35. An audience recording of this performance from February 11, 1998, may be viewed at http://www.youtube.com/watch?v=KuFMoWV1cns.

36. Rachel E. Seiler, "When I Look at the World: Viewing the Impact of U2's Music on Listeners' Consciousness and Activism through the Lens of Narrative Inquiry—Preliminary Dissertation Research Findings" (paper presented at "The Hype and The Feedback," a conference exploring the music, work, and influence of U2, Durham, NC, October 2–4, 2009).

37. Josh Tyrangiel, "Bono's Mission," *Time* (February 23, 2002), http://www.atu2.com/news/bonos-mission-1.html.

38. Schmemann, *For the Life of the World*, 34–35.

39. An audience recording of this performance from November 5, 2009, may be viewed at http://www.youtube.com/watch?v=cZfUAMehb24. This representation of a past narrative to a current-day audience to foster a powerful uniting experience hints at another feature of *leitourgia* less prominent in U2's work than the five considered directly in this chapter. *Leitourgia* understands itself as empowered to evoke past groundbreaking and community-shaping events, such as the Exodus or the Last Supper, in a way that calls forth their power into the present. This active memorial process is technically called *anamnesis*.

40. Band interview with Serbian television station TV B92, broadcast August 2009, http://www.youtube.com/watch?v=AcWKg_uWt24.

41. Neil McCormick, ed., *U2 by U2* (New York: HarperCollins, 2006), 309.

42. McCormick, *U2 by U2*, 309.

43. An audience recording of this performance from October 27, 2001, may be viewed at http://www.youtube.com/watch?v=-3Wtdux2rDI.

44. McCormick, *U2 by U2*, 309.

45. Christine Sams, "Inside Bono's Dressing Room," *The Sun-Herald* (November 6, 2006), http://www.atu2.com/news/inside-bonos-dressing-room.html.

46. Fagerberg, *Theologia Prima*, 16, 228.

Bono *v.* Nick Cave Re: Jesus **11**

GREG CLARKE

C HRISTIAN KITSCH IS THE KITSCHIEST of all kitsch and perhaps the most profound. Artist and author Betty Spackman defines kitsch in *A Profound Weakness: Christians and Kitsch* as a lie that tells the truth: it "both conceals and reveals the vestiges of wonder, the underlying mysteries of faith. . . . In a way, kitsch represents a closet desire for spiritual reality, and the creative longing to manifest mystery."[1]

Songwriter, performer, and author Nick Cave has been bringing his Christian kitsch out of the closet in Australia recently, with a national traveling exhibition of his artwork, lyrics, and various paraphernalia associated with his art.[2] A circa-1950s bust of Jesus often features prominently in photographs of Cave, its bleeding heart just to the right of his eye line as he sits at his piano composing some of the most poignant and spiritually aggressive songs of the past few decades. "I don't believe in an interventionist God," he famously sang in "Into My Arms," perhaps the most theologically uncompromising opening line of any rock song.

Since the orthodox Christian teaching is precisely the opposite to the opening line of "Into My Arms"—that is, that God intervened in the world in the person of Jesus Christ in the event summarized as the Incarnation—Cave's Jesus bust cannot be for its owner an object of spiritual devotion. It plays some other role. In his celebrated 1996 BBC lecture "The Flesh Made Word," Cave explores his movement from reading the Old Testament as an arts school student in his twenties to reading the Gospels in his thirties and finding that Christ embodied an emotional movement from self-loathing (the allegedly brutal, capricious Old Testament God's judgment on the world) to self-divinizing. The lecture startled a number of his long-term fans and critics, who wondered if Cave was going insane. He explained:

> The more I read the Gospels, the more Christ called to my imagination, for his journey was, it seemed to me, just that: a flight of the imagination. Christ, who [called] himself both the Son of Man and the Son of God as the occasion warranted, was exactly that: a man of flesh and blood, so in touch with the creative forces inside himself, so open to his brilliant flame-like imagination, that he became the physical embodiment of that force: God. In Christ, the spiritual blueprint was set so that we ourselves could become Godlike.[3]

In contrast, when challenged by journalist Michka Assayas that believing Jesus to be the Son of God was "farfetched," Bono replied,

> No, it's not farfetched to me. Look, the secular response to the Christ story always goes something like this: he was a great prophet, obviously a very interesting guy. . . . But actually Christ doesn't allow you that. . . . So what you're left with is either Christ was who He said He was—the Messiah—or a complete nutcase.[4]

This very orthodox position outlined by Bono, itself a variant of C. S. Lewis's "Lord, Liar or Lunatic" options,[5] is fleshed out in the conversation with Assayas, as I explore. But it contains the crux of the difference between Cave's and Bono's understandings of Jesus. Bono receives the biblical story as the church has done down the centuries, with the chief aim being glorification; Cave morphs it into something else, with the chief end being creative expression. The differences in their positions are significant, but that is not to say there are not similarities. Cave's position on the nature of Christ may be a long way from creedal Christianity, but he and Bono have in common that Christ is an inspiration, an exemplar, an elevator, a liberator. Cave admires and appropriates Christ, sometimes to the point of identification with him. Bono worships, follows, and emulates Christ, albeit with the faltering steps of any who claim to do so.

In what follows, I examine the different ways in which the Christ story informs the texts of these two artists: their songs, their speeches, Cave's novel, and Bono's social justice works.

Sons of the Father

Cave and Bono are about the same age, and both lost a parent when they were teenagers. The effect seems to have been similar: both young men were driven to express their rage and emptiness in rock music. Both seem to have been singing and writing the story of loss ever since. Cave has made no secret of the connection between his art and his sonship: "The loss of my father created in my life a vacuum, a space in which my words began to float and collect and find their purpose. . . . Like Christ, I too come in the name of my father, to keep God alive."[6] Cave has come to understand his role in life to fulfill the misguided and unfulfilled creative desires of his father, Colin Cave, an English teacher in 1960s Australia. It is startling that this "patriphilial" drive is still with him (at age fifty-two), and his most recent novel (*The Death of Bunny Munro*) is a startlingly bleak portrayal of father-son relationships, albeit with a glimmer of hope that they are renewable and redeemable.

Likewise, Bono's difficult relationship with his father is well documented, along with the poignant weeks before Bob Hewson's death and the song connected with it all, "Sometimes You Can't Make It on Your Own." Bono told Neil McCormick, as recorded in *Killing Bono*, that great performers play for the back of the room, but really driven ones "are playing to one person. It might be a lover. But it might be your father."[7]

The father-son dynamic is therefore significant in the song writing of both artists and is often connected with Jesus as a son. For Cave, the title Son of Man is more relevant, and it is Christ as a man that directs Cave's depictions of him. Christ "walks in grace and love"; he speaks wonders; he opposes the System; he is the image of capital-M Man. But he is not the living hope of the world, sent from God the Father; he only sees himself that way. Perhaps he best captures this enduring view of Jesus in the song "The Mercy Seat," with the lyric on the lips of a condemned man:

> I hear stories from the chamber
> How Christ was born into a manger
> And like some ragged stranger died upon a cross
> And might I say it seems so fitting in its way
> He was a carpenter by trade
> Well, at least that's what I'm told.

This last line throws dusts of doubt in the air over the whole project of Christ's divinity, challenging the veracity of the Gospel stories while borrowing the ethical and dramatic power of the "rags to nails" story of the crucifixion.

For Cave, the manifestation of God remains a mystery, one that he cannot resolve and whose sense of peace and fulfillment eludes him. In "Nobody's Baby Now," he sings that he has tried to unravel the mystery of Christ, but the answer refuses to be found; God, in the words of another powerful song title, is still "Hiding All Away." Cave's God is not revealed in Christ; rather, Christ can become God through intense creative acts.

For Bono, the mystery of God taking on flesh becomes increasingly satisfying as an expression of divine Love:

> To me it makes sense. It's actually logical. It's pure logic. Essence has to manifest itself. It's inevitable. Love has to become an action or something concrete. It would have to happen. There must be an incarnation. Love must be made flesh.[8]

He may have sung that he still hasn't found what he's looking for, but that was never an expression of doubt or unacceptance, as it appears to be for Cave. For Bono, it is one of certainty about where love lies and that the singer is journeying toward it.

In U2's "The First Time," we have another cryptic rendering of the Prodigal Son story, as the rich Father hands over the keys to the Kingdom to his wayward Son, who refuses them and leaves by the back door. But the Son still says, "That for the first time / I feel love." This is the unconditional love of the Father for the Son. In contrast, for Cave, the Son is trying to make up for the Father's failures. In a reexpression of the second-century Marcion heresy, Cave says in his lecture,

> Christ, the Son, came as an individual, the Word made flesh to set right the misguided notion of his Father, or as Paul wrote to the Corinthians, "God was, in Christ, reconciling the world to himself." Christ came to right the wrongs of his father.[9]

The same theological sentiment is sung out in Cave's "The Good Son," his own warped riff on the Prodigal Son parable, where Jesus doubles for the wayward son:

> He lays down his queer plans
> Against his brother and against his family
> Yet he worships his brother
> And he worships his mother
> But it's his father, he says is an unfair man,
> The Good Son.

Both Bono and Cave find rich creative resources in the father-son dynamic, both in its human structures and in its theological formulations. It explains or explores psychological drives as well as providing a genealogy of creativity. However, for Bono, the power of the father-son relationship is rooted in belief in the logic and reality of the Christian Trinity, whereas for Cave such a doctrine is only the background for individual striving for significance.

Jesus the Word

Bono and Cave feed lyrically not on bread alone but on the words of Jesus. The words of Jesus are an urtext for Western songwriters, since they have such influence on English language, ethics and storytelling. Everywhere in the lyrics of both men we find traces of the words of Jesus.

The band Nick Cave and the Bad Seeds probably gets its name from Jesus's parable of the seeds (despite the fact that none of the seeds themselves are bad in the parable—they just fall on bad ground). For Cave, Jesus's words matter most not for their content but for their impact; he aestheticizes the religious teachings. He has a fascination with the sound of words, and he finds joy in prolixity. His theory of language seems also to owe something to Jesus. In his public lecture "The Secret Life of the Love Song," Cave said,

> Jesus Christ himself said, in one of His most beautiful quotes, "Where ever two or more are gathered together, I am in your midst." He said this because where ever two or more are gathered together there is language. I found that language became a poultice to the wounds incurred by the death of my father. Language became a salve to longing.[10]

Language makes up for, or satisfies, the need for communication, and if the communication is one way and God is silent, then those who want to hear from God will find themselves busy with language, aiming it upward. "Any true love song," says Cave, "is a song to God."

He take this even further to suggest that artists speak for God, following Christ's example:

> Just as we are divine creations, so must we in turn create. Divinity must be given its freedom to flow through us, through language, through communication, through imagination. I believe this is our spiritual duty, made clear to us through the example of Christ.[11]

Christ is here the exemplar but not the object of devotion. Contrast this with Bono in "Magnificent." Some early reviewers mistook the lyric as the ultimate act of self-importance—"I was born, I was born to sing for you; I didn't have a choice"—as if Bono were telling his audience that he was God's gift to them, a Theo Vox perhaps. But unlike the humanistic philosophy developed by Cave, Bono in "Magnificent" is in fact addressing God. It is an act of praise and worship. The lyric finishes, "I didn't have a choice but to lift you up." The allusion to Mary's Magnificat in Luke 1:46–55 makes this meaning even more obvious.

Jesus's words, for Bono, are often the moral motivation for human striving. In "Crumbs from Your Table," he most likely cites the parable that Jesus tells of the Canaanite woman who begs Jesus for "crumbs" when the religious of the day are ignoring him. Those in great need understand what really matters, while those who are complacent in their blessings feel like they never have enough.

Cave finds archetypal truths in Jesus's parables, drawing a connection between biblical and mythical storytelling and contemporary culture. For example, the song "The Good Son" is written from the point of view of the "nonprodigal" son in the Jesus story recorded in Luke 15. Nathan Wiseman-Trowse suggests that Cave borrows both the biblical story of the jealous, obedient son who feels his father is unfair to favor his wayward brother and the archetypal power of good versus evil siblings.[12]

Significantly, the notion of Jesus as the incarnate Word of God plays a role for both artists. For Cave, Christ is a messenger of God, performing the message through not just his words but his body. He is not divine in being but divine in expression. This heterodox notion of incarnation elevates humanity to a godlike condition: "The essential humanness of *Mark*'s Christ provides us with a blueprint for our own lives, so that we have something that we can aspire to, rather than revere," Cave writes in his introduction to *The Gospel according to Mark*.[13] Cave's Word of God liberates humanity from lowliness and mundaneness but is not himself an object of worship.

For Bono, Christ is incarnate in a more orthodox theological sense. It is fitting for the triune God to take on flesh, to "explain itself and describe itself by becoming a child born in straw poverty."[14] The message of Christ is found in the drama of the Incarnation, in the scene into which God took on flesh: lowliness, ordinariness, neediness. "Looking for baby Jesus under the trash," as Bono sings in "Mofo," is precisely the appropriate place to look.

The Man of Sorrows

> *I heard a man say once that Christians worship sorrow. That is by no means true. But we do believe there is a sacred mystery in it, it's fair to say that.*
>
> —MARILYNNE ROBINSON, *GILEAD*[15]

Cave identifies most strongly with Christ as the Man of Sorrows. Roland Boer describes Cave's spiritual journey as going from raging Old Testament prophet to someone softer and sadder because "the New Testament brings out the dim, sad light of Christ knocking on the door of his heart, as in the Holman Hunt painting."[16] The image of Christ weeping for Jerusalem, as the Israelites wept by the river of Babylon, informs one of the songs that broke Nick Cave into the mainstream "The Weeping Song."

In his lecture "The Secret Life of the Love Song," Cave cites a favorite poet of his, Federico Garcia Lorca, on the importance of *duende*, which is a term in the Spanish arts referring to the "origin" or "soul" of an artwork. It might be best thought of as a virus, or a demon of the bloodstream, a kind of inner shadow self of the Muse. Whereas the Muse visits like an angel, *duende* flows through an artist like a taunting, teasing demon. Lorca writes: "The Duende . . . will not approach at all if he does not see the possibility of death, if he is not convinced he will circle death's house."[17]

Sorrow, death, and violence seem to be in Cave's blood and arguably generate most of his lyrics; his is an angry, enduring sorrow that leads to violence. Lyn McCredden has suggested that Cave's sorrow parallels the notion of abjection in religion, as articulated by Julia Kristeva: "This 'religiosity' is apparent in Cave's enduringly melancholic encounters with the abject limits of the human—the violence done to a corpse, the entanglement of innocence with darkly erotic drives."[18]

Cave admires the "actor" Jesus, the creative Jesus who can find within the strength to rail against his enemies and the "established order." There is something Nietzschean in Cave's image of Jesus, the *Übermensch* being held back by petty pharisaic preoccupations. His sorrow is complex, partly a sorrow at the horror of the world but also an angry pity for its weakness.

Recently, an Australian radio journalist wrote a book tracing "emo" culture back to Nietzsche, who preferred the violent self-aggrandizing heroics of the old Greek gods. The book *Hey! Nietzsche! Leave Them Kids Alone!* claims that Nietzsche's vision of a new religion of man, in which "all truly noble morality grows out of triumphant self-affirmation,"[19] represents the direction of pop culture from the Buzzcocks to today (e.g., My Chemical Romance). Cave's violent sorrow belongs within this lineage.

The song "Sorrow's Child," from the album *The Good Son*, significantly ties the death drive with the creative instinct. It is perhaps Cave's clearest expression of the *duende* philosophy of emotion and creativity: "Sorrow's child grieves not what has passed / But all the past still yet to come." The mode of existence is sorrow; weeping is never done, and weeping is all there is to do.

For Bono, the place of sorrow in the life of the artist and the individual is very different. Bono identifies with the sorrow that Christ feels for others, but this is a personal sorrow, not an existential one. Bono's is not an angst-ridden sorrow, nor is it a muse; rather, it is a sorrow that motivates social response alongside art. It is not the *duende*, but something more akin to biblical accounts of sorrow: David weeping in sackcloth and ashes as penitence for his adultery with Bathsheba (Psalm 51); Christ weeping over Jerusalem before acting to redeem it (Luke 19:41); the apostle Paul's sorrow for his unbelieving brethren (Romans 9:2). This is not to aggrandize Bono's vision but rather to emphasize the nature of the sorrow found in U2's music: it is the mourning for what could be, before living in a manner that seeks it.

In the song "Wave of Sorrow," written about the horrors of famine and war in Ethiopia, Bono calls out to Jesus in faith and hope that the sorrow might be relieved. The song ends with new Beatitudes, raining blessings on those who are suffering most. "Blessed is the spirit that overcomes" is not for Bono a call for Nietzschean dominance but a call of endurance in confident faith.

In the song "Until the End of the World," the protagonist is "drowning my sorrows," but his sorrows swim and overwhelm him with regret. This might be the point at which a Cave song would conclude, but Bono's greater Christian confidence generates the rest of the lyric: "I reached out for the one I tried to destroy." This seems to be an act of contrition or penitence and an attempt to make amends for wrongs and to alleviate the sorrow. For Bono, sorrow is not the condition of life but the consequence of wrongdoing; it needs to be killed off.

The difference between Cave's sorrow and Bono's is not that one is an unrealistic vision of God's care for the world while the other acknowledges the tragic truth; on the contrary, it is the purposes of sorrow that distinguish them. For Cave, sorrow is in the blood like a virus; for Bono, it is like singing out the blues. Whereas a majority of Cave's songs grow from sorrow and remain in it, Bono's sorrow leads to change and generates faith, hope, and love, as indicated in 2 Corinthians 7:10: "Godly sorrow brings repentance that leads to salvation and leaves no regret, but worldly sorrow brings death."

The Cross and the Bloodied Lamb

The death of Christ continues to focus artistic interest, whether it is Andres Serrano's controversial *Piss Christ* or the latest fashion jewelry, the cross is never far from Western creative sensibilities. It is central, too, in different ways to Nick Cave and to Bono.

There are fascinating deposition scenes in Cave's "Loverman" video, as the Bad Seeds "take down" the limp body of Cave "the Christ," and it is this image of a defeated man through whom a violent God is victorious that shapes Cave's understanding of this event. The crucifixion, for Cave, is a sacrifice for the sake of ideals but not a victorious one. The song "Foi Na Cruz" on Cave's album *The Good Son* is a Brazilian Protestant song proclaiming that Jesus takes our sins on the cross, punished for us. But this is not liberating in any spiritual way for Cave; instead, it is evidence of the dark power of God, an expression of vengeance and grief.

For Cave, Christ is associated with vengeance rather than sacrifice. Cave repaganizes the Christian gospel of Christ's death for others so that the vengeance wreaked upon the world by murderers becomes a means of exonerating Christ. Cave explores the "red right hand" of God, his vengeance (a phrase taken from Milton's poem *Paradise Lost*[20]): "You're one microscopic cog in his catastrophic plan / Designed and directed by his red right hand." Oxford University literature professor Peter Conrad suggests a different interpretation of Cave's fascination with the cross, focusing on the father-son dynamic: "On the cross, Christ asked God the Father to forgive his human tormentors; Cave's Christ, recovering from his wounds, asks the parent's forgiveness for surviving."[21] Cave's notion of the cross might be summarized as horrific and nonsalvific.

For Bono, in contrast, the cross is clearly the unlikely instrument of grace. As he said to interviewer Michka Assayas, "I'm holding out that Jesus took my sins onto the Cross."[22] In songs such as "When Love Comes to Town," "I Still Haven't Found What I'm Looking For," "Tomorrow," "Sunday Bloody Sunday," and more, the historic teaching of the atoning power of the cross is heard in lyrical forms. There is little that is Gothic about Bono's depiction of the cross—there is no garish Mel Gibson–style focus on physical pain. Instead, the emphasis is on spiritual liberation without denying the high cost to God, Father, and Son.

It is possible to contrast the two artists' visions of Jesus's death through their various images of the sacrificial lamb. In Cave's "Darker with the Day," a haunting song of yearning and spiritual sorrow, the singer finds himself in church:

> Inside I sat, seeking the presence of a God
> I searched through the pictures in a leather-bound book
> I found a woolly lamb dosing in an issue of blood
> And a gilled Jesus shivering on a fisherman's hook.

This comment on the kitschiness and bizarreness of Bible illustrations is also an insight into Cave's low view of the theology of the atonement: a bloodied lamb does nothing to communicate God's love and forgiveness for Cave. Instead, it is an image of both domestication and conquest of Jesus. In contrast, on the recent album *No Line on the Horizon*, U2 produces a gentle song of hymnlike reverence to "the lamb as white as snow," where the lamb is the source of forgiveness. "I love the idea of the sacrificial Lamb," Bono told Assayas. "It should keep us humbled. . . . It's not our own good works that get us through the gates of Heaven."[23]

For Bono, the cross is "nonsense that makes sense";[24] it is the beginning of something wonderful; it is the pathway from Sunday Bloody Sunday to Easter Sunday;[25] a victory won by Jesus that we have only begun to claim (as the final lyric of "Sunday Bloody Sunday" asserts). For Cave, the cross is one more instance of the negative energy of *duende*; for U2, there is a powerful positivity around this awful event. U2's foot-stomping cover version of Woody Guthrie's "Jesus Christ" captures the band's gospel enthusiasm, with its chorus of "hallelujahs" after the line "and they laid Jesus Christ in his grave."

Getting beyond the Grave—Resurrection and Return

Cave's characters ask to be judged. His recent novel *The Death of Bunny Munro* begins with the main character saying, "I am damned." And he, Bunny Munro, is indeed on a road to destruction but not without a hint of mercy. When the "Mercy Seat" death row inmate of Cave's song "The Mercy Seat" says that he is not afraid to die, he lies. He wants the electric chair really to be the Mercy Seat. But he is fearful that he is going to "hide in death a while." The anxiety over afterlife is a significant element in both Cave's and Bono's work.

In the 2006 U2 single "Window in the Skies," Bono sings a line best understood as a theology of the cross and resurrection:

> The rule has been disproved, the stone it has been moved
> The grave is now a groove, all debts are removed

It is possible to imagine Cave attracted to the lyric in one sense: the rule is disproved, the nitpickers and hypocritical power mongers lose; something more transcendent, more real, wins. But the concepts of sins forgiven, death's power broken, and resurrection seem distant in Cave's work. A very haunting minor track originally on the *X-Files* album called "Time Jesum Transeuntum Et Non Riverentum" (Dread the passage of Jesus, for he will not return) captures the fear that death is the end by focusing on the nonreturn of Jesus. Similarly, the very quiet and contemplative "Brompton Oratory" chronicles the singer sitting in church reading from Luke 24 about Jesus "returning to his loved ones"; the very unmoved manner of the singer suggests that there is nothing to believe here, and only the *pathos* of the story remains.

The question of what lies beyond is often on Bono's lips: it's the refrain of the song "Wake Up, Dead Man!" from the album *Pop* ("Tell me the story about eternity, and the way it's all gonna be"); it's what every audience at the end of a U2 concert has sung in "40" ("How long to sing this song?"); it's the destination of "One Step Closer" ("I just watch the taillights glowing"); it's the marvelously ironic "The Playboy Mansion" ("Then there will be no sorrow" and "It's who you know that gets you through the gates of that mansion"); and it's what he is waiting for "In a Little While" ("In a little while / surely you'll be back").

Bono promotes a particular Christian vision of the future in the notion of "kingdom come," revealing to Assayas that he takes Jesus at his word when he tells his disciples to pray for God's will to be done "on earth as in Heaven." This is not an overrealized eschatology on Bono's part but a view that the resurrection of Christ inaugurates the Kingdom, and so now "in science and in medicine" (as he sings on "Miracle Drug") as in other "rectifying" areas of human exertion, we find partial fulfillment of Jesus's command to welcome the stranger, heal the sick, restore the blind to sight, and return the Creation to its proper, joyful balance. It's the cry of "Peace on Earth," and it's the challenge of "Stand Up Comedy": if life is a comedy, not a tragedy, with a happy ending in love, then people need to get up and walk the talk and take a stand. I suggest "Stand Up Comedy" is written to provoke the real-life outcomes of accepting Bono's particular views on Jesus.

Your Own Personal Jesus

In *Hey! Nietzsche! Leave Them Kids Alone!* Schuftan chronicles the spiritual unraveling of Dave Gahan, singer for Depeche Mode, who abandoned his Christian faith to embrace philosophical and practical Hedonism and himself as its Messiah. In the song "Personal Jesus," he invites his listeners to "reach out and touch faith"; he has become the desired Lover, Father, Redeemer; he knows he's second best, but he says call him: "lift up the receiver and he'll make you a believer." Unlike the Jesus you pray to, he is "someone who hears your prayers/someone who cares."

This *emo* appropriation of the idea of a personal relationship with Christ is simultaneously both mocking satire and serious spiritual realignment. Cave takes the idea further into the realm of Gothic to suggest that by becoming Christlike, we create God. But both Gahan and Cave are making a profound theological—or antitheological—statement: there is no personal encounter with the spirit of God available in Jesus Christ. In one of his most beautiful songs, "(Are You) The One That I've Been Waiting For?" Cave refers to Jesus, singing, "There's a man who spoke wonders though I've never met him," and then goes on to replace the absent divine with the very present lover:

> There's a man who spoke wonders though I've never met him
> He said, 'He who seeks finds and who knocks will be let in'
> I think of you in motion and just how close you are getting
> And how every little thing anticipates you
> All down my veins my heart-strings call
> Are you the one that I've been waiting for?

This erotic song is affirming the loss of Christ in reality, though he be kept in his words. The Derridean "apocalypse *sans* apocalypse" is invoked in the sense that the messiah will never come and that this must somehow be sublimated with art and love.

But for Bono, his lyrics are like a call, a phone call, between Jesus and humanity. In "The Saints Are Coming," he "cries to his daddy on the telephone, how long? How long?" But in the recent track "Unknown Caller," Bono finds another way of expressing the "he who knocks will be let in" teaching: he who picks up "God's telephone," as Bono has described it, will be listened to, loved, and reassured. The "Unknown Caller" is surely a play on the Unknown God of Acts 17, whom the apostle Paul wants to make known to those at the Areopagus that day. When the recipient of God's call will "cease to speak" that God may speak, then Christ, the now-known Caller, has an ancient message spoken in contemporary, perhaps even corny, language:

> Restart and reboot yourself
> You're free to go
> Shout for joy if you get the chance
> Password, you, enter here, right now
> You know your name so punch it in.

This is the offer of a fresh start, a born-again moment, for the digital age. It's Christ's offer of a system reboot, the chance of freedom and joy, without losing your identity. You know your name, and your name is known.

In the open Bible that forms part of the traveling Nick Cave exhibition, Cave has added his penned notes above the Gospel of John chapter 17, asking, "Why is faith essential to eternal life, why the need to believe?" In other words, his question is, why the appeal from Christ to be more than an admirer and to be a follower and worshipper?[26] I suspect Bono answers Cave's inquiry in the lyric of "Unknown Caller" by suggesting that each of us has a password, a unique identity, that establishes a real connection with the Caller who becomes known to us when we pick up the phone.

Notes

1. Betty Spackman, *A Profound Weakness: Christians and Kitsch* (Carlisle, UK: Piquant Arts, 2005), 17.

2. Nick Cave, "The Exhibition," created and presented by the Arts Centre, Melbourne, 2007–2009. Much of the exhibition is chronicled in *Nick Cave Stories* (Melbourne, Australia: Victorian Arts Centre Trust, 2007).

3. Nick Cave, "The Flesh Made Word" (BBC Radio 3 Religious Services, 1996).

4. Michka Assayas, *Bono on Bono* (London: Hodder & Stoughton, 2005), 204–5.

5. See C. S. Lewis, *Mere Christianity* (London: Collins, 1952), 54–56.

6. Nick Cave, "The Flesh Made Word," quoted in Peter Conrad, "The Good Son," *The Monthly* (August 2009), 31.

7. Bono in Neil McCormick, ed., *Killing Bono: A True Story* (New York: VH1 Books, 2004), 334.

8. Mark A. Wrathall, ed., *U2 and Philosophy: How to Decipher an Atomic Band* (Chicago: Open Court, 2006), 38.

9. Cave, "The Flesh Made Word."

10. Nick Cave, *The Secret Life of the Love Song / The Flesh Made Word*, CD (King Mob, 2000).

11. Cave, *The Secret Life*.

12. Wiseman-Trowse's suggestion that an Elvis myth is also in operation here seems a stretch. See N. Wiseman-Trowse, "Oedipus Wrecks: Cave and the Presley Myth," in *Cultural Seeds: Essays on the Work of Nick Cave*, ed. K. Welberry and T. Dalziell (London: Ashgate Press, 2009), 157–59.

13. Nick Cave, introduction to *The Gospel according to Mark* (Melbourne: Text,1998), xi.

14. Assayas, *Bono on Bono*, 125.

15. Marilynne Robinson, *Gilead* (London: Virago, 2004), 156.

16. Roland Boer, "Under the Influence? The Bible, Culture and Nick Cave," *Journal of Religion and Popular Culture* 12 (2006).

17. Federico García Lorca, "Play and Theory of the Duende," in *Deep Song and Other Prose*, trans. C. Maurer (New York: New Directions Books, 1980), 47–48. See also Amanda G. Michaels, "Digital Duende: Reading the Rasp in E-Poetry," *Shifts: Queen's Journal of Visual and Material Culture* 2 (2009): 1–18.

18. Lyn McCredden, "Fleshed Sacred: The Carnal Theologies of Nick Cave," in *Cultural Seeds: Essays on the Work of Nick Cave*, ed. K. Welberry and T. Dalziell (London: Ashgate Press, 2009), 171.

19. Nietzsche in *On the Genealogy of Morals*, cited in Craig Schuftan, *Hey! Nietzsche! Leave Them Kids Alone* (Lowfield Heath, UK: 2009), 270.

20. Book II: "What if the breath that kindled those grim fires / Awaked, should blow them into sevenfold rage, / And plunge us in the flames; or from above / Should intermitted vengeance arm again / His red right hand to plague us?"

21. Conrad, "The Good Son," 31.

22. Assayas, *Bono on Bono*, 204.

23. Assayas, *Bono on Bono*, 204.

24. Chris Heath, *Rolling Stone* interview, quoted in Robert Vagacs, *Religious Nuts, Political Fanatics: U2 in Theological Perspective* (Eugene, OR: Cascade Books, 2005), 6.

25. See Christian Scharen, *One Step Closer* (Grand Rapids, MI: Brazos Press, 2006), 34.

26. *Nick Cave Stories*, 84.

Fallen Angels in the Hands of U2   **12**

DEANE GALBRAITH

THE FIGURE OF THE FALLEN ANGEL has a pervasive presence in the U2 songbook—and this is particularly so during the band's efflorescence in the late 1980s to early 1990s. From "Angel of Harlem" to "Trip Through Your Wires," from "Bullet the Blue Sky" to "The Fly," a fallen angel is frequently found haunting a U2 song. And when it appears, it presents us with a powerful and sublime collision of opposites: a creature at once transcendent yet earthbound, purely spiritual in form yet supremely corrupt. As the literary critic Harold Bloom observed, "'fallen angels' . . . retain a pathos and a dignity and a curious glamour. . . . However fallen, they remain angels. . . . They provoke in us . . . mingled delight and horror."[1] We are simultaneously attracted to and repulsed by fallen angels because while fallen and earthbound, theirs is a fall that is writ large—a fall, quite literally, of cosmic proportions.

What lies behind the ambivalence that we often feel when contemplating a fallen angel? Bloom's compelling explanation is that the fallen angel mirrors a major conflict at the heart of the human predicament. According to Bloom, we are beings in search of transcendence, humans who wish to be more than human, a wish paradigmatically portrayed in Milton's *Paradise Lost*, where the great fallen angel, Satan, and then Adam lament their loss of Paradise and long for return.[2] If we are fallen angels, writes Bloom, it is that "we share Satan's dilemma of what it means to be a fallen angel," having to negotiate our own loss of Eden.[3] Fallen angels represent "something that was ours and that we have the potential to become again."[4] We want to become evermore godlike, and that which is godlike about the human imagination, Bloom romantically suggests, is humanity in its pure potentiality, in wonder of what is "evermore about to be."[5] Despite Bloom's tendency to universalize what today is a peculiarly Western and especially Christian conception of humanity, he persuasively identifies the essential rationale for the mythic importance of fallen angels in the Western narrative of the human. Our intimate relationship with fallen angels rests, most crucially, on a perceived mutual conflict between our potential transcendence and actual mortality—a conflict that rages at the heart of the music of U2.

U2's Fallen Angels: Angels or Devils?

As Stephen Catanzarite observed, U2's 1991 masterpiece *Achtung Baby* is formally and thematically suffused with musical and lyrical meditations on the consequences of the Fall. The musical distortions, layered voices, and lyrical ambivalence combine to recall "the paradoxes, contradictions, inconsistencies and hypocrisies that permeate our existence" as a result of that Fall.[6] The characters in *Achtung Baby* are murky, irreducible combinations of both good and evil. We see this, for example, in "So Cruel," where a woman is unable to receive love without also hating those who love her. She acts simultaneously as tender lover and cruel sadist. The lyrics that describe her "like an angel" are immediately juxtaposed with a more sordid description that pictures her love as an addictive and manipulative drug. Instead of the subtle and vivifying transcendence of a heavenly angel, when she offers to take her lover higher, he is forced to watch her while she controls him "from above." For this is a fallen angel, not purely good or evil, but a lover whose best intentions are insidiously corrupt, a "head of heaven with fingers in the mire."[7]

During U2 concerts in the early 1990s, Bono directly confronted the fallen angel lurking within his human psyche by dressing up in the costume of his demonic alter ego, letting the devil come out and perform a few songs onstage. His inner demon sometimes took the form of "the Fly," a caricature in whom the majestic flight of a pure angel is reduced to no more than the vacuous buzzing of a dirty pest. In Christian tradition, the devil or Satan is the leader of all the fallen angels, the first to descend from his former position as a leading angel in the highest heaven. One of Satan's titles, Beelzebub, is popularly translated as "the Lord of the Flies"—a fact that suggests that Bono's Fly is in service to the devil.[8]

The structure of the chorus to U2's song by the same name, "The Fly," adds further to U2's intertwining of the angelic and the demonic within the human heart. For in the chorus, while Bono employs his normal (human) speaking voice to predict the rise and fall of man, his (angelic) gospel falsetto overlays these words with lyrics that compare man to a shining, burning star falling from the sky. In this vocal combination, the character of the Fly is shown to represent humanity in its lost potential, that is, subsequent to Adam's original sin and its cosmic consequences: "It's no secret that the stars are falling from the sky / The universe exploding 'cause of one man's lie."[9] Within the chorus's complex musical layering, therefore, the fallen human and the fallen angel are revealed to be intimately interconnected. Yet neither the human nor the angelic voices are simply identified as either wholly good or wholly evil. For the fallen human is ever reaching upward for a lost glory, "like a fly on a wall," while conversely his shining angelic potential is "falling from the sky." The character of both fallen humans and fallen angels are alike in that their goodness is utterly contaminated by evil.

The culmination of Bono's parodies in the early 1990s was the character Mr. MacPhisto—a washed-up campy cabaret singer cum devil, influenced by Faust's Mephistopheles and Screwtape, the fictional devil invented by fellow Irishman C. S. Lewis.[10] Bono's MacPhisto was as tragic as he was evil. He acted thoroughly devilish in renditions of U2's "Desire," lusting after money "like a preacher stealing hearts at a traveling show."[11] And then he revealed a pathetic innocence in his falsetto chorus of Elvis Presley's "I Can't Help Falling in Love," which Bono explains is intended to portray "the little boy inside the corrupt man breaking through for a moment."[12] In this manner, the ambivalent, conflicted figure of the fallen angel that determines the representation of the human ended up being projected back onto the great fallen angel himself.[13]

There is, of course, a fairly long history of sympathy for the devil in rock and roll—that is, for the heroic, iconoclastic, authority-defying Romantic devil. Romantic poets such as William Blake have exalted both human desire and satanic self-determination in ways that approximate rock music's glorification of "raw human emotion," unrestrained sexual desire, and rebellion.[14] Yet in MacPhisto, Bono blatantly parodies this side of the rock singer and, thus, himself—well aware of the history of hubris and decadence in rock and roll but equally aware of the futility and vanity of any person who claims to rise completely above his or her inner fallen angel. So the one-sided, Romantic, and rock culture emphasis on the devil as a heroic "rebel without a cause" is balanced by U2's portrayal of MacPhisto as a pathetic, self-centered, and ultimately evil figure. In this, U2 stands squarely with Milton and C. S. Lewis rather than with William Blake. As a result, any alleged glory that this fallen angel cum fallen rock star possesses is exposed as illusory. And in the costume of a washed-up rock star, ironically portrayed on U2's own rock concert stage, Bono also clearly mocks his own human inability to be wholly good, acknowledging the complex mixture of good and evil, angel and devil within any human being.

The Jewish and Christian Apocalyptic Origin of the Fallen Angel

From where does U2's conception of fallen angels ultimately derive? Although the idea of good and evil angels has precedents in ancient Persian religion, the most formative and influential formulations are to be found in the apocalyptic writings of early, pre-Rabbinic Judaism and in early Christianity. The earliest surviving account of fallen angels is found in the *Book of Watchers*, written no later than the third century BC and possibly even earlier. In this account, a group of twenty angels conspire to descend from heaven when they find themselves unable to resist the beauty of human women and desire to have sexual intercourse with them. After the fallen angels had satisfied their desire, their human wives give birth to monstrous hybrids, giants who tower 450 feet tall and devour all the produce of the land, prompting the giants to turn their substantial appetites to human flesh and even on one another. The rebellious angels wreak further havoc on Earth, teaching their wives forbidden magical knowledge, not to mention various beauty tips such as the application of eye shadow and the wearing of jewelry. The fallen angels also teach humanity the art of making weaponry and the secrets of astrology. But in the end, God intervenes by destroying the giants in the Great Flood and imprisoning the fallen angels below Earth, where they await his final judgment.

There are many versions of this story that have survived from Hellenistic and later periods—a testimony to the story's ongoing authority and popularity. In the many retellings of the myth of the fallen angels, a number of variations emerged, some of which should be briefly mentioned to illustrate the breadth and scope of the tradition. In one variation, the rebellious angels wage war in heaven in an attempt to dethrone God.[15] For example, in *The Life of Adam and Eve* (ca. 100 BC–AD 200), Satan and a group of angels are cast out from the presence of God after they refused to worship Adam. Satan pompously protests to the archangel Michael, "I will not worship one inferior and subsequent to me. I am prior to him in creation." When Michael threatens God's wrath, Satan declares his intent to wage war against God himself, to "set [his] throne above the stars of heaven and . . . be like the Most High."[16] But instead, Satan is cast out of heaven. In another variation of the myth, the fallen angels are identified with the so-called wandering stars—that is, the planets, which, as ancient astronomers observed, took a course across the night sky that was different from the path traveled by the majority of constellations. In early Jewish texts, stars were frequently identified as angels. So it was a small further step to identify these wandering stars as the rebellious angels who had departed from the paths prescribed by God.[17] In one further variation, the angels are originally sent to Earth by God himself to teach knowledge and justice and to have authority over humankind. But the angels later rebel against God by abusing their authority, either by acting as tyrants over the nations or by mating with human women.[18] Although there are many differences between these fascinating accounts, we can discern a number of common and recurring elements. We almost always find a description of a rebellion against God by a group of angels, an explanation for the introduction of violence or illicit knowledge or death into the world, an account of the descent or expulsion of the rebellious angels from heaven, and notice of their eventual punishment and imprisonment either on or below Earth.[19]

One of the most notable aspects of the earliest of these narratives is that they assign the ultimate blame for the origin of death and evil—not to humans—but to fallen angels. As such, human sin is only a secondary consequence of prior angelic evil. Furthermore, fallen angels are blamed as the ultimate cause of all subsequent evil in human history, due to the actions of their sons, the giants. For after the Great Flood, while the bodies of the giants have been destroyed in the flood waters, the spirits of the giants survive. These spirits become known as "demons," which are responsible for all the temptations faced by human beings.[20] This account of evil might come as a surprise to those more accustomed to the narrative of Adam and Eve in the Garden of Eden. For in the Genesis account, it is humans who are responsible for the first sin, for the loss of Eden, and for the introduction of death and suffering. Ancient Judaism therefore had two competing explanations for the origin of evil and death. It is very difficult to determine which tradition was earlier, and in all probability, given the lack of any clear signs of dependence, they may have developed in parallel.[21]

However, from about the second century BC, the narrative of a human responsibility for the Fall began to prevail. We begin to read accounts stating that angels only fell to Earth after Adam and Eve had sinned, and we learn that demons appeared on the scene only after humans had already been sinning for some time.[22] In Genesis 1–11, as in the second century–BC book Jubilees, Adam and Eve sin before any provocation from the fallen angels. The serpent that tempts Eve in Genesis 3 is never identified as a fallen angel (instead, it is merely a talking snake), and the Fall of the angels does not occur until a much later period, in the time of Noah (Genesis 6).[23] Furthermore, the demons in Jubilees only begin to tempt humans after the Great Flood, by which time humans had already been committing evil acts for some time.[24] Each of these accounts reverse the chronology of the Fall, place the human Fall before the angelic Fall, and shift the primary responsibility from the heavenly/angelic to the earthly/human realm.

Yet despite this shift of emphasis, the authority of the fallen angel tradition was so great that for centuries afterward almost every substantial account concerning the Fall of humans also featured elements from the account of the fallen angels. The most important contribution of the fallen angel tradition was to create an emphasis on the cosmic dimension to human, earthly sin—which in Christian (though not Jewish) tradition later led to the doctrine of Original Sin.[25] Thus, Bloom's identification of the intimate relationship between humans and fallen angels can also be understood as a consequence of the complex transmission of the two traditions, in which the human Fall narratives were interpreted and rewritten in light of the angelic Fall narratives. The Fall may be presented as the responsibility of humankind in books such as Genesis and Jubilees, but traces remain of a further, angelic cause that shifts the blame far beyond human responsibility.

Fallen Angels in U2's Apocalyptic Vision

This cosmic dimension to the Fall of humanity has both spatial and temporal dimensions. The earthbound, evil, fallen angels oppose the heavenly, good angels in a battle fought throughout the span of universal history, which will culminate in a final end-times battle and divine judgment. This conception of reality is usually referred to as an "apocalyptic" worldview.[26] U2's music displays fundamental continuity with this apocalyptic vision of good and evil, frequently projecting human ethical struggles onto a cosmic canvas. In "I Still Haven't Found What I'm Looking For," the moral choices that Bono has made throughout his life are alternately aligned with the ranks of benign or evil angels: "I have spoke with the tongue of angels; I have held the hand of a devil."[27] U2's lyrics are filled with allusions to an invisible cosmic dimension existing behind earthly ethical and existential struggles. The lyric "If you just close your eyes you can feel the enemy" refers to this unseen dualistic battle as well as the invisible moral battle waged within.[28]

U2's apocalyptic mind-set, as articulated by Bono in 1981 at a seminar for Christian bands, is made more clear in his explanation of how he understood the band's ongoing battle with the great fallen angel, Satan:

The same Satan that is evident in Kampuchea, in the starving peoples there, is the same Satan who is working in the Marquee clubs, through drugs, whatever, here, right, in this country. It is the same Satan. He is waging war on the Lord and on us. And by fighting him, by getting involved in *battle*, you're fighting Satan. Getting involved in battle doesn't necessarily mean running off to the obvious areas, like Kampuchea or whatever it is. There is a battle to be fought at home. And the battle for us was in U2, just being what we are, just Christians.[29]

From Bono's description of this perceived satanic attack on U2, one might expect that he is referring to plagues and pestilences of biblical proportions. But in fact, the context was a dispute that Bono had with the band's own manager, Paul McGuinness, over the length of time U2 was taking to record a song. An annoyed McGuinness had provocatively asked how a Christian band could justify spending thousands of pounds recording a single when there were people starving in Kampuchea. From Bono's description of the conflict, we see that he aligns himself on the side of "the Lord," fighting a battle that not only had an earthly dimension in the recording studio and the impatience of their manager but also a spiritual dimension in an ongoing satanic war being waged against God.

Although at the time Bono was likely speaking with the fervor of youth and was still very much under the fundamentalist influence of the Shalom Fellowship, U2's lyrics continued to evidence an essentially apocalyptic worldview throughout the ensuing decades, with the spiritual battle lines becoming more nuanced and interiorized. This is even evident in "Fire," the very song that U2 was recording at the time McGuinness challenged them to hurry it up. The song is filled with end-times apocalyptic imagery culled from Revelation 6:12–13, which describes the sun turning black, the moon turning red, and stars falling from the sky. Yet U2 utilizes this imagery to paint a picture of the interior battle between one's God-given spiritual passion and one's tendency to "fall down," knocked down to the ground by the falling stars. In this particular sense and despite Bono's protestations to the contrary about "Sunday Bloody Sunday," this song can rightly be called a rebel song. For the lyrics subvert the militant's focus on external enemies by pointing inwardly to "the trenches dug within our hearts," where the real battle is believed to be fought.[30] In U2's perspective, the cosmic battle takes aim at our own television-numbed immunity that prevents us from pursuing justice. It is not, primarily, a battle between "us" and some external "them."

Likewise, U2's fallen angels are ambiguously good *and* evil and ambiguously human *or* angelic. For they are combatants in an ongoing cosmic battle focused on interiority—cosmic projections of human spiritual war-fare. In "She's a Mystery to Me," which Bono and the Edge wrote for Roy Orbison, a woman likened to a "fallen angel" behaves as sweet savior of the night and demonic succubus.[31] She is heavenly in the dim nightlight yet hellish in the full light of day. Her love is ethereal yet so sharp that it tears her lover apart. As her lover melts under the power of her love, heaven becomes darkness. Reminiscent of the woman in "So Cruel," the battle lines are not so much between heaven and hell but between the heaven and hell that battles within us all.

Another famous, ambivalent angel in the U2 catalog is the real-life angel Billie Holiday, who is described in "Angel of Harlem" as "a star exploding in the night; filling up the city with broad daylight."[32] Just as in early Jewish apocalyptic literature, a fallen angel appears here in the guise of a fallen star. The song juxtaposes Holiday's almost infinite ability to transform and enlighten everyone around her by the power of her ethereal voice with the swollen eyes that betrayed her mortal struggle with alcohol-ism. The contradictory mix is inherent in the song's title, which conjoins the angelic to an image of the grim ghettoes of early-twentieth-century Harlem. As an "angel in devil's shoes," Holiday transforms her pain into sublime music, transcending her Harlem beginnings yet never fully resolv-ing her inner hurt and pain. As Bono sings in "Crumbs from Your Table," with more than a sideways glance at himself, "From the brightest star / Comes the blackest hole."[33] U2's stars are usually dazzling and dying, both angelic and fallen.

(Re)Negotiating the Tensions

At this point, I could proceed by producing a whole host of comparisons between fallen angels in early Judeo-Christianity and in U2. But such an approach tends to reinforce the commonly held distinction between an original, static text and its subsequent stream of reception—which is to some degree artificial. In his analysis of the Revelation of John, James Harding comments that the book's meaning "is inextricably bound up with the entire odyssey of its use, reception, and effect" so that any analysis of the so-called original meaning is "not different in kind from the study of its reception and subsequent construals."[34] Any construal of the biblical and extrabiblical texts concerning the Fall is merely an arbitrary freeze-frame in an ever-flowing stream of negotiated meaning that extends to the poetry of Milton to the music of U2 and to U2's listeners. So a better approach may be to ask not only how ancient Jewish and Christian texts shed light on U2's lyrics but how U2's negotiation of the tensions in the tradition helps us to read those ancient texts.

Slavoj Žižek observes that these narratives of the Fall, which tell the story of a certain loss that occurred between two points in time, in fact "obfuscate the *absolute synchronicity* [emphasis added] of the antagonism in question. . . . When a certain historical moment is (mis)perceived as the moment of loss of some quality, upon closer inspection it becomes clear that the lost quality emerged only at this very moment of its alleged loss."[35] That is, only when the narrative of the Fall was created did Paradise come into being, as an ideal constructed from the fabulous gap between present reality and our imagined utopian potential. If this is so, the many ongoing reformulations of the fallen angel tradition never aim to overcome the tradition's inherent tensions; they in fact *sustain* them. Valorized as "paradoxes," the tensions are integral to the very conception of the Fall so that to address these tensions *directly*, to expose them, would result in the collapse of the entire tradition.

I have already alluded to what I see as the major tension within the tradition: if there was an angelic Fall at the beginning of time, this implies that—even before humanity came along—the world was already corrupted, already imperfect. So on the one hand, all these references within the tradition to fallen angels, cosmic battles, and so on, amplify the sinfulness of humanity in the Fall—by painting human sin with dark satanic brushstrokes. But on the other hand, the role given to fallen angels tends to *de-emphasize* human responsibility, by suggesting that the real reason for evil is so much bigger than us. The successful maintenance of the tradition is dependent on emphasizing the former effect while obfuscating the latter.

Steven Harmon rightly notes in "U2: Unexpected Prophets" that orthodox Christian doctrine admits a tension between "the not-yet transformed nature of the world on the one hand and hope for its transformation on the other."[36] The orthodox Christian formulation explains the tension in terms of the cosmic effects of human sin, which require an apocalyptic end-times transformation of the cosmos and humanity for their full eradication. This theme is taken up in some detail by Stephen Catanzarite, who introduces his position with a quotation from Augustine: "Whatever we are, we are not what we ought to be."[37] Catanzarite's commentary on *Achtung Baby* interprets each song on the album in light of the Christian and, in particular, Catholic doctrine of the Fall. He is surely correct that the doctrine of the Fall is central to the themes, moods, and musical dynamics of *Achtung Baby*. But his book has the primary aim of commandeering the album for a heavily theological elucidation of Catholic doctrine. This is not to fault the book on its own terms but only to acknowledge the limitations of the particular lens through which he explores *Achtung Baby*—as is, in fact, openly admitted in the book's introduction, which rather candidly and playfully admits, "This is not a book about U2."[38]

U2's hope for an end-times reversal of the Fall—for restoration of justice and of humanity itself—is certainly voiced with startling regularity in their lyrics.[39] Yet the manner in which U2 expresses this hope should not be too quickly assimilated to the catechism of the Catholic Church, as does Catanzarite.[40] As Michael Gilmour discerningly points out, "a pervasive ambivalence is hard to miss" in U2's particular expression of that hope. The confidence with which Bono prays, "Jesus, throw a drowning man a line," is matched by the despair that drives him to lament that he just "can't wait any longer" in "When I Look at the World."[41] U2 does not fail to ponder whether the ultimate responsibility for evil may reach beyond humanity altogether. Bono's deeply felt appreciation of the immediacy of human suffering drives him to question, much like the psalmists of old, whether even God himself is responsible for this "fucked-up world." While in "Wake Up Dead Man" he expresses the hope that the problem of evil can be resolved at the end of time, as simply as rewinding a tape recorder, we should not miss the despondent if not sarcastic tone in which he voices that hope.[42] The dissonance between vocal tone and lyrical meaning leaves room for doubts that continue to challenge orthodox tradition, to which Bono still tenaciously holds. The U2 listener is in a very different position from the reader of a Catholic catechism. For U2's music does not intend dogmatic closure but remains open ended and intentionally ambiguous, both expressing orthodox Christian hopes while posing challenges to those same traditions.

What I suggest is that this tension concerning the nature of evil is not something that can be so easily resolved by appealing to the orthodox Christian doctrine of the primeval Fall or to humanity's end-times restoration—and that this very fact is reflected in the ambivalent nature of U2's artistic renegotiations of the tradition. The tension is integral to the tradition itself—in which the fallen angel is both a sign of the seriousness of human sin and a hint that evil extends beyond human responsibility to an ultimately heavenly origin. It adds to our appreciation of the artistry of U2 that we detect a similar tension in their music; for U2's music is not simply an assimilation of the tension in orthodox Christian doctrine but is also poking and prodding at the very limitations of orthodoxy's construction. The ambiguities in U2's music are never fully reduced to the tension between "the not-yet transformed nature of the world" and the future hope for restoration but also indicate a residual unease with the doctrines themselves.

U2's Fallen Angels: "Faraway, So Close!"

The complex relationship between the human and the fallen angel is explored in detail in the lyrics and video of one of U2's finest compositions, "Stay (Faraway, So Close!)."[43] The song introduces us to a woman who is seeking deliverance from the violence of her domestic life. Hope is "faraway, so close," like the modern technologies of radio and "satellite television," which have the ability to take her anywhere in the world without really taking her anywhere at all. While she can talk along with people on television talk shows, she cannot receive any genuine human contact. This "faraway-closeness," which is all that the medium of television has to offer, is paralleled by a figure in the song who is indistinguishably human or angelic and who offers her salvation while also being hopelessly out of reach. While this angelic figure asks her to stay just one night with him, to effect her salvation by removing her from the violent relationship, it is never clear whether he has made his offer audible to the woman. The climax to the song is beautifully ambiguous. At three o'clock in the morning, there is a bang and a clatter "as an angel hits the ground." *An* angel—the article is indefinite, and so is the angel's identity. Is this "hit" the final, fatal hit resulting from the strike of the abusive partner from the opening verse? Is this hit the self-induced suicidal hit on the ground which ends her pain? That is, is the woman the broken, fallen angel? Or, alternatively, is this the unseen angelic protector, who has always been present throughout the song but has remained impotent, unable or unwilling to intervene? Has he given up his divine distance, fallen from the heavens, and come to provide help that is both close and real?

Further interpretive options are presented by U2's video and the feature-length film on which it was based, *Wings of Desire*, both produced by Wim Wenders. In the film, two guardian angels are responsible for watching over the residents of a gray and bleak divided Berlin, only able to observe and record the suffering endured by people on Earth but unable to intervene or to provide any tangible assistance. It is only by giving up their immortality, by falling to Earth, immersing themselves in contingency, that the angels can establish real contact with human beings, to assist by sharing in their pain. The song itself was written for the film's sequel, *Faraway, So Close!*, and the music video also portrays the members of U2 as angels, invisibly inspiring members of a young rock band—until the angelic Bono falls from the heavens and hits the ground in synchronization with the sudden ending to the song. Yet the song "Stay" retains a polysemy that is not matched by the music video. And adding to the complexity of it all, the angels in Wenders's own films are themselves symbolic of the fragmentation and homelessness of the modern urban *human*. Therefore, it is in this very excess and intertextual crisscrossing of potential meanings that "Stay" reveals, first, the complexity of the relationship *between* humans and fallen angels; second, the complexity within the human, as one who desires transcendence and yet must plunge into absolute finitude to fully embrace life; and, third, the ambiguous responsibility for the human predicament. For the evils of modern life represented in "Stay" are capable of being interpreted in two quite opposite yet equally legitimate ways: either as the fault of human actions and modern independence or as a fault of the divine distance and remoteness that preordains this situation.

"If There's an Order in All of This Disorder"

In U2, as in early Jewish and Christian narratives, the ongoing reformulation of the fallen angel motif preserves and even further complicates rather than overcomes the tensions that are inherent to the tradition of the human Fall. The intertwining of both angelic and human Falls has two opposite effects in respect of human responsibility for evil: the angelic Fall both heightens human blame by lending it a cosmic dimension; it also excuses humans by indicating a further, angelic cause of evil in which humans are the victims rather than the perpetrators. While U2 continues to affirm the orthodox doctrine of the Fall and its apocalyptic end-times reversal, the multivalent dimensions of the band's music also poke and prod at its very construction. U2's music and performances renegotiate the parameters of the tradition, opening up spaces for a wide range of listener responses and elucidating both the orthodox formulations of the Fall and its inherent tensions. Yet, in the final analysis, it would appear that U2 never wishes to finally dissolve those tensions and always stops short at the attempt to do so, secretly wanting the paradox to continue—without going so far as to admit its nature as a fatal contradiction that would collapse the entire tradition. Indeed, U2's lyrics and performances generate much of their artistic power and energy—whether consciously or unconsciously—from probing and exploiting tensions in the conception of humanity, angels, and evil, which have existed at the heart of Western tradition for the last two thousand years.

Notes

1. Harold Bloom, *Fallen Angels* (New Haven, CT: Yale University Press, 2007), 13, 17.

2. Bloom, *Fallen Angels*, 46. Bloom's contention is that "angels have always been metaphors of human possibilities either unrealized or thwarted." He lyrically describes our "angelic mode of apprehension" as "the anticipation that, in exalted moments, seems to stand tiptoe in us" (47). Milton is indebted to late medieval narratives that describe the Fall of the angels, themselves deriving from the early Jewish and Christian narratives.

3. Bloom, *Fallen Angels*, 46.

4. Bloom, *Fallen Angels*, 23.

5. Bloom, *Fallen Angels*, 47.

6. Stephen Catanzarite, *Achtung Baby: Meditations on Love in the Shadow of the Fall* (New York: Continuum, 2007), 3–4.

7. U2, "So Cruel," *Achtung Baby* (Island Records, 1991).

8. Bono's familiarity with the term *Beelzebub* is demonstrated in U2's early song "Shadows and Tall Trees," *Boy* (Island Records, 1980), the title of which is taken from a chapter in William Golding's *Lord of the Flies* (1954). Golding's novel frequently alludes to Beelzebub/Satan and allegorically portrays the Fall of humanity.

9. U2, "The Fly," *Achtung Baby* (Island Records, 1991).

10. Bono acknowledges that his main inspiration for Mr. MacPhisto came from his reading of *The Screwtape Letters*, by C. S. Lewis; see Steve Stockman, *Walk On: The Spiritual Journey of U2* (Orlando, FL: Relevant Books, 2005), 106. In fact, in the video to "Hold Me Thrill Me Kiss Me Kill Me," Bono is portrayed reading a copy of *The Screwtape Letters*, and his intent to mock the devil (so as to cause him to flee) derives from the same book.

11. U2, "Desire," *Rattle and Hum* (Island Records, 1988).

12. Bill Flanagan, *U2: At the End of the World* (Toronto: Bantam, 1995), 208.

13. Cf. Jeffrey Burton Russell, *Mephistopheles: The Devil in the Modern World* (Ithaca, NY: Cornell University Press, 1986), on the humanity and depth of character of the Mephistophelean (64–65) and Miltonic (97–99) Satans.

14. Laura Lunger Knoppers and Gregory M. Colón Semenza, eds., "Introduction," in *Milton in Popular Culture* (New York: Palgrave Macmillan, 2006), 9.

15. 2 Enoch 29:4–5; Ascension of Isaiah 10:13; Questions of Bartholomew 4:53–57; cf. Qur'an 2:34.

16. *The Life of Adam and Eve*, 12–15.

17. The ancient Jewish identification of stars with angels: Daniel 12:2–3; LXX (the ancient Greek translation of) Job 38:7; Book of Dreams 86; Epistle of Enoch 104:2–6; Revelation 19:17. The regularity of the stars as a model for human behavior: Book of Watchers 2:1–5:7; Sifre Deuteronomy 32:11. The identification of wandering stars as fallen angels: Book of Watchers 18:13–16; Astronomical

Book 80:6–7; Irenaeus, Proof, 16; Against Heresies 4:40.3; 5:24.4; Tertullian, On Patience, 5; Gregory of Nyssa, Catechetical Oration, 6.

18. Apocalypse of Abraham 13:9–11; Book of Dreams 89:59–90:1; Jubilees 3:15, 5:1–2; 7:21–22.

19. See Book of Watchers 6–7; cf. Genesis 6:1–4; Similitudes of Enoch 69:4–5; 2 Enoch 18:4; Justin, 1 Apology 5; Athenagoras, A Plea for the Christians, 24.

20. Book of Watchers 19; Book of Giants.

21. The Book of Watchers can date no later than the third century BC, because its influence can already be traced in works that date to the early second century BC—including Jubilees and the Book of Dreams—and the work itself appears to be the result of the compilation of even earlier stories. This contrasts with the story of the disobedience of Adam and Eve from Genesis 3, of which there is no citation elsewhere in the biblical books and which is still regularly overlooked in biblical paraphrases and rewritings from Qumran. Cf. 1 Enoch 32:6, which clearly refers to a similar story but with differences concerning the identification of the trees, which suggests that it may be an earlier, pre-Genesis 2–3 variant. Most significantly, none of the biblical passages that catalog the sins of humankind ever refer to the Adam and Eve story. Margaret Barker concludes, "The most likely explanation is that the story [of Adam and Eve] was added to the Old Testament at a very late stage in its compilation, and placed as a preface to the whole work." *The Lost Prophet: The Book of Enoch and Its Influence on Christianity* (Sheffield, England: Sheffield Phoenix Press, 2005), 37.

22. Angels fall after human sin: Genesis 2–3, 6:1–4; Jubilees 3, 5; demons appear after human sin: Jubilees 10; cf. Apocalypse of Abraham 23:11–13; 4 Ezra 7:1; 2 Baruch 48:42, 54:15–19. The Christian Testament of Reuben, from approximately AD 100, even claims that women tempted the angels to descend from heaven, by treacherously charming them with their feminine beauty (5:1–6). See also Annette Yoshiko Reed, *Fallen Angels and the History of Judaism and Christianity: The Reception of Enochic Literature* (Cambridge: Cambridge University Press, 2005).

23. Genesis 2–3, 6:1–4; Jubilees 3, 5.

24. Jubilees 10.

25. Augustine, *City of God,* 14, 16.

26. The seminal definition of apocalyptic is given in *Semeia* 14 as "a genre of revelatory literature with a narrative framework, in which a revelation is mediated by an otherworldly being to a human recipient, disclosing a transcendent reality which is both temporal, insofar as it envisages eschatological salvation, and spatial insofar as it involves another, supernatural world." John J. Collins, "Introduction: Towards the Morphology of a Genre," *Semeia* 14 (1979): 1–20, 9.

27. U2, "I Still Haven't Found What I'm Looking For," *The Joshua Tree* (Island Records, 1987).

28. U2, "Acrobat," *Achtung Baby* (Island Records, 1991). Quoting Bruce Cockburn, U2's "God Part II," *Rattle and Hum* (Island Records, 1988), envisages a struggle of good and evil in terms of a battle between the forces of darkness and

the forces of light: "Heard a singer on the radio / late last night / Says he's gonna kick the darkness, 'till it bleeds daylight." The battle of the forces of light against darkness recalls the apocalyptic tone of the Dead Sea Scroll known as The Community Rule (1QS), in which all good humans are ruled over by an unseen angelic "Prince of Light" and all evil humans by an equally invisible "Angel of Darkness." Only after a prolonged battle against the forces of evil and darkness will righteous humans be reincorporated into the divine light originally intended for Adam. Spatially, the battle reaches through the different levels of the heavens, in which fallen angels or their demonic offspring are in continuous battle with good angels. And, temporally, this battle is ongoing, until the end of the age, at which time all will be restored to the Edenic conditions that prevailed at the beginning of time.

29. Bono, "U2's Vision," CD (Littlehampton, England: Dream Depot, 2005), author's transcription (emphasis is Bono's own). I am most indebted to Beth Maynard for alerting me to its relevance for this chapter.

30. U2, "Sunday Bloody Sunday," *War* (Island Records, 1983).

31. Roy Orbison, "She's a Mystery to Me," *Mystery Girl* (Virgin, 1989).

32. U2, "Angel of Harlem," *Rattle and Hum* (Island Records, 1988).

33. U2, "Crumbs from Your Table," *How to Dismantle an Atomic Bomb* (Island Records, 2004).

34. James E. Harding, "The Johannine Apocalypse and the Risk of Knowledge," 123–50, in William John Lyons and Jorunn Økland, eds., *The Way the World Ends: The Apocalypse of John in Culture and Ideology* (The Bible in the Modern World, 19; Sheffield, England: Sheffield Phoenix Press, 2009), 125. The fallen angel myth has never been a unity or a complete myth, but to employ Claude Lévi-Strauss's phrasing, "simply a transformation, to a greater or lesser extent, of other myths," where he is referring to the Bororo myth. *The Raw and the Cooked*, Introduction to a Science of Mythology 1, trans. John Weightman and Doreen Weightman (Harmondsworth, England: Penguin, 1986), 2. Cf. Jacques Derrida, "Structure, Sign and Play in the Discourse of the Human Sciences," in *Writing and Difference*, tr. Alan Bass (Chicago: University of Chicago Press, 1978), 286. If we are to examine a fallen angel tradition in its openness to other texts then, as Claude Lévi-Strauss advises, it is necessary to examine all the available versions of the tradition. "There is no single 'true' version of which all the others are but copies or distortions. Every version belongs to the myth." "The Structural Study of Myth," in *Structural Anthropology*, tr. Claire Jacobson and Brooke Grundfest Schaepf (New York: Basic Books, 1963), 218.

35. Slavoj Žižek, *The Plague of Fantasies* (London: Verso, 1997), 12–13.

36. Steven Harmon, "U2: Unexpected Prophets," *Christian Reflection: A Series in Faith and Ethics* (January 2006): 81–88, 85.

37. Catanzarite, *Achtung Baby*, 1. He is apparently quoting Fulton John Sheen's purported quotation of Augustine from *Peace of Soul* (New York: McGraw-Hill, 1949), 38, as Catanzarite goes on to quote Sheen at length on the following page.

The alleged quote is probably a paraphrase of Augustine's thought (e.g., *City of God,* 12–14).

38. Catanzarite, *Achtung Baby*, xii.

39. For example, U2, "Tomorrow," "With a Shout (Jerusalem)," *October* (Island Records, 1981); "New Year's Day," "40," *War* (Island Records, 1983); "The Unforgettable Fire," *The Unforgettable Fire* (Island Records, 1984); "The Playboy Mansion," *Pop* (Island Records, 1997); "In a Little While," "Peace on Earth," *All That You Can't Leave Behind* (Island Records, 2000); "Yahweh," *How to Dismantle an Atomic Bomb* (Island Records, 2004).

40. For example, Catanzarite, *Achtung Baby*, 13.

41. Michael J. Gilmour, "The Prophet Jeremiah, Aung San Suu Kyi, and U2's *All That You Can't Leave Behind*: On Listening to Bono's Jeremiad," *Call Me the Seeker: Listening to Religion in Popular Music*, ed. Michael J. Gilmour (New York: Continuum, 2005), 34; U2, "Peace on Earth" and "When I Look at the World," *All That You Can't Leave Behind* (Island Records, 2000).

42. U2, "Wake Up Dead Man," *Pop* (Island Records, 1997). Cf. Bono, "The Book of Psalms," 133–40, in Jamie Byng, *Revelations: Personal Responses to the Books of the Bible* (Edinburgh, Scotland: Canongate, 2005); Brian J. Walsh, "Wake Up Dead Man: Singing the Psalms of Lament," in *Get Up Off Your Knees: Preaching the U2 Catalog*, ed. Raewynne J. Whiteley and Beth Maynard (Cambridge, MA: Cowley, 2003), 37–42.

43. U2, "Stay (Faraway, So Close!)," *Zooropa* (Island Records, 1993).

WHEN I LOOK AT THE WORLD   IV

Bono's Rhetoric of the Auspicious   **13**
Translating and Transforming Africa for
the Consumerist West

BRUCE L. EDWARDS

MARSHALL MCLUHAN, THE LATE, GREAT, FEARLESS, imperious chronicler of mediadom, gave away the secrets of the Internet age more than fifty years ago in books full of maxims, paradoxes, and puns, including *The Mechanical Bride*, *The Gutenberg Galaxy*, and *Understanding Media*.[1] McLuhan saw the future: image rules, persona is everything—not as an extrapolation of who you really are but as a simulacrum of the who you prefer to project. Good morning, meet my "avatar."

Critical terms such as "global village" and "the medium is the message" and concepts such as "media are extensions of the five human senses" and the acute differences between "hot" and "cool" media—these we all owe to the provocative offhand neologisms tossed out by Professor McLuhan. (Serendipity was the source more often than not of his asides cum insights: a fourth book planned after *Understanding Media*, its title intended as *The Medium Is the Message*, came from the publisher misprinted as *The Medium Is the Massage*. Keep it as is, McLuhan demurred, for it fortuitously captured even more of his meaning: "Now there are four possible readings for the last word of the title, all of them accurate: 'Message' and 'Mess Age,' 'Massage' and 'Mass Age,'" he quipped.[2])

The quirky vocabulary and unique phraseology associated with McLuhan's work have perhaps outlived the actual substance of his thesis—that is, that we live in a mediated age, our senses overrun, our worlds created and interpreted for us by Mad Men from Madison Avenue. Yet, they continue to drive much of our academic discourse about media, diagnosing the effects of pervasive advertising on our consciousness and our consciences. Academics of his time and since have tended to invest these elliptical terms with whatever stipulative content they wished to foreground and then use their vague explanatory power to bring gravitas to their analysis.

Which is exactly my plan.

As I offer my pro bono defense of the transformative rhetoric of Bono's autophilanthropic enterprise to reduce AIDS, poverty, violence, and despair in the real villages of Africa, I lean on and take liberties with siphoned resources from McLuhan. To recognize Bono's genius, we need to understand essentially that he turns McLuhan's project inside out to achieve his laudable humanitarian goals. Bono manages, if you will, a kind of ethical ventriloquism that equips people to do the right thing despite their bad habits, despite their natural tendencies, redeeming the consumeristic lifestyle they have embraced rather obliviously for good.

McLuhan positioned us to recognize that we're clumsy and halfhearted and hypocritical about the way that we pretend to negatively analyze certain kinds of persuasive discourse—for example, advertising copy. We know that we are not supposed to be susceptible to manipulation, but we so enjoy the chase; there is pleasure in consumer surrender. He exposed the carefully constructed art of being tricked willingly into purchasing things we don't want or really need, because in the act of being a dutiful consumer, we sense it somehow transfers a value to us, albeit an illusory one, that we think we seek, a range of products whose image conveys a life or lifestyle we aspire to embrace and to be known for embracing.

Our eyes, ears, nose, fingers, tongues serve as conduits and envoys for goods that we think ennoble us before the watching world. In McLuhan's milieu, that meant primarily a public audience of some sort. But the privatization of public behavior that can now be broadcast afar, the expansion of "my audience" into millions of strangers who may look or listen in, this phenomenon awaited the Internet age, proving the validity and prescience of McLuhan's sometimes overheated pronouncements. What was once mere living for one can now be a performance before millions.

America's Super Bowl is the most-watched television event of the year, and some even watch the game. But the bigger, more diverse audience assembles for the commercials that play between game action, priced anywhere from $1 million to $2 million for as little as thirty seconds of airtime, depending on placement during the broadcast, thirty seconds of powerful image and sound saturation and insidious voiceovers. You can hardly pass through the video or audio section of a Big Box store these days without noticing that it sells—and people are buying, mind you—items such as "The 100 Greatest TV Commercials" or "The 50 Most Beloved Advertising Jingles." How is it we would deliberately choose to obtain and consume wistful reminders of what once amused or distracted us while captive of their product lines? As consumers it seems that we even like to recall and thereby relive the feelings we once had of owning and being owned by a prior buying adventure. These are Bono's people.

Famously defamed in Vance Packard's 1957 "subliminal advertising" expose *The Hidden Persuaders*,[3] romanticized in today's *Mad Men* AMC series, denounced by hundreds of commentators on the left and on the right as ingeniously commodifying vicarious sex or domestic violence or homoeroticism or what have you, today's manipulation by advertisement becomes tomorrow's beloved nostalgia. We want to be seduced, and if it is something wearable—all to the good. That famous director, the one whose esoteric interview about aesthetics we want to catch—why he cut his teeth making sexy music videos and sexist television commercials. The tools for art and the tools for sales are indistinguishable. How could anyone expect virtue to arise from these despicable scenarios in which we are deliberate victims as well as perpetrators, our jail doors locked on the inside?

Surveying the culture of the 1960s, Walker Percy, the brilliant twentieth-century modernist fiction writer and erstwhile Christian apologist, once observed that a man with a distinct and urgent message, the primary merit of which was that it was true, could nevertheless suffer from its becoming too well believed, too well known, thereby losing its power to convict and thereby becoming impossible to be heard in the cacophony of advertising and mediaspeak in the modern age. The truth is mistaken for something else: an ineffective beer commercial, perhaps, or, worse, a product that inexplicably did what it claimed to do and thus is more threatening than one that promises everything and nothing. We want to believe that blondes do have more fun. Thus, Percy:

> The Christian novelist is like a man who goes to a wild lonely place to discover the truth within himself and there after much ordeal and suffering meets an apostle who has the authority to tell him a great piece of news and so tells him the news with authority. He, the novelist, believes the news and runs back to the city to tell his countrymen, only to discover that the news has already been broadcast, that this news is in fact the wealthiest canned spot announcement on radio-TV, more commonplace than the Exxon commercial, that in fact he might just as well be shouting Exxon! Exxon! for all anyone pays any attention to him.[4]

Percy found himself wondering, as the 1960s ended, whether anybody would ever again be able to distinguish between genius and mere cleverness, between authentic news from home, our true home, and the latest, artificially hyped delivery of "data" that have the merit of being neither true nor false, all in the eye and ear of the beholder. The commonplace. Believed by all and therefore, as Percy's spiritual mentor Kierkegaard said, believed by no one. Too many voices all saying the same thing, or one voice saying the one, unique thing, have the same effect: incredulity. "I have news" means "Exxon! Exxon!" And vice versa. (And Percy, like McLuhan, didn't witness the Internet Age.)

Enter Bono, the Armchair Anthropologist

And so let us say that things are as pundits McLuhan and Percy distantly observed but with greater stakes, for we have reached a time of the apotheosis of their prophecies, not only a time in which it is likely that we are yielding willingly and with aforethought to become the enablers of our chosen advertisers but a time in which we have also become able producers of advertising ourselves, capable of turning all things and everything into, in Norman Mailer's terms, "advertisements for myself." Let us also say that we have come to the time when the machineries of state production do now indeed belong to the proletariat, as we are poised to take ourselves captive, writing ransom notes to ourselves for our soul's release, self-deception as self-actualization mediated through our amateur command of the technology that we inhabit as host or that inhabits us as parasite.

Bono has in fact discerned that we do live in such a time as this. As a public figure, a celebrity, Bono has himself participated in many reincarnations and self-creations; that is, he has been a rock musician. Bono has lived through and profited by several eras of human media experiments. And he has mastered its grammar. And through becoming self-aware, unlike most of us, he uses this new sentience for nefariously good purposes. The hidden persuaders are no longer so hidden if you and I can see them and embrace or reject which ones we want to choose to manipulate us. The romanticization of product placement and advertisement by favorite fetish is not a theory to Bono; he has embodied it, onstage and in the recording studio.

My contention is that Bono has successfully demonstrated within a hypercritical landscape the effectiveness of a rhetorical platform little observed by friend or foe—carefully subverting our tendency to reject rock star do-gooders and guilty appeals to share the West's profound wealth by deliberately proposing novel, mercantile solutions that mesh seamlessly with our deeply embedded consumerist lifestyles. He understands the deep structure of buying. Simultaneously exemplifying and inverting McLuhan's and Percy's insights, Bono's campaign and U2's music each propose a self-consciously maddening method and platform for inculcating redemptive, eleemosynary mass behavior amid people ill disposed to it. Note Bono's misdirection here at the end:

> So much of the discussion today is about value, not values. Aid well spent can be an example of both, values and value for money. Providing AIDS medication to just under four million people, putting in place modest measures to improve maternal health, eradicating killer pests like malaria and rotaviruses—all these provide a leg up on the climb to self-sufficiency, all these can help us make friends in a world quick to enmity. It's not alms, it's investment. It's not charity, it's justice.[5]

It's not alms, it's investment. It's not charity, it's justice. In this phrasing, these are these juxtapositions: alms = appeal to conscience; investment = appeal to pocketbook; in turn, charity = guilt mongering, while justice = contributing out of an ethical alignment. What breathtaking realignments!

To assist in saving the lives of actual inhabitants of the African continent, Bono has deliberately chosen to move incognito as the informed armchair anthropologist that he is among the affluent and the politically powerful, taking good notes, cataloging what makes them tick, what persona motivates their action. The verdict here: the investor who also seeks justice is the persuading persona.

Bono does this while all the while masquerading himself, humbling himself as it were, in the arch capitalist role, all to divert the First World's resources to the most disadvantaged and, thus, the most impervious to manipulation by media. Is it possible to be ethical and generous against one's will? Bono aims to find out as an insider. Shouting "Exxon! Exxon!" he, too, has made his peace with commoditization if it will save lives: Product (Red), his coinvention with Bobby Shriver of the Kennedy clan, depends on a host of suppliers and collaborators as part of his "rebranding Africa" effort, not as a tactic to sell Africans his wares but as Africa as a warehouse to which the profits can flow. As he explains in the editorial preface to the *Vanity Fair* issue that he guest edited in July 2007:

> Without our corporate partners—American Express, Apple, Emporio Armani, Converse, Gap, and Motorola—we could never afford such bright neon, or the acres of bold billboarding. These companies are heroic (and—shock, horror—we want them to make money for their shareholders because that will make (Red) sustainable). In the project's first nine months, $25 million has gone directly from (Red) partners to the Global Fund, which grants money to health-care organizations around the world to fight aids, tuberculosis, and malaria. That is more than Australia, Switzerland, and China contributed last year.[6]

This is Bono's transformative rhetoric at work: turning CEOs and stockholders into "heroes" for doing what comes naturally to them, making money. Eliminating the "middle man" and asking for direct donations instead misses the point, drawing water from a well that will soon dry up. The middle man is he or she whom Bono wishes to capture in his net; for it is the ease with which the consumer who buys the product he or she is going to buy anyway—that is the key. The exchange of images and personas at the point of sale is the epitome of McLuhan's masterful phrase *the medium is the message*; the purchase is the donation; the nobility of the purchase is the value added. As Bono told the *New York Times*, for whom he has written a series of op-eds over the last several years that lay out his transformative project, "Africa is sexy and people need to know that."[7] By which he means,

> I've played that tune. I've talked of tragedy, of emergency. And it is an emergency when almost 2,000 children in Africa a day die of a mosquito bite; this kind of hemorrhaging of human capital is not something we can accept as normal.
>
> But as the example of Ghana makes clear, that's only one chord. Amid poverty and disease are opportunities for investment and growth—investment and growth that won't eliminate overnight the need for assistance, much as we and Africans yearn for it to end, but that in time can build roads, schools and power grids and propel commerce to the point where aid is replaced by trade pacts, business deals and home-grown income.[8]

Africa is herein (re)galvanized as a place of value, of opportunity, by being certified as a place worthy for transactions that benefit both parties to the deal. The goal therefore is twofold: (1) rebrand Africa, no longer let it be seen primarily as a place of "emergency," a place of devastation (war, poverty, disease, tyranny) but rather of "adventure" (i.e., investment and growth) and (2) diagnose the Western consumer conscience and move to recalibrate it to warrant the alignment of personal mercantile success and ebullient self-image with debt relief, economic justice, and return on investment. That's the theory, at least. Let's look at the practice.

The Rhetoric of the Auspicious: A Kairotic Sensibility

U2's "I'll Go Crazy If I Don't Go Crazy Tonight" suggests quizzically, "Every beauty needs to go out with an idiot." How so? It seems that both can learn something from the experience.

For the beauty, the idiot delivers perspective while still captive of her enchantments, keeping her properly skeptical about her good looks, honest about their effects. The beauty, however, provokes in the idiot momentary inspiration all the while leaving behind a residue of wistful longing for her permanent company. Indulge me, then, in a playful analogy derived from the lyrics of this song to explain my own motivations and point of view: every anthology needs a tour de force. Count me a respectful idiot amid the camp of true believers, the beauties, one might say. I can get away with saying things that the true believer can't, for it would seem untoward and disrespectful to the beloved. Regard me as one whose incipient faith in U2 rests less on the companionship and expert testimony of the faithful themselves and rather more upon the remonstrance of their chosen redeemers, the appeal of their public personas.

I am a congenial inquirer wanting to peddle my discovery of something in Bono's volumes of words about Africa I've never seen accounted for elsewhere. I believe this discovery can be useful among his knowledgeable admirers but especially among his detractors. I find there to be something of incalculable and surprising value at work in Bono; thus, I offer my perspective on his long public campaign to bring attention and relief to Africa and its multiple challenges as a continent.

My aim here is to provide a slightly more nuanced explication of Bono's notable command of what best can be described as the rhetoric of the auspicious. Our phrase serves our postmodern Internet age as a concept roughly akin to what classical rhetoricians called *kairos*, a term that rhetorical historian Sheri Helsey eloquently capsules as "right timing and proper measure—directly related to the rhetorical importance of time, place, speaker, and audience, the proper and knowledgeable analysis of these factors, and the faculty of using the proper means in a particular context to arrive at belief."[9]

In classical study, kairos is typically juxtaposed with *chronos*, another Greek word for time, as sometimes a complementary, sometimes a competing, conception of "time": the eternal versus the now, the everlasting versus the temporary. Kairos is comprehensive auspiciousness: how and why and when and to whom and for whom something should be said. Chronos represents, one might say, mere chronology: registering that something was said, without context or conditions. Kairos captures a moment in time, so to speak, that somehow stands for all moments; chronos accounts for and pinpoints a particular moment as but one in a succession of endless moments.

In some ways, my use of this concept in connection to Bono is even better epitomized in the New Testament in the Book of Ephesians 5:15–16, where Paul exhorts, "Walk circumspectly . . . redeeming the time, for the days are evil" (King James Version). That the days are evil and full of troubles suggests an urgency to speak and to act; thus, time (and here it is the noun form of our Greek term *kairos*) must be "redeemed," taken advantage of, used to the fullest, while we can, as we can—because walking circumspectly also means walking redemptively, demanding that we operate with high seriousness, integrity, and purpose. This, in essence, forms my central contention in this chapter: Bono possesses unique rhetorical prowess in positioning us to see how lives and civilizations in peril—but not helpless—may be assisted and rescued with the resources of those who have previously lacked vision or motivation to do so, by seizing the occasion to provide that vision and that motivation by the most unusual acts of reimaging and sleight of hand.

Let's imagine that you have only "heard" of Africa, never seen it, but the building blocks that you have been given consist solely of words such as *famine, poverty, disease, corruption, catastrophe, burden.*

Vision requires basic literal sight and not only metaphorical, or what McLuhan would identify as "mediated," sight; I must see what is clearly and unromantically there yet without the prelabeling that would block one's line of sight. To take unmediated or direct action, I cannot just see what I plan to see or hope to see. When we lack the ability to see this way, we must have help; we must have an alternate source of images and a different way of entering the constellation of images out there. Bono talks frankly about obstacles of incurring vision, of rejecting the portrayal of Africa only as a "burden," and thereby he challenges his audience to resee and thus reify Africa as opportunity, as adventure.[10] How is it that he, his activism, and his music enable us to witness and acknowledge that which we otherwise could not have glimpsed, recognized, embraced? By auspiciousness, timeliness, and kairos. Auspicion requires the seizing of timing and opportunity, the wherewithal and the courage to speak and act, to regard an audience empathetically and projecting them as capable of vision and capable of action in spite of themselves.

What here rivets my rhetorical attention is Bono's willingness to spend the capital of his fame and fortune on those and for those whose health and safety and acclaim and glory may await a world to come if we fail to act. What Bono remarkably manages to do is translate and transform the image of Africa from one of helplessness and devastation and thus perpetually in need of the West's self-prepossessing rescue and intervention to one of hopefulness and a continent naturally positioned by its vigorous meekness to inherit Earth, wealth, and prosperity of the twenty-first century. Not at the expense of anyone but to the advantage of all. The rhetoric of auspiciousness delivers an Africa not full of parties to be pitied but of partners to be engaged.

What is controversial and deemed suspicious by the undiscerning is the fact that Bono has coyly injected elements of Western consumerist assumptions and behavior into his "redeeming of the times," his reimaging of Africa. The goal is to reframe our Western notions of Africanness, by admitting, without erasing, the continent's diversity, historical complexity, and undeniable exploitation, as well as its images of perpetual victimhood and its presumed and primary helplessness—but then confronting and complementing this extant image base of the prior environment through intentional substitution of new imaging: images of potential, images of talent plentitude, images of indigenous "opportunity" and "adventure," not in an exotic Indiana Jones or Allan Quartermain sense but in an economic and politically liberating sense, Africa recommissioned for the benefit of both audiences, the African and the Westerner.

Rhetorical auspiciousness is the art of choosing when and what to say to the high and to the low about momentous, complex, divisive, world-wearying issues that confound undersecretaries of state departments, theologians, pundits, world economists, local economics, noneconomists, even everyday ordinary listeners to music. Auspiciousness itself honors a certain attention paid and acknowledgment made that the spokesperson indeed has chosen the right and ripe time to speak and that he or she has successfully assembled by hook and crook a private and public audience of appropriately astonishing diversity and authority to act that makes the effort to communicate the new Africa worthwhile, its strategic plan marshaled among kings and queens who bestow credibility, perhaps even achievability.

In Bono's case, this auspiciousness also comprises the audacity and courage it takes (let alone the capacity to absorb and deploy) to turn the economics of globalization or universal health care on its head and demand from those possessing their jurisdiction to accomplish them through application of justice and due mercy. This auspiciousness embodies the temerity not only to sing the truth to power on behalf of the powerless in arenas and concert halls amid the corps of idolizing audiophiles but to pull up a chair beside the heads of nations and churches and to ask expectantly, "May we reason together?"

It is one thing to pen a stirring anthem or deeply reflective meditation on the fate of the poor, the catastrophically disenfranchised, the imprisoned, the marginalized, or the sick and dying. (Nearly every entertainer with the slightest conscience has once or twice in his or her career joined a telethon or a sing-a-thon or fashioned a foundation of this or that sort to funnel "aid" and emotional reparations to the destitute or dispossessed.) It is another thing entirely to have made it one's aim not just to be the funnel or financier but rather to become the informed, driven exemplar of good faith and, what is more, practical strategy.

They who command the rhetoric of the auspicious seize the day to help articulate modest proposals of all sorts and to broker remedies on behalf of those who cannot determine whether they will eat on a given day, let alone plan a banquet for dignitaries a month ahead of their humanitarian fact-finding visits. Bono, in fact, has deployed this kairos-saturated rhetoric of the auspicious but has done so not from a perch or a palace or some perfectly safe haven, by remote control as it were, but in the midst, down there, hands on, incarnate, not from theory but from determined, quotidian practical grace.

Bono's skill and conviction, the shrewdness and the cunning, may be linked to his understanding of Jesus of Nazareth's admonition to be "wise as a serpent, harmless as a dove." I am still learning how to grasp and to delineate what qualities Bono possesses to enable him to be at once a rock star, a diplomat, a psalmist, a dad, a husband, and a witness. And if I am a bit late to this daunting task, perhaps it is fortuitous; for it seems on the surface that it would be much easier, though perhaps even more daunting in the end, simply to isolate a pivotal period in U2's career and analyze/ interpret a selective compendium of lyrics and themes and symbols that inevitably point us to this epiphany of philanthropy that Bono and U2 have reached.

I have already charted what something like this would look like in my head: emerging from their lucrative but principled vocations, album by album, their work is premised on the task of moving listeners from their protected self-image onto painfully realized historical self-awareness, leading to redemptive self-analysis, leading to risky public self-commitment, and, finally, to a premium self-identification with those less poised for privilege, so notoriously "other" than themselves.

Powerful as that analysis may prove to be for those better prepared to produce it, the more interesting portrait to sketch over time is how one crosses (or even chooses to cross) the line from clueless celebrity to artful problem solver, risking the opprobrium of a media who specializes in hypocrisy detection and the backlash of potentially fickle fans who tire of causes and charities. From my preliminary observation, Bono acknowledges no such sense of career risk, nor any concession to careerist cynics whose job is to ignore what is perfectly obvious to him and those who have looked through his eyes: the immediate needs of the afflicted, the orphaned, the hungry, the wounded, and the dying when the West continues to prosper and stabilize, recessions and stunted recoveries notwithstanding.

But this is the unique challenge that he does recognize amid the early decades of the twenty-first century: we are prone to compassion fatigue over the immediate needs of the afflicted, orphaned, hungry, wounded, and dying. Those exploits must be, as my title attempts to capture, translated into opportunities, then transformed into adventures even for the West to see them, to acknowledge them, and to reach out to them, and they to us, reciprocally. To do this, one must acquire then exercise the rhetoric of the auspicious.

Strategies and Tactics: Addressing Bono's Cultured Detractors

"We needed help in describing the continent of Africa as an opportunity, as an adventure, not a burden." This is Bono detailing how and why he had assembled the crew of writers who contributed to the *Vanity Fair* issue he edited. With this phrasing, Bono leapt for the first time into the very public project of rebranding Africa and redeeming our consciences, his motive explained elsewhere: "We need to get better at storytelling. . . . Bill Gates tells me this all the time. We've got to get better at telling the success stories of Africa in addition to the horror stories. And this magazine tells great stories."[11]

But it was not his first time that he had used his rock celebrity status to commandeer an editorship. The United Kingdom's *The Independent* granted Bono the editorial reins of its May 16, 2006, edition. In early January 2006, Bono had explained a rudimentary form of the rhetoric of auspiciousness to a European correspondent for *MTV News*:

> Red is a 21st century idea. I think doing the Red thing, doing good, will turn out to be good business for them. . . . This is not a rock star cause, it's an emergency. . . . We launch this today with four companies, we want 40, then 400, we are looking for the best and the brightest to work with us.
>
> Red is about *doing what you enjoy and doing good at the same time* [my emphasis]. It's not philanthropy, it's business. Philanthropy is hippy, this is punk rock, even more it's hip-hop, they want to make money in the ghettos.[12]

Notice how "emergency" has slipped in, to distinguish it from a mere "rock star" cause, but as we know, this will later be explained away, edited out of his presentations to emphasize his proposed new imaging for Africa. Or, rather, it will be inverted: the emergency becomes ours, not Africa's; it is our souls that are at stake. He's careful also to distinguish this "business" venture from "philanthropy," which is a hindrance, a headache, portrayed as an antiquated idea. Here it is: It's simply "doing what you enjoy and doing good at the same time," an appeal that menaces no one but buoyantly lifts up the person attentive to its effects. But it is important to note how deep the roots for Bono's campaign really are and how early these strategic notions were present in an embryonic form in Bono's previous encounters with the rich and politically famous.

James Traub has helpfully drawn the curtain back from one revealing episode in his lengthy 2005 profile of Bono, "The Statesman," for the *New York Times Magazine*, to show one of Bono's earliest, direct engagements with the powerful using his incipient grasp of the rhetoric of auspiciousness:

> By the summer of 1999, Bono was ready to take on Washington. The Clinton administration was already committed to canceling two-thirds or so of the $6 billion that the poorest African countries owed the United States, but Bono wanted 100 percent cancellation—not only because he thought it was right, but also because you can't sing about two-thirds of something. "It has to feel like history," he says. "Incrementalism leaves the audience in a snooze." [Bobby] Shriver arranged for Bono to meet with Gene Sperling, President Clinton's chief economic adviser, and with Sheryl Sandberg, chief of staff to Lawrence Summers, who had just been named secretary of the treasury. Summers himself was not about to waste precious time meeting with a rock star. He did agree, however, to "drop by" while Bono spoke to Sperling. Bono laid out his argument. "He was deeply versed in the substance," Sandberg recalls. "He understood capital markets, debt instruments, who the decision makers were."
>
> Summers tried to give Bono the polite brush-off. "These are complicated issues," Summers told him. "I'll have to take it up with the G-7 finance ministers." And now this earnest, impassioned rock star with the accent of a racetrack tout issued a call to destiny. "You know what," he told Summers, "I've been all over the world, and I've talked to all the major players, and everyone said, 'If you get Larry Summers, you can get this done.'" "It was," Sandberg says, "a really important moment. I think we were all inspired and motivated."[13]

Several things stand out from this account. First, Bono understands the language and the substance of global economics and thereby disarms an audience that might otherwise not take him seriously, someone like Larry Summers, for instance. He rejects the notion of "incrementalism," which lacks momentousness and the "kairotic," or timely, urgency. It has "to feel like history." Bono appeals here to another kind of image exchange; those who concur with debt relief stand with those who are reversing centuries of oppressive colonialism and, best of all, preventing a benevolent form of neocolonialism in which First World bankers hold them hostage. Finally, Bono recognizes the vanity of a leader like Summers, detecting what ego massaging must take place to get his consent; as it turns out, it's the simplest, most basic appeal, one as old as the Garden: "Ye shall be as gods." Larry Summers needs to know that his peers on the other side of the world think he's the lynchpin for the whole enterprise.

Traub later explains how Bono had gotten "attached" to African issues originally:

> Why Africa? Why not, say, global warming? Part of the answer is happenstance: Africa is what Bono got swept up into. But Africa, or so Bono feels, needs what only a certain kind of world figure can give—a call to conscience, an appeal to the imagination, a melody or a lyric you won't forget. The cause of ending extreme poverty in Africa speaks to Bono's prophetic impulse. Rock music, for him, is a form of advocacy, but advocacy is also a form of rock music. His definition of "sing" includes speeches and press conferences, and his arenas include Davos and Capitol Hill. Among his best work is the rallying cry. He often says, "My generation wants to be the generation that ended extreme poverty." There's not much evidence that this is so; but Bono has helped make it so, in part by repeating such resonant phrases.[14]

Traub may be understating the case for the success of Bono's "rallying cry"; it is hard to name another rock celebrity of Bono's stature who has sustained his advocacy and refused to shrink back from public disdain regarding his insistent call for generational greatness. Bono's achievement is not only that he has generally "raised consciousness" but has among the mighty and the lowly, the affluent, and the nearly rich, stirred them to conversation about Africa and then to action, action that may be buying a mocha latte or a (Red) T-shirt, but action all the same that was not taking place before he raised his voice.

Later that year, Paul Theroux, famed travel writer, novelist, and Africanist, wrote a piece that is representative of many a critique offered by those offended by Bono's bravado in seeking economic remedies for Africa's plight. Here, Theroux attempts to elucidate "the rock star's burden," an allusion to Rudyard Kipling's infamous poem, "The White Man's Burden." In his essay, Theroux excoriates the presumption and wrongheadedness he sees afoot in Bono's efforts.

> It seems to have been Africa's fate to become a theater of empty talk and public gestures. But the impression that Africa is fatally troubled and can be saved only by outside help—not to mention celebrities and charity concerts—is a destructive and misleading conceit.
>
> Africa has no real shortage of capable people—or even of money. The patronizing attention of donors has done violence to Africa's belief in itself, but even in the absence of responsible leadership, Africans themselves have proven how resilient they can be—something they never get credit for. [15]

Theroux's broadside is essentially a strong reaction to all kinds of Western do-gooders, including missionaries, and can stand for a dozen other jibes and diatribes against celebrityhood and coercive philanthropy. But it also shows that Theroux is not really paying attention. In point of fact, in large measure Bono agrees with him that the false notion that "Africa is fatally troubled" is indeed "a destructive and misleading conceit." It is clear that Bono continues to learn from his dialogue in country with African colleagues and understands perhaps even better than Theroux that "Africans themselves have proven how resilient they can be." In a recent *New York Times* op-ed, he has described his sojourn with such "resilient" Africans:

> These are not victims and do not demand such attentive pity. What they desire is collaboration, partnership, self-determination.
>
> Over long days and nights, I asked Africans about the course of international activism. Should we just pack it up and go home, I asked? There were a few nods. But many more no's. Because most Africans we met seemed to feel the pressing need for new kinds of partnerships, not just among governments, but among citizens, businesses, the rest of us. I sense the end of the usual donor-recipient relationship.
>
> Aid, it's clear, is still part of the picture. It's crucial, if you have HIV and are fighting for your life, or if you are a mother wondering why you can't protect your child against killers with unpronounceable names or if you are a farmer who knows that new seed varietals will mean you have produce that you can take to market in drought or flood. But not the old, dumb, only-game-in-town aid — smart aid that aims to put itself out of business in a generation or two. "Make aid history" is the objective. It always was. Because when we end aid, it'll mean that extreme poverty is history. But until that glorious day, smart aid can be a reforming tool, demanding accountability and transparency, rewarding measurable results, reinforcing

the rule of law, but never imagining for a second that it's a substitute for trade, investment or self-determination.

I for one want to live to see Mo Ibrahim's throw-down prediction about Ghana come true. "Yes, guys," he said, "Ghana needs support in the coming years, but in the not-too-distant future it can be giving aid, not receiving it; and you, Mr. Bono, can just go there on your holidays."[16]

A more severe and academic criticism appeared in the *Journal of Pan African Studies*, in September 2008, in an article by Teresa Barnes, whose own opening summary lays down all her cards:

> The Product Red campaign rests on a quartet of mistaken assumptions. The first is that the consumption of commodities in the Western world has no particular relationship to Africa's problems and therefore increasing such consumption is a neutral exercise, free from side effects. The second mistaken assumption is that AIDS rages through Africa at pandemic strength due mainly to a lack of funds for medicines. Next, the campaign assumes that it is permissible to continue to cast the African continent in the role of passive recipient of First World largesse. Finally, Red broadcasts the idea that social change is easy.[17]

Barnes's article is marred by several fundamental misunderstandings or misconstruals: Red was never a program to fund Africa; rather, it was a way to rally Western consciousness to encounter a new and different Africa. In a sense, she takes Bono too literally. Bono is advocating that in the act of "doing what they enjoy" or "doing what they were already going to do," consumers might as well buy that coffee or those T-shirts so that the brand generates and confers its own honorific. Nowhere does Bono make the mistake of assuming that consumption is neutral; rather, he argues it can be redirected, its agency rewarded with serving a dual purpose: self-satisfaction and covering the cost of an antiretroviral dose.

Neither does Bono equate the increased availability of medicine with an overall solution to the pandemic of HIV/AIDS; instead, he must be seen as making the simple appeal that one more dose keeps one victim alive one more day and that in itself is an unalloyed good. No one knows better than Bono that we must keep the reality of individual dilemmas before us in acutely drawn, personal narratives, lest we lose the intimate face of suffering—and relief. The needs of the one need not be sacrificed for the needs of the many, for the ultimate solution requires a comprehensive and multifaceted strategy: generational courage and aspiration to rise to greatness. Finally, Bono's campaign is not interested in reaffirming that

Africa must play the role of passive receptor of donor aid; no one who has followed the rhetoric of auspiciousness at work in Bono's presentations could possibly conclude anything other than that he wishes to empower individuals with the choice to determine their own futures.

As to whether the Red enterprise characterizes "social change as easy," one must surmise that Barnes must never have listened to U2's music. In the same song we referred to earlier, "I'll Go Crazy," Bono sings, "Is it true that perfect love drives out all fear? / The right to appear ridiculous is something I hold dear / Oh, but a change of heart comes slow." In reserving "the right to appear ridiculous," Bono acknowledges that what he has been doing, how he has oriented his career and that of his band, would be quite foolish if he didn't believe in his campaign, ready to risk untold millions of income to challenge his audience to respond. He fathoms that "a change of heart comes slow," but undaunted, undeterred, he ventures on. He understands what gets lost behind the headlines. Lives are at stake.

An Auspiciousness for Africa

The modern world owes much of its pseudoknowledge of Africa, its images and metaphors, from the jaded reports of adventurers such as Henry Stanley and Richard Burton. It was their published journals as explorers, alongside the more empathetic and compassionate Rev. David Livingstone, that gave Victorians their thrills and their astonishment at the continent. Their accounts gave Europe its sensory experience of "darkest Africa." How long has their convenient demonization and diminution held sway, through their repetition of images of the presumed exoticism and primitivism of Africa, proffered by raging social Darwinists such as Thomas Huxley?

Truth be told, we see Africa not much differently from the times and days and images that were represented in the breathless reports of these Victorian social desperados. But there was an active counternarrative, starting from William Wilberforce, the great antislavery crusader, through to William Booth, founder of the Salvation Army. Wilberforce begins and extends the narrative of equality; Booth appropriates the metaphor of darkest and writes a provocative tract called "in Darkest England," a rebuke to our instinctual tendency to elevate ourselves by diminishing others. Part satire, part diatribe, part environmentalist, Booth's over-the-top performance enraged Huxley, who denounced Booth as a dangerous socialist who would essentially undermine Western civilization with a basic egalitarianism that impedes and reverses the march of progress toward en-lightenment and the ascension of the human species.

These social reformers, practicing their own version of the rhetoric of auspiciousness, arrested the development of these sentimental Africana images to point out that African men and women were also men and women like themselves, deserving of respect and autonomy. It is in this line of descent that I believe we can place Bono, whose efforts to translate Africa for Western eyes and transform its possible futures within the historical tradition of Christian controversialists mirrors the tremendous achievements of these social reformers.

There is one other comparison to be made that may be even more salutary. Bono implicitly shares with his spiritual mentor and fellow Irishman C. S. Lewis the view that we are the "quarantined planet"—"unique" and demanding a redemptive visit from God, not because we merit it, but precisely because we demerit it. Like Edwin Ransom, Lewis's hero in his science-fantasy novel *Out of the Silent Planet*, who stands to thwart the sinister Earth-based imperialists exporting their love of torture and environmental destruction across the galaxy, Bono too attempts to dramatize the human condition using melodies and lyrics to assist in rescuing humanity from itself, a world drunk on its own alienation from its creator. Bono's humanitarianism is thus intrinsic to his Christian conviction that while we may, even in our better moments, not regard humankind as worth saving, God continually does, for He made us in His image. And if God chooses to act on our behalf, against his own "self-interest," so to speak, how can we not feel compelled to share from our bounty the "cure" with those who may not generate it on their own?

In closing, let me give Bono the last, literally eschatological word that once more foregrounds this kairotic moment:

> There are some things where the scale of the problem has you just in a spin. For me, and for others, I think you try on all fronts to fight this war. And I would be, personally speaking, in the blackest despair were it not for my faith in people and in God, and actually my faith even in people who don't believe in God. You see over the years impossible situations have been turned around, the idea that women would vote . . . the idea that what happened in southern states of the United States, with the civil rights movement, it's an extraordinary thing. We look back at periods where humankind looked barbaric, really barbaric. Slavery is barbaric. And yet, economic slavery is what we're talking about here in Africa. Sending our church plates but not letting them trade, there's something noxious about that to God.

When we're holding children to ransom for the debts of their grandparents, it just blows smoke up the nostrils of God, the God I believe in, and I really see this as not only about the lives of our sisters and brothers in Africa but about our own souls. This is the defining moment of our generation. This is what we're about. We'll look back in 50 or 60 years, people will say did you really let 20 to 30 millions of people die whilst you had medicines that you could easily manufacture and distribute? And people are going to swallow hard. If the questions are not asked in schoolbooks in the future, they're certainly going to be asked when you meet your maker.[18]

Notes

1. Marshall McLuhan, *The Mechanical Bride: Folklore of Industrial Man* (New York: Vanguard Press, 1951); *The Gutenberg Galaxy: The Making of Typographic Man* (Toronto, Canada: University of Toronto Press, 1962); *Understanding Media: The Extensions of Man* (New York: McGraw Hill, 1964).

2. http://marshallmcluhan.com/common-questions/ (accessed January 10, 2011).

3. Vance Packard, *The Hidden Persuaders* (Philadelphia: McCay, 1957).

4. Walker Percy, "Notes for a Novel about the End of the World," in *The Message in the Bottle* (New York: Farrar, 1975), 117.

5. Bono, "It's 2009. Do You Know Where Your Soul Is?" *New York Times*, April 18, 2009, http://www.nytimes.com/2009/04/19/opinion/19bono.html.

6. Bono, "Message 2U," *Vanity Fair*, July 2007, http://www.vanityfair.com/magazine/2007/07/bono200707.

7. David Carr, "Citizen Bono Brings Africa to the Idle Rich," *New York Times*, March 5, 2007, http://www.nytimes.com/2007/03/05/business/media/05carr.html.

8. Bono, "Rebranding Africa," *New York Times*, July 9, 2009, http://www.nytimes.com/2009/07/10/opinion/10bono.html.

9. "Kairos," in *Encyclopedia of Rhetoric and Composition*, ed. Theresa Enos (New York: Garland, 1996), 371. For more information, also see "Kairos: A Neglected Concept in Classical Rhetoric," in *Rhetoric and Praxis: The Contribution of Classical Rhetoric to Practical Reasoning*, ed. Jean Dietz Moss (Washington, DC: Catholic University Press, 1986), and James Kinneavy and Catherine Eskin, "Kairos in Aristotle's Rhetoric" *Written Communication* 11, no. 1 (1994): 131–42.

10. Bono, "Message 2U."

11. David Carr, "Citizen Bono."

12. http://www.mtv.tv/news/Bono-sees-red-over-Aids-12628/ (accessed January 12, 2011).

13. James Traub, "The Statesman," *NY Times Magazine*, September 18, 2005, http://www.nytimes.com/2005/09/18/magazine/18bono.html.

14. Traub, "The Statesman."

15. Paul Theroux, "The Rock Star's Burden," *New York Times*, December 15, 2005, http://www.nytimes.com/2005/12/15/opinion/15theroux.html.

16. Bono, "Africa Reboots," *New York Times*, April 17, 2010, http://www.nytimes.com/2010/04/18/opinion/18bono.html.

17. Teresa Barnes, "Product Red: The Marketing of African Misery," *Journal of Pan African Studies* 2, no. 4 (2008): 71, http://www.jpanafrican.com/docs/vol2no6/2.6_Product_Red_Marketing_Of_African_Misery.pdf.

18. David Yonke, "Keep Africa Pledge, Says Bono," *Toledo Blade*, July 8, 2003, http://www.toledoblade.com/apps/pbcs.dll/article?AID=/20030708/NEWS10/107080058.

Boy, Baby, and Bomb   **14**
U2's Use of Antilanguage

JOHN HURTGEN

ANTILANGUAGE IS LITERALLY "BACK TALK." However, it is not sass for sass's sake. Antilanguage was originally the theory of British linguist M. A. K. Halliday (as he articulated in *Language as Social Semiotic*, 1978), which describes the counterreality-generating system and language of a cultural subgroup. A subgroup registers opposition against a dominant group—often the only way it can, with words—while at the same time creating an alternative reality for itself.[1] Antilanguage is always more than an alternative reality; it is always language in conscientious opposition to a dominant group.

According to Halliday, antilanguage is characterized by *relexicalization*, in which the old words of the dominant culture will be given new meaning; *overlexicalization*, for which multiple words will be used for important concerns of the subgroup; and all kinds of verbal play (from puns to intertextuality), which will be used to generate an alternative conceptual reality over against a dominant culture. A perfect example in US American culture is the antilanguage of rap, which at least initially arose in poorer urban neighborhoods: words were relexicalized, that is, given different meanings (the word *rap*, for one, and *hood*, for another); words were overlexicalized, that is, multiple words were used for focal concepts (money, cars, drugs, women); and rap is now known the world over for its creative, stinging verbal play.

How, you might ask, could one apply this linguistic category to "the greatest rock group in the world," whose lyrics more often than not are of justice, faith, struggle, and God? One of the few rock-and-roll bands to do so positively, U2 has sought (implicitly and explicitly) to create an alternative reality for its hearers. "The goal" is not "sex, drugs, and rock 'n' roll" but—as Bono would declare during the Elevation tour in "Beautiful Day"—"the goal is soul," life lived and pursued on a different plane. Yet, that different plane generates tension from U2's first song on the first album to the last song on *No Line on the Horizon*. And that tension is in turn generated by and given expression in the antilanguage it has consistently created. First, I look a little closer at antilanguage, then I consider the ingredients that initially went into the creation of a community known as U2, and, finally, I look briefly at three U2 songs to demonstrate songs of U2 as antilanguage.

Sociolinguistics and Antilanguage

At the heart of Halliday's theory is the idea of language as a signaling system (or, semiotic), which is embedded within an encompassing cultural matrix. Language thus becomes "a resource, a meaning potential."[2] Language has a meaning-generating potential and possesses the ability to encode information on at least three levels: content, form, and expression—that is, in linguistic terms, semantics, lexicogrammar, and phonology.[3] When we employ language—at the sounds, words, sentences, and meanings levels—we are encoding social information that simultaneously generates and maintains a given reality or worldview. When you do this, as someone either disaffected or marginalized by a dominant group, Halliday theorizes that often persons (always a subgroup) will use language in such a way as to register opposition against someone else. Their language, the antilanguage, is for group use only and for in-group use only (not for outsiders).

The functional components (or metafunctions) of all languages are, according to Halliday, the ideational (language as reflection), the interpersonal (language as action), and the textual (language as actual verbal expression, in relation to the environment).[4] We employ language, first, ideationally to construe a model of experience or to construct logical relations between things and/or persons. We want to speak of doing and happening (what's going on), of processes of sensing (how someone feels about something), and of other relational notions (who has or doesn't have, who is or is not). We employ language, second, interpersonally to enact social relationships. Halliday was never one to do linguistics by just looking at sample sentences to get at structure and meaning. The interpersonal component (or metafunction) of language means that there is always some social exchange with another, or others, in view. We employ language, third, textually to create relevance to context. If we're going to tell a fairy tale, then we'll begin by saying, "Once upon a time," because we know that how you say something vis-à-vis its social context is vital (right down to intonation, register, even regional dialect [assumed or genuine]). The textual component (or metafunction) of language no doubt emphasizes the innate and socialized abilities that we have to create with our soundings, wordings, and meanings powerful (but also sometimes boring) speech acts.

Yet, Halliday again theorizes, when a group begins to create an antilanguage, it focuses on the latter two components—the interpersonal and the textual—because of prime importance is the interpersonal and the textual. The two functions are prime: interpersonal (language as it stresses the tension between two groups) and textual (language as it creatively registers opposition and generates alternative reality with all kinds of wordplay). Antilanguage is language, but it is pathological language—that is, language that evinces that something is wrong with the dominant culture and something right with a subgroup (or that at least needs to be heard).

What does antilanguage look like? Halliday's initial study included linguistic samples from the counterculture of vagabonds in Elizabethan England, antisociety in modern Calcutta, and the subculture of Polish prisons and reform schools.[5] Examples of other studies of antilanguage include Roger Fowler's analysis of Anthony Burgess's *A Clockwork Orange* (with its lead character Alex), Bruce Malina's analysis of the Fourth Gospel (with the communities that made up the Johannine response in earliest Christianity), and my own analysis of antilanguage in the Apocalypse of John (with the other Johannine communities that responded apocalyptically in Asia Minor at the end of the first century).[6] In my analysis of antilanguage of the prophet John and the communities for whom he was the spokesperson, I detected relexicalization (new words for old) in the form of a pregnant woman for Israel, a Lion and a Lamb for Jesus, a dragon and a snake for the devil; overlexicalization (multiple words for focal concepts) in the form of multiple descriptors for Jesus, God, Spirit, people of God, and opponents. The voice whose sound was like a trumpet (Revelation 1:10) set the "puny inexhaustible voice" (to borrow Faulkner's words) of the prophet John to languaging in such a way as to effectively register opposition to ungodly powers.

The Genesis of U2's Antilanguage

Višnja Cogan makes a convincing argument that among the many elements that explain U2 is fundamentally its Irish experience, which finds expression in, among other things, the band's community, independence,

imagination, spirituality, social consciousness, and ambition.[7] The genesis
of the alternative language- and reality-generating system that became U2
is to be found, at least minimally, in the matrix of the death of loved ones,
the Lypton Village gang, and the Shalom Charismatic Christian community, experiences that set the stage for Bono, the Edge, Larry, and Adam to
form a tight community indeed and, I argue, an anticommunity.

A good place to start is the experience of the death of loved ones for not
only Bono but for the other members of the group. The death of Bono's
mother, Iris, when he was fourteen (1974) was, as Bono himself describes,
the single event that made him an artist: "I think my whole creative life
goes back to when my world collapsed, age fourteen. . . . The first thing I
started writing about was death. What a bummer the boy is! Actually, *Boy*,
our first album, is remarkably uplifting, considering the subject matter."[8]
Bono's mother's death would find its way into Bono's lyrics on a number
of occasions. It certainly provides the backdrop for the first song on *Boy*,
"I Will Follow." It led to a period of not only rage in his adolescent years
but for a search for community, for family. Larry Mullen's sister, Mary,
died as a child, but it was the early death of his mother, Maureen, in a traffic accident (in 1978 when he was seventeen) that provided a moment of
decision for him: "I am not saying I would have jumped [i.e., left the band]
had she lived but, after her death, there was nowhere else I wanted to be."[9]

A near death, the suicide attempt of a friend (Sean d'Angelo), provided
further backdrop to the material for U2's first album as Bono wrote what
would become its seventh song, "A Day without Me," in which he dealt
with the aftermath of suicide for those whom the victim has "left behind."[10]
Ian Curtis, the lead singer of the postpunk group Joy Division, committed
suicide in 1980 just as *Boy* was to be recorded, which meant two things
for U2: the tragic loss of the powerful voice behind its favorite band at
the time and the loss of the producer who was working closely with Joy
Division, Martin Hannett, who apparently could not bring himself to work
with U2's first album at that time.[11] For Bono personally and for the band
members corporately, death added to the tension—and the need to express
that tension in language—that would create its antilanguage.

Second, Lypton Village, the alternative reality "gang" in which Paul
Hewson and David Evans found a home in the mid-1970s, provided fertile
soil for tension between the adolescent and adult world of Dublin. As John
Waters describes,

> Lypton Village was an extreme case, a revolt against banality. It was not a
> petulant, ideological revolt, but a weary, existentialist one against both the

tackiness and emptiness of the lower middle-class culture around them, the way in which their immediate environment seemed to embody the isolation and alienation they felt from society as a whole, and also against the fatalistic jocularity, the Cheer Up It Might Never Happen syndrome, that lay like a damp sheet under everything.[12]

Lypton Village was the genesis of what would become the U2 community (as Cogan and others have said, as well as Bono himself).[13] Bono describes the construction of a community set up in conscientious opposition to the prevailing Dublin culture:

> We invented a Village, which was an alternative community, called Lypton Village, and we used to put on arts installations, when we were sixteen, seventeen, with manic drills and stepladders. See, the alcohol level in our neighborhood was so high, people going to the pubs a lot, and we were young, arrogant, and probably very annoying kids, but we didn't wanna go that route. The pub looked like a trapdoor to somewhere very predictable, so we wouldn't drink. We used to watch *Monty Python*. We invented our own language, gave each other names, and we'd dress differently. We would put on these performance-art things, and in the end we formed two bands, the Virgin Prunes and U2.[14]

Relexicalization took place in Lypton Village: Paul David Hewson became Bono Vox (named after a local hearing aid shop); David Howell Evans became the Edge (because the shape of his head and/or his analytical nature).[15] Overlexicalization also was to be found in the multiple names given to Paul Hewson, as Bono explains: "Before Bono, I was 'Steinvic von Huyseman,' and then 'Houseman,' then 'Bon Murray,' 'Bono Vox of O'Connell Street,' then just 'Bono.'"[16] Relexicalization as well as overlexicalization is also noticeable in the name of the band itself: from the Hype to the Feedback to U2, which all suggest playful interaction and tension. Verbal play of all kinds—indicative of antilanguage, according to Halliday—was part of the experience. U2's membership in the social subgroup that was Lypton Village was the context for the kind of lyrics and music it would create. It would be a rock band that did not act like your normal rock band.[17]

Third, the experience of Bono, Edge, and Larry in Shalom, a Charismatic Christian prayer meeting, gave the three the tension of being a distinct sect of believers in a strongly Catholic and Protestant country. They became tightly connected with a group that would eventually, to hear members of the band tell it, demand sole allegiance, even to the point of exhorting them to leave the worldly rock 'n' roll scene. They traded Lypton Village for another kind of subgroup, complete with its own (anti) language, which set up a great tension among dominant Catholic, Protestant, and certainly secular elements of Dublin life. U2 was a band at this time, having just released the album *Boy* (in 1980). Bono explains:

> We were doing street theatre in Dublin, and we met some people who were madder than us. They were a kind of inner-city group living life like it was the first century AD. They were expectant of signs and wonders; lived a kind of early-church religion. It was a commune. People who had cash shared it. They were passionate, and they were funny, and they seemed to have no material desires.[18]

Shalom meant serious Bible study, prayer, worship, and spiritual commitment for its members. Again, Bono explains: "At that point, we were angry. We were agitated by the inequalities in the world and the lack of spiritual life."[19] Steve Stockman argues for the seriousness of this charismatic subgroup of Irish religious life:

> The idea of being radical attracted U2. In any other city of the western world, this kind of Christian behavior would have been seen as old fashioned and almost nerdish. In any other city, Bono would have laughed at such middle class, respectable, religious behavior. But in Dublin, this was radical stuff. To take Jesus seriously was far out. In some ways, Shalom was an out-there kind of gang on parallel lines with the Lypton Village gang. It wasn't as if one of them was dangerous and the other one safe.[20]

The worldly denial of Shalom was eventually denied (never to be embraced by Adam), and the future of U2 would continue. After all, being a rock band would require everything and more. However, the experience did affirm the spiritual and world-denying set that would serve as the imprint of the band so that it might function as "the rock band with a conscience." Also, it would leave Bono, the major writer of the group, with an even firmer grasp of the language and themes of the Bible, the sine qua non of its version of antilanguage.

Antilanguage in the Songs of U2

I propose to show the shape that antilanguage takes in the songs of U2 by examining three songs that represent U2 at its beginning (*Boy*), middle (*Achtung Baby*), and penultimate (*How to Dismantle an Atomic Bomb*): from its earliest album, *Boy* (1980), the song "I Will Follow"; from a middle album, *Achtung Baby* (1991), "The Fly"; and from what was its latest release at the time of my study, *How to Dismantle an Atomic Bomb* (2004), "Vertigo." All three songs were first releases for each album.

"I Will Follow" is the first song on U2's first album and is a song that U2 has performed on every concert tour. The boy loses his mother. The boy enters a period of "terror and confusion,"[21] "rebellion":[22] "my mother's death threw petrol on the fire."[23] While there may be a hint of suicidal urge in the chorus ("If you walk away . . . I will follow"), it is clear that the song wants to reflect not only the experience of adolescent angst (particularly) in the loss of a mother but of the experience of an anticommunity that trumps any urge to self-violence and self-negation. The most immediate background to the song is not only the mother's death but that of the family and alternative reality that, first, Lypton Village, then Shalom, and now U2 had become. U2 provides an antilanguage that sets up tension against adolescents in community who would say, "I'm content with just looking at myself," "being blind," "having four walls come falling down," "being lost." From the very beginning, U2 is the "band of social consciousness," and the forcefulness of the label is that U2 demonstrated in its honesty and group cohesion that the alternative reality was possible for others to "follow."

Relexicalization is seen particularly in the word "follow." "Following" expresses the notion that, rather than aloneness, I choose relatedness: "If you walk away, walk away, I walk away, walk away. I will follow." Next to "follow," I point to "Your eyes," which again points to life lived in community. Rather than aloneness, again, "Your eyes make a circle" that encompasses me, includes me, you see me.

Overlexicalization of the "U2 community" is seen in the multiple verbs, nouns, and adjectives that indicate alternation between being outsider/lost and being insider/found:

Outsider/Lost: "I was on the outside," "I was looking at myself," "I was blind, could not see," I was there when the walls came crashing down, "I was lost."
Insider/Found: "I am found," "Your eyes make a circle [that encompasses me]," "I see you when I go in there," and—most important—"I will follow," where you go, I will go (whether Ruth 1:16 is seen as a footnote or not).

The chief wordplay of this brief song of three minutes, thirty-seven seconds, is the chorus, repeated three times: eight "walk away's" and three

"I will follow's." The repetition is wordplay, meant to move the hearer, who may identify with blindness and lostness. There are, of course, musical touches that indicate movement from outsider to insider—for example, when the song begins, there is distinct volume effect from less loud (farther away) to more loud (closer), with a corresponding increase in the volume of the two-note chord and pounding drum rhythm that speaks throughout the song (sometimes without lyrics), "I will follow." Bono shouts near the song's beginning, "I will follow," signaling to the hearer his intent from the get-go. Life has dealt a cruel deal: a mother is supposed to be helping you make the journey to manhood ("his mother takes him by the hand"); but she's dead, and whenever the boy remembers this, "he starts to cry." The verbal play of the chorus (again, along with a driving drumbeat that insists that the hearer get up and walk away as well) summons the hearer to catch the rhythm of movement and be swept away by it. It is a simple movement: if you walk away, I walk away. Life hurts, but a life of community is possible. One final wordplay in the song just may make another implicit connection with Bono's mother. The reference to "Your eyes" (repeated five times in the bridge) may be a veiled reference. Iris, Bono's mother's name, by metonymy indicates the eye.

"The Fly" (*Achtung Baby*, 1991) was also a first-single release. Bono explains the song in general: "The whole track is a high-energy sonic barrage but with an angelic chorus."[24] Then, he explains it specifically: "As we moved from the eighties to the nineties, I stopped throwing rocks at the obvious symbols of power and the abuse of it. I started throwing rocks at my own hypocrisy. That's a part of what that work was about: owning up to one's ego. These characters in the songs like 'The Fly' are owning up to one's hypocrisy in your heart, your duplicitous nature."[25] The latter explanation of the song does not dispel the notion that U2 is ideally the "band with a social conscience," ready to boldly go morally where no rock band has gone before. Truth remains, and aphorisms abound in the song, the numerous nonsecrets: for example, "it's no secret that a friend is someone who lets you help." But it's one thing to know the truth and quite another to do it.

Thus, here is a song about owning up to your own hypocrisy. Wherever there is "one man's lie," "it's no secret that the stars are falling from the sky." In "The Fly," U2 employs antilanguage to set up tension against themselves, or as Stokes quotes Bono, the song may be described "as the sound of four men chopping down *The Joshua Tree*."[26] Antilanguage in "I Will Follow" clearly has the backdrop of trying to create an honest yet hopeful response within adolescence. Antilanguage in "The Fly" sees the boy grown up to be a man, able to continue to acknowledge his truth, his "secrets." Yet he does so knowing the great hazard. So Bono: "It's saying: Scale this rock face at your peril. Lots have tried before you and have been left on the fly paper."[27]

Relexicalization, I would suggest, takes the forms of "the fly" (although flies typically have a better time at sheer wall faces than do human beings). Yet when you add the "fly paper" metaphor, as does Bono, it helps to see where the song is going. "The secret" would be another relexicalization: secret is now understood as the aphorism, the truth so common, so general, that it does not need explanation. However, truth can use affirmation in life lived because humans have the tendency to aphorize and then to apostasize.

Overlexicalization is seen in multiple, truthful aphoristic expressions (too numerous to list here). However, there is overlexicalization in the way that a man or a woman struggles with "Love" (the capital "L" sort): beg, crawl (on the sheer face of love), rise, fall (from sheer face of love). Yet at our best we are like a shooting star. Would that we could burn purely, brightly, and at length for Love. We cannot. Yet, when we do shine, burn brightly, the poet says.

The chief form of wordplay is the two voices that, at least on *Achtung Baby*, singing at the same time, produce a strong tension against each other. Bono said that it took them fifteen years to learn how to sing the song correctly, with the first voice ("Love, we shine like a burning star") followed by the second voice ("A man will beg, a man will crawl").[28] Either way, the "social conscience of rock" has shown the more excellent way, burn brightly for love but acknowledge faults.

The first song on U2's *How to Dismantle an Atomic Bomb*, 2004, was "Vertigo." The song had its genesis as a hard-driving song with a classic rock guitar riff and remained so after a most difficult birthing process. Edge described it as "just a great visceral rock 'n' roll song."[29] The image of vertigo, dizziness, is simple enough to grasp. As for the basic story line behind the dizziness, Bono sums it up thus:

> In the case of "Vertigo," I was thinking about this nightclub we've all been to. You're supposed to be having a great time and everything's extraordinary around you and the drinks are the price of buying a bar in a Third World country. . . . And it felt like the way a lot of people were feeling at the moment, as you turn on the telly or you're just looking around and you see big, fat Capitalism at the top of its mountain, just about to topple. It's that woozy sick feeling of realizing that here we are, drinking, drugging, eating, polluting, robbing ourselves to death. And in the middle of

the club there's this girl. She has crimson nails . . . a cross around her neck, and the character in this stares at the cross to steady himself. And he has a little epiphany and you don't know what the epiphany is.[30]

Again, the alternative reality that the antilanguage sets into play is grounded in social consciousness that is part and parcel of the U2 community—and, actually, even cross consciousness (even though Bono asserts that, even with crimson and cross, the "epiphany" remains inconclusive).

As for relexicalization, "vertigo" itself connotes a life ruled increasingly by "the jungle" that is "your head," by the "mind" that can "wander." The moral life wasted, the resulting dizziness leaves us with the sense that "it's everything I wish I didn't know." "The girl with crimson nails" (and "Jesus round her neck") represents, as in the (presumably female) "eyes" of "I Will Follow," the opportunity for life as it could be, salvation, restoration, and, at least, some kind of epiphany that just might reduce or diminish the dizziness attendant with giving in to the temptation to "want it all" and sell your soul to the devil ("just give me what I want, and nobody gets hurt"; certainly a reference to Jesus's temptation by the devil [Matthew 4, Luke 4]).

Overlexicalization certainly would include lexical items that connote life that results in moral and social imbalance (you just know that something's wrong!): dark, jungle, soul can be bought, mind can wander, vertigo, can't stand the beats, everything I wish I didn't know, boys know they can't dance, all this can be yours, no one gets hurt, checkmated, hours of fun. The antilanguage sets up a strong tension by positing that there is a better way, a way that a person by sheer grace may experience: "except *you give* me something I can feel, feel" ("feeling" preferable to "thought" because "a feeling is so much stronger than a thought"). However, this "feeling" (emotion) paradoxically acquires cognitive substance: "I can feel your love teaching me how to kneel, kneel." Kneeling, or humility, a second reference back to Jesus's paradigmatic form of prostration, even to the point of death. Thus, there is overlexicalization for the possible remedy that is held out: your soul can't be bought (perhaps a connection to the later reference of Jesus's death for sinners, a là crimson nails, Jesus [presumably on a cross] round the neck), that is, your soul—if you recognize it—has already been bought.

Wordplay abounds to convey the sense of vertigo: not a verbal cue, but the opening guitar line ends repeatedly with a quick descent (the person with vertigo getting ready to fall down?); Spanish played off against English (even the counting is off, "uno, dos, tres, catorce!"; "hola" and "que pasa?"—phrases that assume that something is off kilter); presumably the satanic promise comes with blinding dizziness, "all this can be yours, all this can be yours, all this can be yours" . . . and with the promise that is also threat, "just give me what I want and nobody gets hurt." Ironically, vertigo gives way to falling of a sort; however, not the "leaping off the pinnacle of the temple" (as in the Gospel temptations) but the learning to kneel. Humility, prayer (in the kneeling position), and the cruciform epiphany resolve dizziness. "Fat capitalism"—and presumably fat capitalists of all sorts—has an answer in the antilanguage of U2, which is solidly affirmed with sixteen "yeah's."

A Return to the Heart

As a conclusion, one last question: How does an internationally successful yet very wealthy aging group of Irish rockers continue to earn the right to speak to the world on issues of morality and the spiritual journey? A partial answer is that they have adjusted their message along the way to better suit their maturity level and their social context. They are no longer an advanced form of Lypton Village, and they have—however imperfectly—put their money and action where there message is. Finally, their language from the beginning maintained a strong tension against the dominant culture, first as adolescents and then, as they matured, adults who continued to behave as adolescents. They have maintained the tension from the beginning, as in this fourth song on their first album, *Boy*:

> Into the heart of a child
> I stay awhile
> But I can go there.
> Into the heart of a child
> I can smile
> I can't go there.
> Into the heart, into the heart of a child
> I can't go back
> I can't stay awhile.
> Into the heart.
> Into the heart.[31]

It is an albeit improvised lyric, but there is important wordplay here. Indeed, the goal is soul and a return to the heart of a child. Yet it is a journey that can only be accomplished as the boy becomes a man.

Notes

A similar version of this chapter appeared in the *Campbellsville Review*, vol. 5 (2009–2010), and is reprinted here with permission from the editor.

1. Michael A. K. Halliday represents the London School of Linguistics, which displays a functionalist perspective within the European structural linguistic tradition. Halliday, who is credited with founding an internationally recognized sociolinguistic theory called "systemic functional linguistics," has two seminal works (among multiple other writings): *Language as Social Semiotic* (London: University Park Press, 1978), which is concerned with the social "meaning potential" in language and in which he first developed the notion of "antilanguages," and *An Introduction to Functional Grammar* (London: Hodder Education, 2004; third edition revision by Christian M. I. M. Matthiessen), which represents a complete statement of "the architecture of language" in the systemic functionalist perspective. Two helpful guides to Halliday's theory are Thomas Bloor, *The Functional Analysis of English: A Hallidayan Approach* (London: Arnold, 1995); Geoff Thompson, *An Introduction to Functional Grammar* (London: Arnold, 2004).

2. Halliday, *Language*, 187.

3. Halliday, *Language*, 21.

4. Halliday, *Language*, 186–88; see also Halliday, *Introduction*, 29–30, in which Halliday distinguishes between the experiential and the logical in the ideational metafunction of language.

5. Halliday, *Social Semiotic,* 172–79.

6. Roger Fowler, *Linguistics and the Novel* (London: Methuen, 1977), 130–59; Bruce Malina, *The Gospel of John in Sociolinguistic Perspective*, Center for Hermeneutical Studies in Hellenistic and Modern Culture Colloquy 48 (Berkley, CA: Center for Hermeneutical Studies, 1985), 1–23; John Hurtgen, *Anti-language in the Apocalypse of John* (Lewiston, NY: Edwin Mellen Press, 1993), 89–146.

7. Višnja Cogan, *U2: An Irish Phenomenon* (New York: Pegasus, 2007), 6–7; to those elements listed, Cogan adds a seventh and an eighth, U2's own image and myth and U2's enduring fans (7–8).

8. Michka Assayas, *Bono* (New York: Riverhead, 2005), 16.

9. U2 and Neil McCormick, *U2 by U2* (New York: HarperCollins, 2006), 70.

10. Niall Stokes, *U2 into the Heart: The Stories behind Every Song* (New York: Thunder's Mouth Press, 2005), 18.

11. U2 and McCormick, *U2 by U2*, 92, 96.

12. John Waters, *Race of Angels: The Genesis of U2* (London: Fourth Estate, 1994), 59.

13. Cogan, *U2*, 14–15, 21; Waters, *Race of Angels*, 59–60.

14. Assayas, *Bono*, 127; earlier in the book, he speaks of the other band members in the village, Edge and Adam, who were well suited to such a group, but Larry was more suspicious about the group (68).

15. Cogan, *U2*, 15.

16. Assayas, *Bono*, 54.

17. Steve Beard relates Bono's confession to an interviewer: "'You're in a rock band—what can't you talk about? God? Ok, here we go. You're supposed to write songs about sex and drugs. Well, no I won't'"; *Walk On: The Spiritual Journey of U2* (Lake Mary, FL: Relevant Books, 2001), v.

18. Cogan, *U2*, 22 (quoting Neil McCormick).

19. Assayas, *Bono*, 136.

20. Steve Stockman, *Walk On: The Spiritual Journey of U2*. (Orlando, FL: Relevant, 2005), 20.

21. Assayas, *Bono*, 21–23; Stokes, *U2 into the Heart*, 9.

22. Assayas, *Bono*, 21.

23. U2 and McCormick, *U2 by U2*, 18.

24. U2 and McCormick, *U2 by U2*, 224

25. Assyas, *Bono*, 106.

26. Stokes, *U2 into the Heart*, 102.

27. U2 and McCormick, *U2 by U2*, 224.

28. U2 and McCormick, *U2 by U2*, 225.

29. U2 and McCormick, *U2 by U2*, 321.

30. U2 and McCormick, *U2 by U2*, 322.

31. "Into the Heart" is an improvised lyric; "craft would come later," Stokes remarks (*U2 into the Heart*, 13).

All That We Can't Leave Behind   **15**
U2's Conservative Voice

STEPHEN CATANZARITE

I T IS OFTEN SAID THAT POLITICS AND RELIGION go together like gasoline and matches. To this potentially deadly combination, allow me to add another agent of volatility: rock and roll.

Among the more troubling aspects of American life in the early twenty-first century is the widening political polarization, including the heating up of what, at the end of the last century, came to be known as "the culture wars"—those inevitable battles that break out whenever and wherever the demands of a religiously informed conscience and the claims of secular liberal democracy come into conflict. With so many aspects of our shared life presenting us with serious and complicated challenges—from health care to warfare, the economy to the ecology—do the American people still have the capacity to find common cause and transcend partisan and sectarian bickering through the rediscovery and cultivation of a shared set of values? I believe we do. I also believe, audacious though it may sound, that rock and roll, when fully and thoughtfully considered, can help all of us, regardless of political persuasion or affiliation, recall and reflect on certain principles and values that have long served as the foundation of American liberty, ingenuity, and greatness.

Let me be clear, however, that my goal is not to attempt to claim rock and roll or any of its chief practitioners for the political right; I recognize that rock music has frequently been used to stir up the more revolutionary instincts of humanity and that many of the form's artists have championed both the agitations and the agitators of the political left. I also do not intend to affix a facade of hipness and glamour upon the venerable tradition of American conservatism in hopes of making it more palatable to modern minds. No such efforts are needed, as I firmly believe that the best of rock and roll constitutes a kind of poetic canon that both articulates and celebrates the deepest yearnings of the human soul—yearnings that I maintain resonate most fully with a conservative worldview. I also believe that authentic conservatism transcends mere fashion and trendiness precisely because it is grounded in objective reality and champions eternal verities.

There was a time in my life when people were surprised to learn that I am a conservative. I count myself among its number. I did not decide one day to declare myself a right-winger. Rather, over a period that stretched from my late twenties into my early thirties, I slowly but surely began to discover the conservative impulse—a longing for order and permanence in both the person and the republic—to be a fundamental characteristic of my personality and perspective. And while the process by which such perspectives are formed is to some degree inscrutable, it is possible to identify certain events, occasions, and elements in our lives that pushed or prodded us to embrace a particular worldview. Among the threads that have served to weave the tapestry that is my conservative consciousness is, I believe, my fondness for the music of U2.

Certainly, nobody will ever confuse the members of U2 for the editorial board of *National Review*. In fact, the band's political affections seem to most often favor those on the left side of the aisle. Still, I submit that the songs of U2 betray a state of mind, a type of character, and a way of looking at the civil social order that is undeniably conservative.

Of course defining conservatism has never been an easy task, as R. J. White wrote more than sixty years ago in his introduction to *The Conservative Tradition*: "To put conservatism in a bottle with a label is like trying to liquify the atmosphere. . . . Conservatism is less a political doctrine than a habit of mind, a mode of feeling, a way of living."[1] And after its bastardization and supplanting by the more ideologically hardened term *neoconservatism*, courtesy of the neocons in the administration of George W. Bush and their detractors, and the staggering losses suffered by the Republican Party in the elections of 2006 and 2008, the very meaning of the word *conservatism* appears to be uncertain at this moment in our nation's history—a moment in which the guiding instincts and impulses of conservatism are needed more than at perhaps any other time in the last century.

After decades spent wandering on the margins of political power, those on the left would of course like nothing more than to close the book on conservatism's long and storied supremacy at the heart of American public life. Meanwhile, on the right, there are those who would burn down conservatism ostensibly to save it. Unduly fixated on the quantum mechanics of winning elections (e.g., Republican political strategist Karl Rove's architectural approach to victory through "framing" political "narratives" to "target" certain "demographics"), these bashful tories believe that conservatism needs to be redefined and "rebranded" for the twenty-first century. They have, it seems, lost confidence in the perennial appeal of conservatism and seek to downplay or outright erase from its memory anything that might be perceived as challenging, controversial, or extreme. But if salt loses its saltiness, what good is it, except to be thrown out and trampled by others?

While many brilliant and soulful minds have contributed to my fragile yet ever-deepening understanding of what I call the "conservative voice," one has distinguished himself as the most potent, precise, and graceful prophet of conservatism in America: the late political theorist, historian, and social and literary critic Russell Kirk, who championed conservatism as "an attitude . . . sustained by a body of sentiments, rather than by a system of ideological dogmata." Tracing modern American conservatism's roots back to opposition to the radical innovations of the French Revolution, which overthrew the established order of French society in favor of an abstract theory of human equality, Kirk denied that conservatism was itself an ideology but was in fact the negation of ideology. Throughout his tenure as the dean of American conservatism, Kirk doggedly fought all attempts to bring low the dignity and complexity of human nature and experience for the sake of fashioning a cheap but politically expedient manifesto or creed. *To conserve* means "to save," and Kirk believed that the authentic conservative labors to save what is best about a civilization's traditions and institutions, harmonizing that best with prudent reform and creative progress from time to time.

Now, aside from a penchant for destroying television sets, the shy and bookish Kirk had seemingly little in common with the average rock star. Indeed, unlike the rock star's typically petulant tossing of televisions from hotel windows into swimming pools, Kirk's violence was more visceral: he simply hated television, which he referred to as "Demon TV."

In one of his later books, *The Wise Men Know What Wicked Things Are Written on the Sky*, Kirk recounts with a kind of glee his attempts to exorcise the Demon from Piety Hill, his ancestral home in Mecosta, Michigan. The set in question belonged to the Kirk family's "hobo butler," who had received a special dispensation to keep it in his room. On the day that the butler was buried, Kirk thrust the television into the cellar. Months later, he arrived home to find his wife and four daughters huddled around "the forbidden TV" in a remote corner of the cellar. Kirk recounts that he

> dispersed them in wrath. Then, taking a pair of powerful wire cutters, I did fierce things to the set, and flung portions of it into trash-cans. In the fullness of time, nevertheless, one of the Ethiopians who dwelt with us, young Shale Selassie Makonnen, secretly repaired the mutilated contraption [and installed] it in his room. . . . When I was about to confiscate this shabby article of contraband it vanished again. Presently a secret agent of the gentler sex informed me that our eldest daughter . . . had contrived to transport the set somehow to the top-most room of the foretower of our archaic house, and there sometimes turned it on. . . . When I learned of this, I climbed the ladder to the summit of the foretower, with some difficulty forced open a small octagonal window, and flung the accursed set to its destruction. To my chagrin, the confounded thing caught in a gutter, and there hung like Mahomet's coffin.[2]

I share this story to illustrate that Kirk was neither a staid and placid academic dwelling in the dry environs of an Ivory Tower nor a parsimonious scold wagging a cold and passionless finger at humanity. In fact Kirk, who descended from a long line of seance-conducting spiritualists, wrote and told ghost stories, dabbled in tarot cards, enjoyed good cigars and wine, and opened his home to beggars, students, unwed mothers, and the leading lights of conservatism with equal generosity and fancied himself a "bohemian tory," which he defined thusly:

> A tory, according to Samuel Johnson, is a man attached to orthodoxy in church and state. A bohemian is a wandering and often impecunious man of letters or arts, indifferent to the demands of bourgeois fad and foible. Such a one has your servant been. Tory and bohemian go not ill together: it is quite possible to abide by the norms of civilized existence, what Mr. T. S. Eliot calls the permanent things: and yet to set at defiance the soft securities and shame conventionalities of 20th-century sociability.[3]

With his landmark 1953 book *The Conservative Mind*, Kirk inspired the development of conservatism as a bona fide intellectual movement in America. Before Kirk, the eminent literary critic Lionel Trilling could triumphantly proclaim liberalism as "the sole intellectual tradition in the United States"[4] and summarily dismiss conservatism as little more than a collection of "irritable mental gestures which seek to resemble ideas."[5] After Kirk, the political and cultural landscapes in America were forever altered. Though authentic philosophical conservatism is unlikely to ever be comfortably defined as "fashionable," Russell Kirk made it at least possible for intelligent, culturally sophisticated people to identify themselves as conservatives without embarrassment. From time to time throughout his life, Kirk compiled lists of what he saw as the guiding principles or sentiments of the conservative mind. While each successive list might add a fresh insight or poetic nuance, Kirk remained impressively consistent and his articulation of conservatism remarkably nimble and accessible.

In a similar though not entirely analogous way, U2 has made it possible for at least two generations of fans of contemporary popular music to expect more from the form than the dead end credo of "sex, drugs, and rock and roll." Here was a band born in the ashes of 1970s punk nihilism, singing songs with a distinctly evangelical Christian flavor; songs with choruses proclaiming, in Latin no less, "glory in you, Lord" ("Gloria"); songs with lyrics based on the Fortieth Psalm ("40"); songs that celebrated pride in the name of love, rather than solely in the connubial act of love. In an age when moral relativism, scientific materialism, and biological determinism seek to consign the idea of objective reality to the ash heap of history, U2 has had the audacity and simplicity to proclaim its belief in "three chords and the truth." Armed with this belief, U2 frequently finds itself in the arena of debate and action on some of the most important humanitarian issues of our time.

Perhaps it can be said that, like U2's humanitarianism, Russell Kirk's conservatism is based in large part on what might be termed "Irish realism," for Kirk's great conservative hero was the Dublin-born eighteenth-century statesman Edmund Burke. Burke believed that "the principles of true politics are those of morality enlarged." What strikes me as the uniting substance between the thought and writings of Russell Kirk and the music of U2 is a shared mission to remind us of what the poet Robert Frost called "the truths we keep coming back and back to," Eliot's "permanent things"—truth, beauty, goodness, the infinite and irreducible significance of persons, prudence, temperance, justice, fortitude, faith, hope, and love.

In his 1993 book *The Politics of Prudence*, Kirk sought to summarize those sentiments that he saw as the hallmarks of the conservative attitude into ten conservative principles. For the purposes of this chapter, I constrain myself to discussing just five of Kirk's principles as a means of amplifying the conservative voice in the songs of U2.

Kirk's first principle states that "the conservative believes that there exists an enduring moral order." That order, which signifies harmony, is made for man, and man is made for it: human nature is a constant, and moral truths are permanent. In other words, there are such things as right and wrong, and human beings have the capacity to know the difference between the two. This belief strongly implies the existence of a Creator of the moral order, and Kirk very firmly believed that all political problems are, in the final analysis, moral and religious problems.

I don't think it necessary to spend much time making the case that, from the band's earliest days and right up to the present, the songs of U2 clearly witness to the existence of a wisdom that is more than human and are imbued with a rich understanding of divine justice. From *Boy* to *No Line on the Horizon*, the reality and implications of an enduring, spiritually ordained and infused moral order have been perennial themes in U2's music.

Another of Kirk's principles states that the conservative adheres to custom, convention, and continuity. Old customs enable people to live together peaceably; the destroyers of custom demolish more than they know or desire. When radicals are successful in overthrowing the established order by suppressing local customs and conventions and breaking the continuity of social institutions, they immediately discover the need to create new customs, conventions, and continuities. Time and again, the new order established by radicals is found to be greatly inferior to the old.

While the songs of U2 frequently offer a hopeful vision of a new and profoundly different kingdom to come, they have never proffered the radical's vision for effacing established social institutions in pursuit of an earthly paradise. Indeed, the songs present a traditionally grounded and conventional understanding of the meanings of faith, hope, love, God, man, time, and eternity—along with celebrations of the more mundane habits of life. One of my favorite U2 songs, "Miss Sarajevo," commemorates the determination of a group of people to reestablish some normalcy and order amid the war-fired evaporation of their society by holding that most conventional of contests—a beauty pageant.

Because they feel affection for the proliferating intricacy of long-established social institutions and modes of life—as distinguished from the narrowing uniformity and deadening egalitarianism of radical systems—conservatives pay attention to the principle of variety, according to Kirk. Over the last few decades, "diversity" and "equality" have served as effective rallying cries for the American left. Yet the preservation of a vibrant and authentic diversity in any civilization requires the survival of orders and classes, differences in material condition, and, yes, many types of inequality. The conservative knows that the only true forms of equality are equality before God's judgment and equality before a just court of law and that the destruction of natural and institutional differences in the pursuit of social and material leveling results in cultural and economic stagnation—and the frustration of the individual. Equal opportunity does not guarantee equal outcomes; results, as they say, will vary.

Serious fans of U2, given as they are to taking the band's charitable and humanitarian campaigning personally, may find this aspect of my thesis perhaps the most difficult to swallow. They should consider that, owing to his station in life—which he and his bandmates have earned by way of natural talent, hard work, industriousness, and personal sacrifice—Bono clearly enjoys creature comforts I do not and has access to people, places, and experiences that remain beyond my reach. I in no way begrudge him this. In fact, I applaud him (quite literally), and I certainly don't want some bureaucrat in The Hague to enforce a legislative scheme that might bring our differing lifestyles into a faux parity. We may in the eyes of our Creator be one, but we are most assuredly not the same. Vive la difference!

U2 provides a stark depiction of the central planner's narrowing uniformity and deadening egalitarianism in "Running to Stand Still," a haunting track from its 1987 album *The Joshua Tree*. The song chronicles the heroin addiction of a young woman, a resident of Dublin's Ballymun Flats. The Ballymun Flats were seven high-rise towers built in the 1960s as part of a state scheme to deal with inner-city poverty, but the towers themselves became infamous symbols of poverty, drug addiction, and social alienation in Ireland in the 1970s. In the song, the woman sees

> seven towers
> but I see only one way out
> you've got to cry without weeping
> talk without speaking
> scream without raising your voice.

As Bono described them in the 2006 book *U2 by U2*, the seven towers of Ballymun were "an attempt by Ireland towards modernity in high-rise living—just as everyone else in Europe had found out tower blocks were not a good idea, we started building them. We used to go up and down in the lifts because we weren't used to having lifts. Then they started to break down and the stairs began to stink of piss."[6]

In vivid contrast to this situation is the proliferating intricacy of long-established social institutions and modes of life celebrated in two songs on the band's 2000 album *All That You Can't Leave Behind*. The opening song, "Beautiful Day," which its lyricist describes as being about "a man who has lost everything but finds joy in what he still has," offers this optimistic vision of life, in all its glorious, uneven, and ever-changing complexity:

> See the world in green and blue
> See China right in front of you
> See the canyons broken by cloud
> See the tuna fleets clearing the sea out
> See the Bedouin fires at night
> See the oil fields at first light
> See the bird with a leaf in her mouth
> After the flood all the colors came out.

Similarly, the album's penultimate song, "New York," offers a gritty but no-less-hopeful description of a city teaming with authentic diversity:

> In New York freedom feels like too many choices . . .
> voices on the cell phone, voices from home,
> voices of the hard sell, voices down the stairwell . . .
> Irish, Italians, Jews, and Hispanics
> Religious nuts, political fanatics
> in the stew, living happily.

Conservatives recognize that human nature suffers irremediably from certain grave faults; thus, they are chastened by what Kirk calls the principle of imperfectability. "Whatever we are," Augustine reminds us, "we are not what we ought to be." There is a little good in the worst of us but also a little bad in the best of us. No perfect social order can ever be achieved by imperfect humanity. Because of human restlessness, the search for Utopia will always end in disaster. "Mankind would grow rebellious under any utopian domination," Kirk says, "and would eventually break out in violent discontent—or else expire of boredom."[7]

U2's 1991 masterpiece *Achtung Baby* is an album-length meditation on the imperfectability of human nature. In songs such as "Zoo Station," "Even Better Than the Real Thing," "One," "The Fly," and "Love Is Blindness," *Achtung Baby* chronicles the longing in our hearts for unity between and among God and man, man and woman, brother and sister, parent and child, along with the restlessness, pride, larceny, lust, and fear that disturbs even the happiest of homes. Kirk reminds us that those ideologues who promised the perfection of both man and society "converted a great part of the twentieth-century world into a terrestrial hell."[8] Echoing

Alexander Solzenitsyn, *Achtung Baby* reminds us that all wars, all man-made catastrophes, all crises of civilization begin first as a crisis within an individual human heart.

Finally, Kirk says that the thinking conservative understands that permanence and change must be recognized and reconciled in a vigorous society. Though the great twentieth-century conservative synthesizer and popularizer William F. Buckley famously described a conservative as "a fellow standing athwart history yelling 'Stop!'" the conservative is by no means opposed to social improvement. He is skeptical, however, that there exists any such force as a mystical progress at work in the world. Over and against the Whig view of history, which sees the past as the inevitable progression toward greater liberty, enlightenment, and scientific and material improvement, the conservative recognizes that when a society is progressing in some respects, it is likely to be declining in others. Progress in a society is that spirit of creativity and that body of talents that inspire us to foster reform and improvement. Without such progress, a people will obviously stagnate. But progress must be tempered with a respect for permanence—those abiding interests and beliefs that undergird a society and give us stability and continuity.

Because I've already examined U2's commitment to permanence and those "abiding beliefs" manifest in the subject matter of U2's songs, I want to dwell for a moment on the songs themselves—their musicality and structure. In some important ways, U2 has been musical innovators, creating a distinctive sound by using novel, at times unorthodox, and frequently technology-driven approaches to instrumentation and song arrangements and essentially using the recording studio as an instrument itself. At the same time, U2 has not only respected but revered the conventions of popular songwriting, traditions handed down from rock and roll's roots in folk, country, blues, and gospel music—musical structures that can be traced back further to antiquity. U2 is always at its best when it channels its influences, rather than allowing those influences to channel it. This is, I believe, the band's secret to creating innovative and original music that is also accessible and engaging: U2's best music reconciles permanence with progress. The influence, for example, of Miles Davis on U2 doesn't result in the band playing modal jazz or (God forbid!) some form of jazz-rock fusion but in that searing, hard bop of a guitar solo on "Love Is Blindness," which is set over a simple, folkish chord figure. The influence of hip-hop on U2 does not result in the band encroaching on the territory of Public Enemy but in the polyrhythmic funk of "Mysterious Ways," which follows, for the most part, a very traditional songwriting structure. In *U2 by U2*, Bono recalls a conversation he had with Bob Dylan:

> He said to me "you've got to go back. You've got to look back. You've got to understand the roots." I think we wanted to ground all of the electricity that was going through us and understand the past better. And it really did help us. Listening to black music helped us get the groove ready for *Achtung Baby*. Listening to folk music helped me develop as a lyricist.[9]

"The past," Burke said, "is a great storehouse of wisdom."[10] Far from promoting a radical redefinition of what it means to be human or advocating for the upheaval of civil society in favor of some novel order, the songs of U2, the best of them, serve to remind us what it means to be human and inspire us to improve society not by revolution but through reformation and renewal.

"Rockers against Drugs?" Sam Kinison used to quip. "That's like Christians against Christ. Somebody was high when they came up with that name." Kinison, who sprinted the surprisingly short distance from Pentecostal evangelist to hard-living stand-up comedian, was responding to a late-1980s public service campaign in which some presumably community-minded rock stars extolled the virtues of just saying no. Along with adherents of both rock and roll and modern intellectual conservatism, the late comic might have had a similar reaction to the premise of this chapter. Is it really possible to be a consistent and coherent champion of the conservative mind-set and an unabashed (or at least only somewhat abashed) fan of the "devil's music"? Rock and roll is, after all, purported to be the music of rebellion set to the rhythm of sexual intercourse. The popular understanding of conservatism, however, renders it as the heartless repressor of mankind's baser instincts in the service of a wholesome and well-ordered society. Put another way, rock and roll is taken to be personified by Little Richard and Janis Joplin, while conservatism is embodied by Pat Boone and Anita Bryant.

But after more than sixty years of growing up together (for rock and roll and the modern conservative movement share a genesis in post–World War II America), is it not possible, and even likely, that these two potent, culture-shaping forces will have become, if not wholly reconciled, at least conversant with each other? Might not each grant the other some grudging respect, setting aside a policy of "mutually assured destruction" in favor of the pop culture equivalent of *glasnost* and *perestroika*?

Reflecting on the birth of his first child, Bono confessed just how profoundly becoming a father shifted his perspective: "You understand why wars are fought, you understand why men want to own land, you understand why women are so smart, because they have to be."[11] These understandings are, I submit, the stirrings of the conservative impulse. Authentic conservatives defend, for example, private property, a free economy, and traditional understanding of the family not only for their own sake but because they involve even greater ends: human dignity, human personality, human happiness. Far from being selfish or bigoted, as the popular caricature often renders him, the conservative wishes to pass these things—the "permanent things," the "truths we keep coming back and back to"—to future generations. The authentic conservative seeks not merely to oppose all that we might become but to protect and promote, through rigorous thought and vigorous imagination, all that we can't leave behind.

Notes

1. R. J. White, *The Conservative Tradition*, 2nd ed. (London: Adam & Charles Black, 1964), 1.

2. Russell Kirk, *The Wise Men Know What Wicked Things Are Written on the Sky* (Washington, DC: Regenery Gateway, 1987), 117.

3. Russell Kirk, *Confessions of a Bohemian Tory: Episodes and Reflections of a Vagrant Career* (New York: Fleet, 1963), 3.

4. Lionel Trilling, quoted in George H. Nash, *The Conservative Intellectual Tradition in America* (1976; Wilmington, DE: ISI Books, 1996), 51.

5. Trilling, quoted in Nash, *The Conservative Intellectual Tradition*, 51.

6. Bono, *U2 by U2* (New York: HarperCollins, 2006), 182.

7. Kirk, "Ten Conservative Principles," http://www.kirkcenter.org/kirk/ten-principles.html.

8. Kirk, "Ten Conservative Principles," http://www.kirkcenter.org/kirk/ten-principles.html.

9. Bono, *U2 by U2*, 213.

10. Quoted in Russell Kirk, "The Essence of Conservatism," http://www.kirkcenter.org/kirk/essence-1957.html.

11. Bono, *U2 by U2*, 211.

Across the Universe   **16**
U2's Hope in Space and Time

SCOTT CALHOUN

WHEN U2 PERFORMED "MIRACLE DRUG" on its 2005 Vertigo tour, Bono would often tell a story to introduce the song while the Edge, as if on repeat for the first half dozen or so bars, sounded the song's opening tones. Bono's story usually ran two minutes and, in the telling of it, set both a theme and a mood for the song. Bono would start, with paced pauses between phrases and sentences: "I know some of you know this, maybe everybody knows this, but you know that Edge is from the future, right? And not even our future. . . . He comes from the future from a completely different planet. . . . That's right." Bono would then transport the audience back to U2's genesis in 1976, when it met the Edge: "Myself and Larry and Adam were on the north side of Dublin and before we saw his spaceship we heard those notes. It was the sound of Edge's spaceship as he came to be with us. This is the sound that his spaceship made when it arrived on the north side of Dublin in the mid-seventies. It made those beautiful notes, there . . . listen." At this point, Bono had been speaking for about a minute, and by the power of suggestion, the Edge's chimes, repeating in pairs of threes, indeed sounded otherworldly and had created a tension, by virtue of their repetition, in want of a resolution. The notes, set in Bono's narrative, allude to those expectant moments in history when humankind sensed it was on the verge of contact with another world. More recently for U2's audience, they might invoke composer John Williams's scoring of the alien mother ship's first notes of communication upon arriving at Devils Tower, Wyoming, in Steven Spielberg's 1977 movie *Close Encounters of the Third Kind* ("It seems they're trying to teach us a basic tonal vocabulary. . . . It's the first day of school, fellas," the scientists remarked as they scrambled to decipher a pattern.[1])

Bono has said "Miracle Drug" was inspired by the life of Christopher Nolan, a schoolmate born with cerebral palsy, and the love Nolan's mother had for her son. Nolan could not communicate in conventional ways, but a medical breakthrough produced a drug that gave him the use of one muscle in his neck, allowing him to use a pointer to type out the poems he had been writing in his head.[2] As the song celebrates Nolan's life and poetry—"The songs are in your eyes / I see them when you smile"— along with his mother's love, it is a statement of having confidence in what we know right now and long to experience; for Bono and Nolan's mother, accessing what we can see comes through a potent compounding of medicine and love to make a miracle drug, which Bono expressed as "Of science and the human heart / There is no limit."

Bono has also said that the lyrics capture his excitement about medical advances in treating and arresting AIDS, but in those Vertigo concerts, he prepared the audience to hear "Miracle Drug" as a statement of courage for approaching what we don't yet know, for how to face the unknown. With his introduction, he returned to a story that U2 had started telling long ago. On many of those concert nights, Bono did not tell the story of Christopher Nolan but chose instead to recount the time that the three band members had their own close encounter of the third kind: "We just stood with our mouths open as this spaceship landed on the north side of Dublin. And a door opened and out walked this extraordinary looking man with an Explorer guitar." On the North American legs of the Vertigo tour, "Miracle Drug" often followed "Beautiful Day," placing two songs back-to-back on the set list in which the Edge frames the body of the song with his signature guitar chimes. (In fact, some might hear in "Beautiful Day" an even better reference to Williams's tones for the aliens' hello at Devils Tower.) As the band thundered through the last lines of "Beautiful Day," Bono would often shout that as a young man he listened to John Lennon whispering in his ear ideas about "imagining" and knowing "the world is more elastic than you think," before launching into singing snippets first from Harry Nilsson's "Many Rivers to Cross" and then either the Beatles' "Sgt. Pepper's Lonely Hearts Club Band" or "Blackbird." For two of U2's five shows at Madison Square Garden in October 2005, Bono added an additional snippet from "Across the Universe," and on a third night he sampled "Power to the People."[3] On those nights, invoking the Beatles and Lennon's call to dream was the hinge for swinging the show from an already enthusiastic "Beautiful Day" to a wide open exhortation to hope with "Miracle Drug." After a minute-plus of hearing the Edge's spaceship play its landing song, not just in the distance of 1976 but in the arenas of 2005, Bono released the audience from his story: "out walked this extraordinary looking man with an Explorer guitar. And Larry came up and said, 'Who are you?' and Edge said, 'I am the Edge.' And Adam said, 'Where are you from?' and Edge said, 'I'm from the future.' And I said, 'What's it like there, on your planet, in the future? And he said, 'It's better.'"[4]

Space Travel Turn Me On

For U2, the future and outer space are promised lands or, more accurately, promised realms, to which it has wanted to lead its listeners from its earliest gigs. A leitmotif threads through its catalog of leaving the past for unknown frontiers, with a belief that the future there and then is better than the present here and now. The leaving is sometimes done with great struggle and fear, but it is often also marked by a courageous and exuberant embrace of a new direction. U2 has trafficked in numerous exploration metaphors to illustrate the human on its voyage of self-discovery, cycling through images of the adolescent, the addict, the political visionary, the pilgrim, the cowboy, the channel surfer, the cosmic voyeur, the wanderer, the conspicuous consumer, the globe trotter, the love and peace corps volunteer, the scientist, and the rocket man. Its lyrics and performances are so rich, with well-crafted characters and plotlines that they have generated ongoing and ever-expanding analyses and interpretations among critics, as all great, enduring works of art do. As rock and roll, the band interested one of the largest audiences in the medium's history because it allows for such personalized, and often visceral, engagements with the universal experience of questing for answers to the human condition. But it is in U2's choosing to dwell on the future and explore the universe as its grandest articulation of what is sometimes called the "geographical cure" for human despondency that I wish to examine here, not via close readings of numerous songs or tours, but as a leitmotif present in its early days that has become fully realized on its most recent tour, the 360° tour.

Any critical reading of the music, work, and influence of U2 is well served by seeing the band as carrying on the "Spirit of Possibility" that infused Western culture in the sixties and seventies, the decades spanning the band members' youths. U2 is a band of the space age that fully embraced an optimistic, liberating openness to the future so characteristic of the dialogue in the scientific, technological, social, and artistic communities of

Europe and America. The band members were all born within four years after the launch of *Sputnik* in 1957, and they entered adolescence soon after the *Apollo 11* moon landing in 1969. Those decades were an ebullient time for much of the Western world when it came to space exploration and the promise that it held for humankind. Technology sectors were teeming with advancements fueled by nations' space programs, and popular culture had fully embraced and commoditized the hopes and fears of a future that looked to include space travel as a regular activity. Futurism had started earlier in the twentieth century as an artistic and social movement that regarded progress, speed, noise, cities, and machines as all beneficial catalysts for change, and with the space age's added doses of imagination, research, and development it bloomed into the defining cultural zeitgeist of the West as rock and roll was also coming into its own. The World Future Society formed in 1966 and began publishing its magazine, *The Futurist*, to report on trends, thinkers, and activities aimed at understanding the future and bringing a good one into existence. Dozens of books were published in those two decades, forecasting either exciting or doomsday futures, but those coming from the futurist's perspective fueled the dreams of many optimistic citizens already enamored by what we might discover through space exploration. One such example is the writings of Edward B. Lindaman, a futurist who directed the programming for the *Apollo* space projects while working for North American Rockwell and whom I regard as a great example of using the sort of futurist rhetoric that U2 employs as well. Lindaman was a prominent exponent for actively creating the kind of future that one wanted and for seeing space exploration as ultimately beneficial for improving life on Earth. In *Thinking in the Future Tense*, Lindaman described a futurist as one who "looks beyond the trends and probable outcomes to imagine other possibilities. This is the creative step—inventing one's own hopes. . . . It helps to realize that everything that is now possible was at one time impossible. In every case someone somewhere dared to dream, dared to imagine something a little better, a little different."[5] In all the ways that U2 encourages us to "dream out loud" and live for the future, U2 may as well be card-carrying futurists.

Lindaman also championed space exploration, and in *Space: A New Direction for Mankind*, he suggested,

> Perhaps our species must go on into Space, or perhaps we must suppress our inner nature. . . . Imagine you are in your living room, watching three pet goldfish in a bowl. Suddenly they propel themselves out of their safe fishbowl, up into the air, out through a slightly open window, and away. Somehow they move at a most unfishy, bullet-like speed to a far-distant

city. They tarry there a little while—not in water, but on the forbidden element of the land. Then they rise again into the alien air, find their way back to your window and into your living room and safely down again into the bowl—the single refuge known to them where warmth and food and equilibrium and something breathable are to be found. Unbelievable? Obviously. From a cosmic viewpoint, humanity's trips through Space are just as astounding, and for virtually the same reasons.[6]

Lindaman then presented his thought that from outer space, we can see Earth anew and bring back an enriched perspective for finding solutions to our earthly problems:

> Our grievous shortcomings in the area of social institutions may be found also in a less familiar field: our treatment of Earth itself. Let us return for a moment to our allegorical fish. Having once attained the magical gift of travel through an alien element, they would surely keep using it (as we have done for some years now with our gift of Space flight), and in so doing they would just as surely change their way of thinking about their native element. Their fishbowl would look quite different from the outside. . . . We never really discovered Earth until we got outside it. . . . Once again, life is striving to make itself something better to see the mind-blinding Space beyond the sky. Although it can no more comprehend Space than a fish comprehends land, it has begun floundering up to it anyway. We must pray that the inventiveness and pluck that enabled man to make nature a servant instead of an enemy will enable him to do the same for his own nature.[7]

Curiously, as if having read Lindaman and drawn artistic inspiration from these passages, Bono designed a "Fish Can Fly" T-shirt in 2008, depicting a fish traversing the moonlit, starry sky, for the Hard Rock Cafe's Signature Series 25, which benefited African farmers and wildlife habitats with sales' proceeds. The example of America's courage and enterprise in space exploration during the sixties and seventies was not lost on Bono, who in the early twenty-first century often co-opted the language of the Kennedy administration when lobbying for ending extreme poverty and achieving goals of the ONE campaign. Bono would call these goals the "moon shots" of our generation, and he told of watching the moon landing as a young boy and thinking that Americans were capable of anything they set their minds and hearts to. He contrasted the Western world's ability to put a man in space with its inability to distribute AIDS and malaria medications to the African villages in need of them, and he proclaimed it was now time to "put mankind back on Earth."[8]

U2 was not the only band to take up space images and metaphors, of course: many rock and popular musical artists drew on the medium for their messages. Tellingly, U2 chose for its intro and outro music on the 360° tour two songs by other artists that address the emotionally complicated life of the astronaut from the time of the *Apollo 11* mission: Bowie's "Space Oddity" (1969) was the intro and Elton John's "Rocket Man" (1972) was the outro. But U2 is the only band who has been afforded thirty-five years to continue working out its space travel metaphors to reach a sort of culminating statement on its 2009–2011 360° tour.

To see U2's affections for all things outer space requires only the slightest powers of perception now, with the 360° tour in hindsight. Making it obvious was a point, it seems, of the tour and its media campaign. Bono and the Edge's October 15, 2009, appearance on the cover of *Rolling Stone* showed them superimposed over an image of space, complete with stars and planets and the not-so-subtle headline "U2 Live from Outer Space." Helping even more was the tour's official concert DVD of the October 25, 2009, Rose Bowl show, which starts with animation of U2's now familiar "Spacebaby" (introduced on the Zoo TV tour) piloting its ship toward Earth. Once in Earth's orbit, Spacebaby asks, "What time is it in the world?" and locks into the coordinates for Los Angeles, California, to seek an answer. Spacebaby sees a U2 concert about to start, and we get to watch on its television screen along with Spacebaby. Back on the Elevation tour of 2001, Bono would introduce the Edge as "the scientist of the band," "our Dr. Spock," and "a man who takes sexual pleasure in the collection of data." But on the 360° tour, during performances of "In a Little While," video of a booster rocket jettisoning high above Earth was projected onto the stage's central screen, which gave way to images of orbiting Earth and then a cut to a videotaped recitation by astronaut Frank De Winne aboard the International Space Station of lyrics from the song: "A man dreams one day to fly / A man takes a rocket ship into the skies / He lives on a star that's dying in the night / And follows in the trail, the scatter of light," to which Bono would moan the song's line: "Turn me on, turn me on, turn me on," adding for these performances, "Space travel turns me on."[9]

Both the Spacebaby graphics and Bono saying he is "turned on" by space travel are characteristic of the playful tropes U2 uses to deliver sincere messages in the guise of a tease and challenge the audience to think about concepts of time and space, which U2 expands on in the course of its shows. Preceding the full-on presentation on the 360° tour is thirty-five years of U2 experimenting with the metaphoric power of the future and space travel. In the 1980s, it preferred to appear as spiritual pilgrims walking Earth in search of answers, finding a few good men but ultimately having hope in a future kingdom to come. Starting with *Achtung Baby* and the Zoo TV tour, it made explicit references to the anxieties and hopes of a people living late in the space age. The 1990s were U2's more playful time along these lines, with references to satellites, atmospheric static, and confusing intergalactic communications. It imagined a coming Zooropa world order fashioned from the basest materials of mass appeal culture to deliver the opiates of entertainment, pleasure, and the semblance of virtuous leaders. It experimented with Brain Eno in otherworldly sonics on the *Passengers* album and then indulged in *Pop* with all its efforts to have a good time in a lonely discothèque littered with consumer electronics and space junk. In the twenty-first century, what many saw as U2 reaching back to its 1980s formulas is better understood, I argue, as its presenting itself as having touched down on Earth again after a wearying trip through the heavens. It brings with it the hope of the future but also sees with increased clarity the problems of the present. With *All That You Can't Leave Behind* (2000), the band knows "It's a Beautiful Day" but it doesn't diminish earthly pain and suffering. U2 implores us to pack our bags, call out to God, and find hope in the state of grace. (At this time, the band begins alluding to Jeremiah 33:3—"Call to me and I will answer you, and will tell you great and hidden things that you have not known"—with a reference on the album cover to "J33-3." Bono would again invoke it in 2009 in "Unknown Caller" on *No Line on the Horizon* and on the 360° tour by referring to the time as 3:33). *How to Dismantle an Atomic Bomb* (2005) spoke more directly of hope and belief in a better future amid wars and dizzying displays of incongruity, and then *No Line on the Horizon* (2009) most clearly presented its out-of-this-world reasons for faith, hope, and love.

But back in 1978, in its earliest shows with only a handful of original songs, the band was already on about this. The Edge had written a song called "Life on a Distant Planet," which U2 performed in clubs and for an Irish television music program. The Edge said the song came from "finding a collision of melody and guitar that just inspired me and set me off. . . . It never really got beyond the initial inspiration to become a full-fledged tune. It was really just two or three ideas put together."[10] Lyrically, it gives impressions and statements from a male character. (It's unclear from the Edge's comments if he wrote the lyrics as well.) He sings of living on a distant planet in "another atmosphere" where a boy cannot get a girl's attention due, it would seem, to the disabling conditions of either an uninhabitable world or a sort of war-ravaged Earth. The boy asks Judith if she can hear him (it seems she can't), and Judith also cannot see. Additionally, there are children who "scream and shout, their eyes tore out," and "Judith turns around and stumbles to the ground." There is a mention of a D-day, and then the singer shifts from saying he is on a "distant planet" to being "lost on a silent planet," feeling "so close and yet so far." The song ends with the frustrated laments of "Heard you call out / Can you come out to play / Have you nothing to say / Can you come out to play / Have you nothing to say / In the morning all through the day time / To the evening, D-day and beyond."[11] The ambiguity of locale in the song's lyrics works well for reading it as from a man who feels like the distance between Dublin and the terrorist bombings in Northern Ireland, for example, is literally worlds apart. As he watches the news on the television, perhaps he feels distant, lost, and silent in his cognitive dissonance. His alienation comes from knowing that peace is possible while seeing people choose war. The song says nothing specific about an Irish situation though and so invites us to hear it as an expression of the existential despair that one might feel in any situation in which one cannot be heard amid conflict between love and hatred, health and sickness, riches and poverty—all of which are themes that U2 has explored on every album.

Having noted the lyrical ambiguity regarding time or place, I find it quite interesting, then, that when U2 performed the song for broadcast in 1979 for Ireland's RTE music show, the image projected behind the band during the second half of the song was an illustration of an unpopulated red planet landscape, with dark mountains, a burning sun, and what looks to be a volcano. Following those images is a cut from video of the *Apollo* missions' lunar rover driving on the moon's surface.[12] The conscious use of the planetary imagery and footage of man's drive across the moon elevates a thematic reading of the song, at least in this performance, to the level where Earth's "situation" is presented as frustrated within the universe. While we might have made it to the moon, the problems back on Earth still remain. Read this way, the song's lyrics suggest that Earth is an intergalactic mute, unable to speak, or is simply not playing its part in the cosmic symphony.

U2 has always known the value of a broadcast moment and has seized those opportunities for making some of its grandest statements. It seems quite conscious of the fact that tens of thousands of people are watching; especially, when an official documentary of a tour is being made, the band is keen to package it in a significant way that fixes a context for which the band members would like the audience to see them in. Spacebaby asking "What time is it in the world?" and then watching the 360° tour DVD is an obvious example of framing the viewers' perceptions, but what's surprising is how early in its career U2 seemed to have hit upon doing this, as with its use of the planet and lunar rover images for a television broadcast in 1979 that would reach far more viewers than what would have ever been present for one of U2's club shows. One might question the degree of artistic control that U2 had in its early years on television and think that the show's producer selected the images without consulting U2. If that was the case, the images chosen by RTE were serendipitously brilliant, but I think it's more likely that U2 suggested the images it wished to have associated with its song. One should not question, however, whether U2 had artistic control over its video for "Get On Your Boots," the first single from its 2009 album *No Line on the Horizon*. The first sequence of images behind the band is shots of a galaxy of stars, quasars, purple clouds, lightning bolts, and red rings around red planets. The video progresses with an overload of visual stimuli, much of it related to military iconography, rocket ships, blood, and repeating images of a red planet with firestorms, volcano bursts, and fighter jets flashing by.[13] Mars is the red planet in its appearance to Earth and in our popular imagination; Mars was the Roman god of war; and Mars is, of course, a distant planet. Furthering the associations between "Get On Your Boots" and U2's 1979 performance of "Life on a Distant Planet" is that "Boots" can be read as saying that life in a post–September 11 world, with prolonged wars in the Middle East and multiple incursions in countries throughout Africa and Southeast Asia, is like living on a silent planet. On just one album before *No Line on the Horizon*, Bono conceded in an early version of the jubilant song "All Because of You," "The thunder is loud / But the sun is shining / Up above the cloud / It's not the noise / It's the deafening silence / That drowns God out," and now, in the video for "Boots," comes the culminating chorus of pleas near the end of the song—"Let me in the sound / let me in the sound now / God, I'm going down / I don't wanna drown now / meet me in the sound"—made more clear by images of Bono trying to break through a glass barrier with his microphone stand, as though he is still that boy trying to get Judith—or the universe—to hear him.

"Boots," like "Life," is a song built of statements without an obviously cohesive narrative, giving impressions of characters a little out of focus. Recall the Edge's comment that he was looking for "a collision of melody and guitar that just inspired me and set me off" when writing "Life," and compare it with *Sunday Times* critic Michael Ross's unfavorable assessment after seeing "Boots" and other new songs performed at U2's July 2009 show in Paris: "Between them, the new pieces exemplified the recent predicament of a band seemingly unable to write structured songs, settling instead for riffs and word-salad lyrics arranged across featureless landscapes."[14]

Or, in other words, a U2 song. Ross's criticism aside, there are telling links between these two songs that span a distance of thirty years for U2. As the Edge said, "Life on a Distant Planet" never became a full-fledged tune, but in its lyrics of alienation, dislocation, and longing to be seen and heard, coupled with the conspicuous invocations in both the song and the performance of an "intergalactic angst," I see this as the protosong for all U2 songs. It's as if U2 has been trying to perform this song its whole career and is only lately able to do it justice.

What Do You Want?

"It's better"? Is that all the Edge had to say about the future? It was enough of an answer at the time, though, and it was all Bono needed to hear and all Bono wants to tell us too. His tall tale of his encounter with the Edge worked just as it should: it boils the historical record to a concentrated fiction containing a truth sufficient for action. Bono playfully asks us to believe an alien from the future came to live with the band, telling it the future was better. What's more, Bono, Larry, and Adam took the Edge in as a band member and worked with him, the alien, as an equal member of their new community. The spectacle of the Edge's arrival and his message from the future sufficiently emboldened the rest of the band to approach the unknown. This, in essence, was their epiphany of 1976: a transformative experience conveying that a message of hope best produces the courage to work through the anxieties, fears, and setbacks of the present. Believing that the future is better is the work of a belief carefully defined. It is not belief without or in spite of evidence but a belief borne of thought and feeling. For U2, this kind of belief is no easy state, and much of its songbook is given to acknowledging this. However, belief proper requires the conviction of both head and heart; it comes from equally validating epistemic and emotional experiences and is the result of effective appeals to our senses of logos and pathos—thus, what we think must be accompanied by equally freighted feeling if courage is to have any chance of liftoff. The highly advanced science represented in a capsule atop a rocket ship—the science for life support and navigational control in an atmosphere and on planets different from ours, where we encounter a physics of the "other"— must be matched by a proportionally equal quantity of propulsive energy sufficient for the definition of "mission success." If you wish to travel to the corner of your street, the ordinary ambulatory energy of the human body can get you there. If you wish to travel to the moon or farther, perhaps to the edge of the known universe, you are going to need a rocket ship. The thought-feeling-belief equation is a 1:1:1 ratio, actually, in which the elements are equal not in size but in magnitude. For example, as Bono enigmatically quipped in "Mysterious Ways," "if you want to kiss the sky, better learn how to kneel."

But how can we test that the future is better? What evidence is there? What about the factor of thought in this equation? In U2's history, the Dublin of the 1970s was in an economic and industrial decline, while Northern Ireland was the stage writ large for the literally demoralizing Troubles that had discouraged generations. There would hardly be enough evidence at hand for a fair-minded observer to indicate that the future was better. If evidence were to be persuasive in the absence of tangible proof, one would have to find mitigating reasons in the character of the messenger. The Edge is presented as someone beyond present time who not only experienced the future firsthand but was kind enough to come "back from the future," to live in 1976 amid discouraged Dubliners. That the Edge came "from the future from a completely different planet" points to the loci of U2's message of hope. In hearing from someone from beyond the present who is, in essence, not from our time but who has stepped into our time and who lives in another world but has stepped into our world, we are strangely inclined to pay attention to what he has to say. We allow him a kind of "space-time authority" by giving him the benefit of objectivity and having an experiential knowledge beyond our own. In Bono's conceit of U2's encounter with the Edge, he presents not only the character of this alien as a basis for belief but also his origin in another time and another place as giving him a more comprehensive view of our time and our world. The goal that U2 has, it seems, is to persuade its audience to look to a cosmic point of view for collecting encouraging data. As far back as 1987, in MTV's "Fire and Desire" interviews with U2, Adam said, "We're not going to take on other people's battles. We're merely going to present information to people that encourages them to take on those battles. That's what hope is, you know? And if that's what we produce, well then, it's hope for people to change things themselves. It's not hope for us to change things for other people."[15]

Neither does U2 shortchange the factor of feeling in the calculus of belief. It is oft told that early U2's strength was the passion and conviction it projected into a room such that fans, critics, and Paul McGuinness, U2's manager to be, noticed this above all else. Bono has since seen to it to provide sufficient spectacle to accompany whatever lyric he's singing, though Bono alone is not responsible for the energy of a U2 concert. The Edge came in a spaceship to the north side of Dublin in 1976, Bono would have us believe, which surely was enough of a spectacle to arouse an emotion to match his message. This particular account of the Edge's visit is but one way that U2 presents itself as feeling "strange" or "lost in the universe" when it comes to making sense of the violence, hatred, wars, greed, despair, famine, and suffering it sees. Its sense of alienation comes, presumably, because it knows of another world without this pain and suffering; or, if its world was once similarly despondent, it was long ago in an evolutionary past and had been overcome through heroic efforts. To wit, consider the well-known opening lines of "New Year's Day": "I can't believe the news today / I can't close my eyes and make it go away / How long, how long must we sing this song?" At times Bono will use the language of a terrestrial traveler, and accompanying media will create a visual rhetoric of maps and navigational coordinates, but quite often references to a cosmic point of view are close by too, in his lyrics or in the packaging of a U2 album, performance, or DVD. Other times U2 shifts the motif from being aliens from outer space to being "merely" humans who had a close encounter of the third kind and who then became a passenger on a tour across the universe and now returned to Earth to tell us what it knows to be real.

However it approaches a given performance, U2 has consistently tried to awaken audiences to live simultaneously in more dimensions of reality: where dreams instruct the world of the real and vision carries us beyond only what is visible. It does so not because it wishes with its audiences for there to be more to life than meets the senses but because it actually believes there to be more and it wants to encourage us with this news. The best reason for hope is, in fact, found only in the most comprehensive point of view and accessed through the thrill of contact with another space-time dimension. U2 itself suggests that it has heard from beyond a Euclidean plane where "Time is irrelevant / It's not linear," and it shares this message in "No Line on the Horizon." Objects, including human beings, are events happening along the viewer's own, finite space-time continuum: the object might seem near or far, here or there, young or old. Put another way, where and when an object "is" depends on where and when you are. And with regard to people, as objects in the universe, where and when they are is relative to where and when you are. By implication, then, to define what something or someone requires taking into consideration where and when it is. The more data points available, the more complete a statement of what something is can be. Perspectives limited to, say, the personal, local, or national scale produce limited, small-scale definitions. But great perspectives—360° perspectives—afford a more comprehensive definition, and when you are able to see everything from outside of time, as from an eternal perspective typically allotted to divinities or immortals, you then have the best reason for hope. I suggest that it is this ultimate, outside-of-time eternal view that U2 privileges in all its work, and the band presents this view as embodied in a universe-governing love. This "love divine," if you will, is what U2's seeking characters ultimately look for, as in "North Star," an unreleased song that U2 performed a few times on the 360° tour: "Forty-five light years from home / Is where you are and where I want to be / . . . Looking for directions / Stars are your reflection / To the space between you and me / . . . Here I am, a space cowboy / Looking out for love and logic / In the universe." In "Miracle Drug," Bono presents the power of a "love divine" more clearly: "Love makes nonsense of space / And time will disappear / Love and logic keep us clear." U2 would have us believe that it has seen planet Earth along love's space-time continuum, but the band itself does not dwell outside of space and time. As a passenger returning from its cosmic voyage of discovery, U2 knows Earth both now and in the future, affording the band members a polychronic, multispatial perspective that gives them the data they need for the act of hope.

U2 explores these quantum questions and makes physics into performance art as a part of its rock and roll, and on its recent 360° tour, it created a stadium show that could function as a sort of space lab for probing the secrets of the universe. As Adam Clayton said in 2009 of the band's stage design, "you don't really need this stuff. But part of show business is you have to change people's perceptions, you have to find ways to make the songs touch more people, to disorientate people so they're more open to being touched."[16] It is part of show business for sure, but it is also poetics in the service of recovery. U2 has landed home (Bono would often shout before the first notes of "Vertigo" on the 360° tour, "Honey, I'm home!") with encouraging, though disorienting news from across the universe; its alien aesthetic works as its grandest stage shows do, by compelling us to come closer, pay attention, so we can begin to entertain notions that there is more than meets the eye. It feels, as we do, that "planet Earth is blue," as it intimated with David Bowie's "Space Oddity," played through the PA system to signal the start of its 360° shows. For a discouraged, overstimulated, and alienated people, U2 hopes that we catch its cosmological point of view, and it wants to be the booster rocket to get us there.

That it—the future—is better must be believed if you are going to join a band, start a friendship or a family, run for president, or work to change the world. Believing that it is a worthwhile goal prompts figuring out the means for reaching it, and that belief sustains one's efforts along the way. Recall the scene in *Close Encounters of the Third Kind* when Roy Neary (played by Richard Dreyfuss)—as the blue-collar public utility worker who knew from experience that UFOs had once come to Earth and had been living expectantly, passionately for their return—was asked by the French scientist Claude Lacombe (played by François Truffaut), "Monsieur Neary, what do you want?" Lacombe asked the question as they stood in awe before the mother ship and watched people once abducted walk out through the bay door to return to Earth. *What do you want? What do you want?* It is the question that U2 asked verbatim in the early 1990s on its Zoo TV tour and on the song "Zooropa," and which it reintroduced as a question in the 2011 legs of the 360° tour in a transitional moment of the set list mixed with video and audio of questions submitted by fans played over a recording of "Fez."[17] (Later on the 2011 legs of its 360° tour, U2 also performed the whole of "Zooropa" as part of its set list.) Roy Neary's reply in the movie is simply, "I just want to know that it's really happening."[18] Roy is seeing something, and he is feeling the consolation of his longing to have contact with extraterrestrial life, but when given the chance to ask for anything, all he asks for is complete epistemological satisfaction: Is it real? He wants vindication for his passion and to know that it is worth pursuing into the future. If it is real, as he comes to believe it is, then he will walk onto the spaceship and join the alien community, which is just what he does.

For U2, I maintain that "it's really happening" for the band members and their audience on their 360° tour. Not that the last thirty-five years of performances were inconsequential (not in the least), but I see a culmination on their recent tour of a long artistic journey in the same direction. The 360° tour—with its giant, sci-fi "claw" of a stage, visibly alluding to the Los Angeles International Airport terminal and Spielberg's mother ship, capable of tremendous sound, color, and light—propels U2's career-long motifs of both terrestrial and interplanetary transportation and functions as the answer to a question it once asked itself, perhaps, in its early years as a band: "What do *we* want?" My considered conjectural answer to that question is along these lines: "We want to be the first band to play in space! But more than that, we want to lift our audiences out of their Earth-bound context so they can see the whole picture. The future *is* better and that is best realized from a different perspective in space and time. But until the day comes when we can do a show in space, we want to have the resources to make audiences feel like a stadium concert is taking place in space." I find compelling reasons to think that the 360° tour comes the closest to what U2 has wanted from its beginning. It's really happening for the band members in that they are able to have the stage, the sound, the lights, the smoke, and the motion to complete the effect of a spaceship that has touched down for an evening on Earth to allow U2 to report on what it knows and to invite more passengers to climb aboard before the ship takes off again. U2's intellectual vitality and artistic mastery were in full bloom on its 360° tour and make the case for attending to its work as we would the best poets, philosophers, artists, inventors, scientists, and engineers of an era.

U2 presents Claude Lacombe's question to its audiences because the band thinks that it can elicit the big existential questions, and it thinks that its audiences, like Roy Neary, want to know that "it's really happening." If we do sense that, indeed, it is really happening, we can draw the requisite strength to take the next steps toward a better tomorrow. U2 suspects that we all feel alienated not just from the human race but from the rest of the universe too. There must be other worlds, we suspect, and we wonder what our relationship is to them. We feel trapped and cut off from a cosmic conversation, as if on a silent planet where we are unsure if the universe is for or against us, and we are frustrated in our state of not knowing. How encouraging it is, then, when we hear in the sound of the universe, perhaps from a love divine, that it will be better.

U2's Ode to the Future

U2 considered calling the 360° tour the Kiss the Future tour, according to early reports from March 2009,[19] ostensibly to state the arch theme of hope for the two years it would be on the road. Maybe the band thought it too obvious a name, but it would have been in keeping with one of U2's ever-present messages. Bono had been practicing his lines for his 2005 the-Edge-as-alien shtick since at least the early 1990s, when he wrote the screenplay for *The Million Dollar Hotel*, which Wim Wenders directed and Lion's Gate released in 2000. In it, Mel Gibson plays FBI special agent J. D. Skinner, sent to a skid row hotel to investigate the death of a resident. Skinner projects the energy of a manically focused crime solver who has a mechanical brace fused to the exterior of his spine from a surgery to re-move a third arm. A resident picks up on something special about Skinner and asks, "You're from the future, aren't you?" Skinner replies that yes, he is from the future, to which the resident asks, "What's that like? And how, how is it?" Skinner's answer is, "The future? It's better."

But finally, in 2009, Bono would declare, "The future needs a big kiss" as the first line in "Get On Your Boots," which U2 chose to release as the first single off *No Line on the Horizon*. It was also the first track on the *U2 360° at the Rose Bowl* DVD, despite U2 opening shows with "Breathe," up to and including the Rose Bowl show. It was rumored that the audio recording was compromised during the taping of "Breathe" at the Rose Bowl, thus forcing U2 to cut it from the DVD. That may be so, but a reading of its show's thematic arc of hope works equally well with or without "Breathe" as the first song. With "Breathe," U2 walked onto the stage out of what looks like the cooling steam from a just-landed spaceship to sing out its news: "These days are better than that," meaning better than the earthly worries mentioned before the chorus. The courage to keep going in this life can come through a daily death-and-rebirth process that allows you to breathe, love, walk out, and find "grace inside a sound," the song proclaims. Following "Breathe," U2 played "Get On Your Boots." But on the DVD, the same ecstatic spirit prevails with "Boots" as the first song, especially with the amplification provided by Bono's clever setup for the song by snipping the melody from Beethoven's Ninth Symphony, commonly called the "Ode to Joy." And not just for the DVD did Bono articulate Beethoven's melody in a series of "da-da-das," but he did so as a regular introduction to "Boots" all tour long.

For fans with memories of U2's early 1990s tricks, the 2009 snippet of "Ode to Joy" should come with a rich irony, as the sample hearkens back to the opening of Zoo TV shows, when U2 mockingly played the tune for its significance as the European Union's anthem. At the start of a Zoo TV show, after the song played and video of the European Union's flag showed one of its stars falling from the circle, Bono would appear on stage, struggling to suppress a goose-stepping salute. But in 2009, the irony comes from U2 reappropriating its earlier use of irony, now in the service of hope: for "Ode to Joy's" lyrics, taken from Friedrich Schiller's poem, are a hymn to the spirit of man and the inspiring wonders that the Creator has placed in the natural world. It is worth consulting the entire song, but here I offer the traditional translation of selected lines for their striking similarity to themes in U2's songbook, especially as it has developed since 2000:

> Oh friends, not these tones!
> Let us raise our voices in more
> Pleasing and more joyful sounds! . . .
> Joy, beautiful spark of the gods, . . .
> All men will become brothers
> Under thy gentle wing. . . .
> All the world's creatures

> Draw joy from nature's breast; . . .
> She gave us kisses and wine . . .
> This kiss for all the world! . . .
> Brothers!, above the starry canopy
> A loving father must dwell.
> Can you sense the Creator, world?
> Seek him above the starry canopy.
> Above the stars He must dwell.

Whatever sarcastic rebuke U2 may have intended in the early 1990s of humankind's belief that it is capable of forming unions for the betterment of all had completely disappeared on the 360° tour. Instead, we find an utterly sincere belief that with the Creator's help, as Schiller said, "all men will become brothers." With no accompanying imagery on the 360° tour to associate Beethoven's melody with any specific political situation, I hear the song offered in further support of the encouragement found in "Get On Your Boots" that a contemplation of a love divine will allow us to hear "You don't know how beautiful you are" and learn that "Laughter is eternity if joy is real." And not only is that the state of the future, but it is a future that will be upon us soon, as indicated in the sample of the band's unreleased "Soon" used as a segue between Bowie's "Space Oddity" and its taking the stage to start the show. From "Soon," we hear the lines "Soon . . . / Soon . . . / Sing yourself on down the street / Sing yourself right off your feet / . . . Sing yourself to overcome / The thought that someone has lost / And someone else has won." Just as Spacebaby watching the DVD of the show asks, "What time is it in the world?" Bono asks the same question early in the show. The answer comes in the display of "3:33" on the video screen and in the song "Unknown Caller," alluding again to Jeremiah 33:3 and that if we call upon the divine, we will hear the secrets of the universe, and this better future can be ours soon, if not now.

Bono would know well, too, that for many in his audience Beethoven's melody would recall for them neither the European Union's anthem nor Schiller's poem (nor even Stanley Kubrick's use of it in *A Clockwork Orange*) but Presbyterian Henry Van Dyke's 1907 hymn "Joyful Joyful We Adore Thee" instead. Van Dyke's lyrics are also worth consulting in full, but consider the first two verses for their uncanny resonance with U2's message in many of its songs that reasons for hope abound:

> Joyful, joyful, we adore Thee, God of glory, Lord of love;
> Hearts unfold like flowers before Thee, opening to the sun
>   above.

Melt the clouds of sin and sadness; drive the dark of doubt
away;
Giver of immortal gladness, fill us with the light of day!
All Thy works with joy surround Thee, earth and heaven
reflect Thy rays,
Stars and angels sing around Thee, center of unbroken praise.
Field and forest, vale and mountain, flowery meadow, flashing
sea,
Singing bird and flowing fountain call us to rejoice in Thee.

First published in 1911 by *The Presbyterian Hymnal*, "these verses are simple expressions of common Christian feelings and desires in this present time—hymns of today that may be sung together by people who know the thought of the age, and are not afraid that any truth of science will destroy religion, or any revolution on earth overthrow the kingdom of heaven. Therefore this is a hymn of trust and joy and hope," Van Dyke said.[20] With all these allusions packed into a fifteen-second sample, Bono offers "Get On Your Boots" as a valediction to take a different space-time perspective and embrace the future, despite the dangers, fears, and wars of the present, because the future already loves you. Believing in the future, then, is not an act of desperation but of hope and reciprocity.

Philosopher and literary critic George Steiner said, "I am unable, even at the worst hours, to abdicate from the belief that the two validating wonders of mortal existence are love and the invention of the future tense."[21] As Bono will do to avoid repeating himself two nights in a row in the same venue—an understandable concern for a mortal showman—he gave a different introduction to the song "Miracle Drug" for the Madison Square Garden audience on the second night of U2's multinight run in 2005. Still, the message was that U2 believes the future to be better. As the Edge played the beginning of the song, Bono said, "These notes make us excited about the future, about being in a band, about the future of just being around in the twenty-first century. It gives us faith in the future. It gives us faith in the people who will shape the future: the scientists, the doctors, the nurses, the right to good health." His speech in New York City was only a slight variation from what he said earlier that year in Chicago for the official DVD concert film of the Vertigo tour: "We don't really look back that much in our music. The best bits of the past we'll try to bring with us. . . . Because we're interested, we're excited, we have faith in the future. That's where we're headed. . . . This is our music, the thing that we're strung out on. This is our drug: 'Miracle Drug.'"[22] U2 has been looking ahead for over thirty-five years, an eon for a rock band, and still believes the future is better.

Notes

1. The scene of the arrival, with the music and these comments, can be viewed at http://www.youtube.com/watch?v=tUcOaGawIW0 (accessed March 7, 2011).

2. Niall Stokes, *U2 into the Heart: The Stories behind Every Song* (New York: Thunder's Mouth Press, 2005), 166.

3. See U2's set list (http://www.u2setlists.com/) and its North American leg I and III listings for the Vertigo tour. See specifically the set list on Vertigo tour leg III for October 7 and 14, 2005, Madison Square Garden, New York City. To hear Bono's statements and these snippets, I recommend downloading the free audio bootlegs for U2's concerts from U2 Start (http://www.u2start.com).

4. I have quoted from Bono's introduction from two concerts—October 4, 2005, at Boston's Fleet Center and October 7, 2005, at New York City's Madison Square Garden—as representative of the introductions he gave on this tour. His remarks come at the end of U2's performance of "Beautiful Day" as a transition into "Miracle Drug." Consult the free audio bootlegs for U2's concerts from U2 Start (http://www.u2start.com/songs/112/1368/) to hear his introductions.

5. Edward B. Lindaman, *Thinking in the Future Tense* (Nashville, TN: Broadman, 1978), 44.

6. Edward B. Lindaman, *Space: A New Direction for Mankind* (New York: Harper & Row, 1969), 10.

7. Lindaman, *Space*, 4, 17.

8. Bono delivered many speeches in the first decade of the twenty-first century using language like this. Two examples for reference are in James Traub's profile for the *New York Times*'s "The Statesman," September 18, 2005, http://www.nytimes.com/2005/09/18/magazine/18bono.html?pagewanted=print, and in his address to the 2008 Women's Conference held by Maria Shriver, http://www.atu2.com/news/bono-speaks-at-the-2008-womens-conference.html (accessed on May 6, 2011).

9. Bono's addition to the chorus for "In a Little While" can be heard on the 2010 DVD release *U2: 360° at the Rose Bowl* and on YouTube clips from this video.

10. Neil McCormick and U2, *U2 by U2* (London: HarperCollins, 2006), 40.

11. Read the lyrics and known performance dates for "Life on a Distant Planet" at U2gigs.com, http://www.u2gigs.com/Life_On_A_Distant_Planet-s251.html (accessed April 28, 2011).

12. Watch "Lost on a Silent Planet" (which is called here by the alternate title "The Magic Carpet") at U2start.com, http://www.u2start.com/

shows/1979-10-00/Dublin,%20Ireland%20-%20Aspects%20Of%20Rock/#video (accessed April 28, 2011).

13. View the video for "Get On Your Boots," http://www.youtube.com/watch?v=INbpkZCoH2k&feature=fvsr (accessed May 6, 2011).

14. Michael Ross, "It Was the Best of Times, It Was the Worst of Times," July 12, 2009, http://www.atu2.com/news/all-that-they-cant-leave-behind.html (accessed May 6, 2011).

15. Adam's comment starts at the 2:18 mark, http://www.youtube.com/watch?v=8_odk_Vs9g4&feature=related (accessed March 9, 2011)

16. Brain Hiatt, "Live from Outer Space," *Rolling Stone*, October 15, 2009, 44.

17. This transitional moment can be viewed with the question "What do you want?" starting at about the 1:00 mark, http://www.youtube.com/watch?v=jSPY71vXkvY (accessed May 4, 2011).

18. This exchange from the movie starts at the 3:38 mark, http://www.youtube.com/watch?v=4zfelpF0Au4&feature=related (accessed May 4, 2011).

19. Ray Waddell of Billboard.com reported on March 6, 2009, that the name for the tour was Kiss the Future, http://www.reuters.com/article/2009/03/07/us-u-idUSTRE5260JX20090307. Billboard.com then changed its report on March 9, 2009, when U2 officially announced that the tour would be called the 360° tour.

20. Albert Edward Bailey, *The Gospel in Hymns* (New York: Scribner, 1954), 554.

21. George Steiner, *Errata: An Examined Life* (New Haven, CT: Yale University Press, 1998), 190.

22. *U2: Vertigo 2005 Live from Chicago*, about 40:50–41:47.

Bibliography
Selected Books, Essays, and Articles for Studying U2

Alan, Carter. *Outside Is America: U2 in the US*. Boston: Faber & Faber, 1992.

———. *U2: The Road to Pop*. Boston: Faber & Faber, 1997.

Assayas, Michka. *Bono: In Conversation*. London: Riverhead, 2005.

Beard, Steve. "The Gospel of Heaven and Hell." In *Spiritual Journey: How Faith Has Influenced Twelve Music Icons*, 237–238, 264. Lake Mary, FL: Relevant Books, 2003.

Beeaff, Dianne Ebertt. *A Grand Madness: Ten Years on the Road with U2*. Tucson, AZ: Hawkmoon, 2000.

Bono. *On the Move*. Nashville, TN: Thomas Nelson, 2006.

Bordowitz, Hank, ed. *The U2 Reader*. Milwaukee, WI: Hal Leonard, 2003.

Bowler, Dave, and Bryan Dray. *U2: A Conspiracy of Hope*. London: Pan Books, 1994.

Brandt, Winston. *U2*. New York: Ballantine Books, 1986.

Brothers, Robyn. "Time to Heal, 'Desire' Time. The Cyber-prophesy of U2's 'Zoo World Order.'" In *Reading Rock and Roll: Authenticity, Appropriation, Aesthetics*, edited by Kevin J. H. Dettmar and William Richey, 237–67. New York: Columbia University Press, 1999.

Calhoun, Scott. "Bono's Prophetic Vox: The Message Author Says U2's Message Is Refreshing, Faithful and Honest." @U2. http://www.atu2.com/news/bonos-prophetic-vox.html. February 9, 2006.

———. "The Legend of Bono Vox: Lessons Learned in the Church of U2." *Books and Culture* (November/December 2004): 10–14.

———. "Where Could We Go from Here? The State of U2 Studies." *Books and Culture* (November/December 2009): 14–15.

Catanzarite, Stephen. *Achtung Baby: Meditations on Love in the Shadow of the Fall*. New York: Continuum Books, 2007.

Chatterton, Mark. *U2: The Complete Encyclopedia*. London: Fire Fly, 2001.

Cogan, Visna. *U2: An Irish Phenomenon*. New York: Pegasus Books, 2007.

Corbin, Anton. *U2&I: The Photographs: 1982–2004*. Munich: Schirmer/Mosel, 2008.

DeCurtis, Anthony. "Bono: The Beliefnet Interview." February 2001. http://www.beliefnet.com/story/67/story%5f6758%5f1.html.

De La Parra, Pimm Jal. *U2 Live: A Concert Documentary*. London: Omnibus Press, 2003.

Dunphy, Eamon. *Unforgettable Fire*. New York: Warner Books, 1987.

Endrinal, Christopher. "Form and Style in the Music of U2." PhD diss., Florida State University, 2008.

Fallon, B. P. *U2: Faraway So Close*. Boston: Little, Brown, 1994.

Fast, Susan. "Music, Contexts, and Meaning in U2." In *Expression in Pop-Rock Music*, edited by Walter Everett, 33–57. New York: Routledge, 2008.

Flanagan, Bill. *U2 at the End of the World*. New York: Delacorte Press, 1995.

Galbraith, Deane. "Drawing Our Fish in the Sand: Secret Biblical Allusions in the Music of U2." *Biblical Interpretation: A Journal of Contemporary Approaches* 19, no. 2 (2011): 181–222.

Garrett, Greg. *We Get to Carry Each Other: The Gospel according to U2*. Louisville, KY: Westminster John Knox Press, 2009.

Garvey, Amy, ed. *U2: The Early Days*. New York: Dell, 1989.

Gilmour, Michael. "The Prophet Jeremiah, Aung San Suu Kyi, and U2's *All That You Can't Leave Behind*: On Listening to Bono's Jeremiad." In *Call Me the Seeker: Listening to Religion in Popular Music*, edited by Michael Gilmour, 34–43. New York: Continuum, 2005.

Gittins, Ian. *U2: The Best of Propaganda*. New York: Thunder's Mouth Press, 2003.

Godson, Lisa. *Stealing Hearts from a Travelling Show: The Graphic Design of U2*. Dublin: Four5One Creative, 2003.

Goodman, Sam. *U2: Burning Desire*. Chessington, England: Castle Communications Place, 1993.

Graham, Bill. *U2: The Early Days*. New York: Delta, 1989.

Graham, Bill, and Caroline van Oosten de Boer. *U2: The Complete Guide to Their Music*. London: Omnibus Press, 2004.

Harris, Paul. "U2's Creative Process: Sketching in Sound." PhD diss., University of North Carolina at Chapel Hill, 2006.

Helme, Deborah. *A Powerful Voice: The Story of Bono from U2*. Norwich, England: RMEP, 2004.

Hewson, Paul. "Elvis: The White Nigger." In *Across the Frontiers: Ireland in the 1990s*, edited by Richard Kearney, 188–91. Dublin: Wolfhound Press, 1988.

Holm-Hudson, Kevin. "Et Tu, U2? 'Wake Up Dead Man' and Bono's Perceived Betrayal of the Faith." *Journal of Religion and Popular Culture* 16, no. 2 (2007). http://www.usask.ca/relst/jrpc/art16-ettuU2.html.

Johnson, Fred. "U2, Mythology, and Mass-Mediated Survival." *Popular Music and Society* 27, no. 1 (2004): 79–87.

Lizie, Arthur. *Dreaming the World: U2 Fans, Online Community and Intercultural Communication.* New York: Hampton Press, 2009.

Luerssen, John. *U2 FAQ.* Milwaukee, WI: Backbeat Books, 2010.

Maynard, Beth, and Raewynne J. Whiteley, eds. *Get Up off Your Knees: Preaching the U2 Catalog.* Cambridge, MA: Cowley, 2003.

McCormick, Neil. *Killing Bono.* New York: Pocket Books, 2004.

McCormick, Neil, and U2. *U2 by U2.* London: HarperCollins, 2006.

McFliker, Todd. *All You Need Is Love to Dismantle an Atomic Bomb: How the Beatles and U2 Changed the World.* New York: Continuum, 2007.

McGee, Matt. *U2: A Diary.* 2nd ed. New York: Omnibus, 2011.

Negativland. *Fair Use: The Story of the Letter U and the Numeral 2.* Concord, CA: Seeland, 1995.

Ponte, Stefano, Lisa Ann Richey, and Mike Baab. "Bono's Product (RED) Initiative: Corporate Social Responsibility That Solves the Problems of 'Distant Others.'" *Third World Quarterly* 30, no. 2 (2009): 301–17.

Quinn, Steven. "U2 and the Performance of (a Numb) Resistance." *Social Semiotics* 9, no. 1 (1999): 67–83.

Ramert, Lynn. "A Century Apart: The Personality Performances of Oscar Wilde in the 1890s and U2's Bono in the 1990s." *Popular Music and Society* 32, no. 4 (2009): 447–60.

Richey, Lisa Ann, and Stefano Ponte. "Better (Red)™ Than Dead? Celebrities, Consumption and International Aid." *Third World Quarterly* 29, no. 4 (2008): 711–29.

———. *Brand Aid: Shopping Well to Save the World.* Minneapolis: University of Minnesota Press, 2011.

Rolling Stone, ed. *U2: The Ultimate Compendium of Interviews, Articles, Facts and Opinions from the Files of Rolling Stone.* New York: Hyperion/Rolling Stone Press, 1994.

Scharen, Christian. *One Step Closer: Why U2 Matters to Those Seeking God.* Grand Rapids, MI: Brazos Press, 2006.

Scrimgeour, Diana. *U2 Show.* New York: Riverhead Books, 2004.

Seales, Chad E. "Burned over Bono: U2's Rock 'n' Roll Messiah and His Religious Politic." *Journal of Religion and Popular Culture* 14, no. 1 (2006).

Shirley, Jackie. *U2.* Stanford, CT: Longmeadow Press, 1993.

Shruers, Fred. "U2." *Music Sound Output* (December 1984): 40, 41–46.

Stein, Atara. "Epipsychidion, *Achtung Baby*, and the Teaching of Romanticism." *Popular Culture Review* 6, no. 1 (1995): 29–44.

———. "'Even Better Than the Real Thing': U2's (Love) Songs of the Self." In *Reading Rock and Roll: Authenticity, Appropriation, Aesthetics*, edited by Kevin J. H. Dettmar and William Richey, 269–86. New York: Columbia University Press, 1999.

Stockman, Steve. *Walk On: The Spiritual Journey of U2.* Winter Park, FL: Relevant Media Group, 2005.

Stokes, Niall. *U2: Into the Heart.* New York: Thunder's Mouth Press, 2003.

———, ed. *The U2 File.* Dublin: Hot Press, 1985.

Stokes, Niall, and Liam Mackey, eds. *U2: Three Chords and the Truth.* New York: Harmony Books, 1989.

Thomas, Dave. *U2: Stories for Boys.* London: Bobcat Books, 1986.

Trachtenberg, Martha. *Bono: Rock Star Activist.* Berkley Heights, NJ: Enslow, 2008.

Traub, James. "The Statesman." *New York Times Magazine* (September 18, 2005): 80+.

Tyrangiel, Josh. "The Constant Charmer." *Time* (December 26, 2005 / January 2, 2006): 46, 47–71.

Uncut Presents U2 (Legends 3) 1, no. 3 (2004).

Vagacs, Robert. *Religious Nuts, Political Fanatics.* Eugene, OR: Cascade Books, 2005.

VanderSpek, Henry. *Faith, Hope and U2.* Toronto: Digory Designs, 2000.

Washburn, Kim. *Breaking through by Grace: The Bono Story.* Grand Rapids, MI: Zonderkidz/Zondervan, 2010.

Waters, John. *Race of Angels.* London: Fourth Estate Limited, 1994.

Williams, Peter, and Steve Turner. *U2 Rattle and Hum: The Official Book of the U2 Movie.* New York: Harmony Books, 1988.

Wrathall, Mark A., ed. *U2 and Philosophy.* Popular Culture and Philosophy Series 21. Chicago: Open Court, 2006.

Subject Index

Song Index

About the Editor and Contributors

Scott Calhoun is the director of "U2: The Hype and the Feedback," a conference exploring the music, work and influence of U2. He's a staff writer for @U2 (atu2.com) and an associate professor of English at Cedarville University, where he teaches nonfiction writing, American literature, and the works of C. S. Lewis.

Stephen Catanzarite is the managing director of the Lincoln Park Performing Arts Center in Midland, Pennsylvania. A graduate of Carnegie Mellon University, he recently received his master's in education from Franciscan University of Steubenville.

Greg Clarke is a founding director of the Centre for Public Christianity in Sydney. He is an honorary associate of the School of Ancient History at Macquarie University, where he lectures on biblical influences on the Western literary tradition. Greg recently became chief executive of Bible Society Australia but is still happiest plunking the bass and listening to U2.

Anthony DeCurtis has written a great deal about U2 over the years, including two cover stories for *Rolling Stone*, where he is a contributing editor. He is the author of *In Other Words: Artists Talk about Life and Work* and *Rocking My Life Away: Writing about Music and Other Matters* and the editor of *Blues & Chaos: The Music Writing of Robert Palmer*. He teaches in the creative writing program at the University of Pennsylvania.

Kevin J. H. Dettmar is W. M. Keck Professor and Chair of English at Pomona College. He has published widely on modernist literature and contemporary popular music, including *The Cambridge Companion to Bob Dylan* and *Is Rock Dead?* He also blogs about contemporary culture and music.

Bruce L. Edwards is professor of English and Africana studies at Bowling Green State University and a former Fulbright fellow to Kenya. He has authored or edited several works on the life and work of C. S. Lewis, most recently, *C. S. Lewis: Life, Works, Legacy* (2007).

Christopher Endrinal is an assistant professor at the University of Massachusetts, Lowell, Department of Music. He earned his doctorate in music theory from the Florida State University College of Music. His dissertation, "Form and Style in the Music of U2," analyzes the structural and aural characteristics that form U2's unique sonic signature.

Deane Galbraith is a founding editor of *Relegere*, a journal exploring the reception history of religious ideas and practices in historical and modern culture, and a part-time lecturer at the University of Otago (Dunedin, New Zealand). He is currently researching the Judaic belief, evident in the Torah and mythological giants.

John Hurtgen is dean of the School of Theology and professor of New Testament at Campbellsville University, Campbellsville, Kentucky. He is the author of *Reading the New Testament* and *Anti-Language in the Apocalypse of John.* John's wife, Pam, and three sons have been to two U2 concerts.

Jeffrey F. Keuss is professor and associate dean in the School of Theology at Seattle Pacific University. A theological and cultural critic, he is the author of *Freedom of the Self: Kenosis, Cultural Identity, and Mission at the Crossroads, The Sacred and the Profane: Current Demands in Hermeneutics,* and *Your Neighbor's Hymnal: What Christians Can Learn from Pop Music about Faith, Hope and Love* and has a monthly podcast on topics of theology and popular culture called "The Kindlings Muse."

Daniel T. Kline is professor of English at the University of Alaska, Anchorage, where he specializes in medieval literature, literary theory, and digital medievalism. Widely published in many venues, his current research concerns children and childhood in late-medieval England and the ethical thought of Emmanuel Levinas.

Sara Koenig attended her first U2 concert when she was a college freshman at Seattle Pacific University, where she is an assistant professor of biblical studies. She approaches the Bible as theology and literature, with special interest in hermeneutics and the history of interpretation.

Beth Maynard serves as an adjunct instructor in spirituality and liturgy at Gordon-Conwell Theological Seminary in Massachusetts. An Episcopal priest, she coedited the sermon anthology *Get Up off Your Knees: Preaching the U2 Catalog* and holds a bachelor of arts from Amherst College and a master of divinity from Boston University.

Neil McCormick is one of the United Kingdom's best-known music critics. He is a columnist for the *Daily Telegraph* and a regular guest on BBC television and radio. He started working for *Hot Press* music magazine in Dublin as a seventeen-year-old punk rock art school dropout in 1978. Neil was a friend of U2 at Mount Temple school and singer in a succession of obscure bands, including Frankie Corpse and the Undertakers, the Modulators, Yeah!Yeah!, and Shook Up! His musical misadventures are laid out in painful detail in the acclaimed 2003 memoir *I Was Bono's Doppelganger*, which has been adapted for the 2011 film *Killing Bono* (directed by Nick Hamm, starring Ben Barnes as Neil, Robert Sheehan as his brother Ivan, and Martin McCann as Bono). Neil collaborated with U2 on its 2006 best-selling autobiography *U2 by U2*.

Michele O'Brien holds a bachelor of arts in journalism and mass communication from New York University. She has worked with agencies in New York, Philadelphia, and Dublin, Ireland, helping brands stand out in their marketplace. A U2 fan for twenty-five years, Michele is delighted to mesh her professional expertise spanning over a decade with her passion for U2.

Danielle Rhéaume was diagnosed with multiple sclerosis soon after drafting her contribution. Since the diagnosis, she has devoted most of her time to patient activism and research of chronic cerebrospinal venous insufficiency, a controversial but promising theory for the cause of multiple sclerosis. Bono helped her understand the difference between charity and activism. She still intends to finish her book.

Rachel E. Seiler is keenly interested in the intersections between popular culture and systemic change; her 2010 dissertation explored the impact of U2's music on listeners' progressive awareness. She hopes her scholarship, teaching, and work in the nonprofit sector can help birth a culture of justice and peace.

Steve Taylor is a senior lecturer at Flinders University, Adelaide, Australia. He is author of *The Out of Bounds Church? Learning to Create a Community of Faith in a Culture of Change* (2005) and publishes widely in the area of theology and contemporary culture.